The 24-Hour Disaster Story with ChatGPT

Andrew Parry

Published by Andrew Parry, 2025.

THE 24-HOUR DISASTER STORY WITH CHATGPT

First edition. May 8, 2025.

ISBN: 979-8231708574

Written by Andrew Parry.

Table of Contents

Introduction: Why Disaster Stories Matter More Than Ever

When you sit down to write a disaster story, you're tapping into one of the most powerful currents running through human storytelling. Disasters, both imagined and real, have always fascinated people. From the moment early humans huddled together and told tales of floods and fires that could wipe out whole villages, disaster stories have been part of how we understand fear, survival, and hope. Today, these stories matter more than ever because the world feels closer to the edge than it has in decades. Climate change, pandemics, wars, economic collapses, political chaos—every headline seems like the beginning of a disaster movie. And that's why disaster fiction resonates so strongly. It doesn't just entertain. It prepares. It warns. It reflects what we're already thinking about deep inside but might be too scared to say out loud.

Writing a disaster story isn't just about blowing things up and throwing your characters into flaming buildings. It's about exploring what people do when the normal rules collapse. How far will they go to survive? What do they cling to when everything else falls away? Disaster strips away the comfortable layers of modern life and reveals what's underneath, for better or worse. It's a chance to show true courage or true cowardice. It's an opportunity to explore human nature in its rawest form. And most importantly, it's a mirror that reflects how societies react under stress—and that mirror is getting more relevant by the day.

In some ways, disaster stories are universal. They work whether you're writing a modern urban thriller where a hurricane traps thousands in a city, a futuristic sci-fi saga about colonies destroyed by alien storms, or a medieval epic about plagues and famine. Disaster isn't confined by genre or era. It's an eternal question: what do you do when the world you knew is gone? That emotional core is what readers or viewers respond to, and it's why, even if you're writing a story set a thousand years into the future or ten thousand years in the past, your audience will still feel deeply connected to it.

Another reason disaster stories are so vital today is that audiences crave catharsis. Watching or reading about other people surviving the worst gives us hope that we could too. It's a way of rehearsing trauma in a safe place. In a time when real-world anxieties are high—whether it's about natural disasters, pandemics, or even existential threats like AI or nuclear war—storytelling becomes a form of emotional preparation. It reminds us that while destruction may be inevitable, resilience is possible. In many disaster stories, the most powerful moments aren't the explosions or the chases. They are the quiet scenes where a character chooses kindness instead of cruelty. Where they choose sacrifice over selfishness. Where they find love or meaning in the rubble.

One thing you'll quickly notice once you dive into writing disaster fiction is how much creative freedom it gives you. You can start small or go big. Maybe it's just one apartment building catching fire and trapping a few residents. Maybe it's a worldwide virus that turns every city into ghost towns. Maybe it's an asteroid hurtling toward Earth. The scale is up to you. The real magic happens not with the size of the disaster, but with the depth of the characters caught in it. The biggest explosions in the world won't move a reader or viewer if the people aren't believable and relatable. Disaster is the backdrop; human emotion is the real story.

And here's where using a tool like ChatGPT becomes an absolute game-changer. Coming up with different disaster scenarios, character ideas, survival twists, plot complications—all those heavy lifting tasks that might have taken you days or weeks before—you can now generate in minutes. It's like having a creative partner who never gets tired, never runs out of ideas, and is always ready to brainstorm with you. This means you can move from blank page to full disaster story in just one day if you want to. The secret is working with intention, having a clear vision for your story, and knowing how to steer the AI to help you craft something gripping, emotional, and memorable.

This book is built around exactly that approach. You'll learn how to use ChatGPT not just to write faster, but to write better. We'll talk about how to start with the end in mind—because in disaster fiction, endings are everything. We'll look at how to reverse engineer a plot that grips from the first line and doesn't let go until the final page. We'll explore different types of disasters, different character archetypes, and different thematic layers you can weave into your story to make it resonate on more than just a surface level. We'll dive into the hero's journey framework and how it can still apply even when the world is falling apart. And we'll walk through how to create pacing, tension, and moments of heartbreaking beauty that make your disaster story unforgettable.

Another thing we'll dig into is why disaster stories don't have to be depressing. Sure, things can get dark—sometimes very dark. But some of the best disaster stories leave you feeling hopeful, not hopeless. They show that even in the worst circumstances, people can still find connection, meaning, and even joy. They show that survival isn't just about breathing; it's about living. It's about carrying something forward into whatever comes next. As a writer, you have the power to decide what kind of emotional impact you want your story to leave behind.

Right now, you might be thinking, can I really write a disaster story in one day? Yes, you absolutely can. Especially when you have the right tools, the right mindset, and a method that focuses your energy instead of scattering it. Disaster fiction naturally lends itself to urgent, emotional storytelling. It thrives on momentum. It demands that you stay in the moment. And that's exactly the kind of intensity that can power you through writing a complete first draft in just a single day. Think of it not just as a writing exercise, but as an act of creative survival—just like your characters surviving in their world, you're surviving the writing process and coming out the other side with a story you can be proud of.

This book isn't just about giving you advice; it's about getting you to write. Quickly. Fearlessly. Powerfully. Whether you want to craft a devastating short story that punches readers in the gut, a sprawling apocalyptic novel that imagines the end of civilization, or a screenplay that turns into the next big disaster blockbuster, you'll find the steps you need here. And you'll find them laid out in a way that's flexible, encouraging, and energizing—because writing a disaster story should feel thrilling, not like homework.

So buckle up. The storm's already brewing. The earth is already shaking. The sirens are already wailing in the distance. You have a world to destroy—and a story to create. Let's get to it.

One Day, One Story: Your Disaster Narrative Game Plan

When you sit down to write a disaster story in one day, you have to think like one of your characters: act fast, stay focused, and keep moving forward even when things get chaotic. Writing a full story in just twenty-four hours sounds impossible if you imagine every moment needing to be polished and perfect. But that's not the point. The point is momentum. You're here to create a living, breathing story, not to sculpt a flawless statue on your first attempt. Disaster fiction is built on urgency, and writing it should feel the same way. You want to get swept up in the energy, ride the adrenaline, and let the rawness of it fuel the emotional truth of the story.

The first thing you need is a clear plan of attack. You're not just typing random ideas and hoping they form a narrative. You're making strategic decisions early that will shape everything to come. Before you write a single line of prose, you'll decide four key things: the disaster event, the protagonist, the ultimate ending, and the emotional tone you want the reader to leave with. If you lock those four things down before you start, the rest of the story can unfold with much less hesitation or second-guessing. ChatGPT is an incredible tool for helping you brainstorm and narrow down these choices quickly if you get stuck.

Start by picking your disaster. Is it a massive hurricane? A sudden pandemic? A nuclear meltdown? An asteroid impact? A slow-burn societal collapse from climate change? Pick one. Stick to it. Don't try to weave multiple disasters together unless that's part of the concept you see clearly from the beginning. A single, clear catastrophic event keeps your story focused and sharp. You're going to lean into that one disaster and let it push all the action forward.

Next, pick your protagonist. This is not a committee decision. One person is at the center of this story. It doesn't matter if you'll later show the perspectives of others—someone has to be the emotional heart. It could be a firefighter racing into the flames. A nurse trying to save patients as the hospital collapses. A child separated from their parents during an earthquake. A scientist frantically trying to warn the world about the incoming asteroid. Whoever they are, they need to have something personal at stake beyond just survival. They have to be trying to save a family member, protect a community, redeem a past mistake, or achieve a lifelong dream before it's too late. That emotional driver will guide every decision they make, and it will drive your story forward too.

Once you have the disaster and the protagonist, you need to know how the story ends. Yes, now. Before you even start writing. Disaster fiction isn't just about the bang; it's about the consequences. Does your protagonist survive? Do they fail? Do they save others but lose themselves? Do they witness the world's rebirth after destruction? Choose the emotional destination before you start. Writing with the end in mind gives your story a natural gravitational pull. Every scene will lean toward that inevitable conclusion, building tension along the way.

And finally, pick the emotional tone. Is your story bleak and hopeless, like the final scenes of *The Road*? Is it gritty but ultimately redemptive, like *Contagion*? Is it tragic but beautiful, like *Titanic*? Knowing what feeling you want the reader to leave with helps you decide what kinds of moments you emphasize during the writing. You want to be emotionally consistent even as the plot goes through its chaos. A hopeful disaster story will frame small acts of kindness and endurance in the foreground. A tragic one will highlight every missed opportunity and cruel twist of fate. Emotional control gives your story impact.

Once those four pillars are in place, you can start shaping your actual game plan for the writing day. Here's how to think about it: imagine your story as a simple arc. It starts with normal life, moves into the disruption (the disaster strikes or is discovered), then escalates as survival becomes harder, culminating in a peak moment of decision, and ending with either survival, loss, or a glimpse of a new future. You're not writing a sprawling epic across twenty timelines. You're focusing tightly on one main event and one main human experience through it.

Break your writing day into manageable chunks. Spend the first hour planning and prompting if needed. Use ChatGPT to create quick character bios, outline possible scene ideas, and get sample dialogue started. Don't fall into the trap of endless prompting though—use it to move, not stall. After that, dedicate a block of time to writing your opening: the normal world your characters are about to lose. Then move immediately to the disruption scene. Get the disaster onstage quickly. Readers come for the collapse, so don't make them wait 20,000 words. By the middle of the day, you should be deep into escalating danger. Smaller disasters should pile onto the big one. Characters should be making tough choices. Tension should be tightening. Every decision should have bigger consequences.

Save a strong, focused chunk of your energy for writing the climax. This is the life-or-death moment, the scene where everything your protagonist believes is tested. Will they run or stay? Save themselves or save others? Rise above fear or be consumed by it? The climax should feel earned, inevitable, and devastating or uplifting depending on your tone. After that, the resolution should be quick. Disaster fiction doesn't need endless epilogues. Show the outcome. Let the emotion settle. Then get out.

One of the best parts of writing a disaster story in one day is that it naturally lends itself to immediate, emotional storytelling. You don't have time to second-guess every word. You have to trust your instincts. You have to ride the emotional wave of your own writing. When you feel scared for your characters, when you feel the weight of their choices, when you're gasping or tearing up or laughing at their triumphs and failures—you're doing it right. That rawness is what disaster stories thrive on. Readers don't come to these stories for polish. They come for heart, terror, courage, grief, and the messy beauty of survival.

Don't worry about whether you're writing perfect prose. Worry about whether the story is alive. Disaster fiction is forgiving in that way. A jagged, breathless style can work beautifully. Short, punchy sentences during action scenes. Longer, aching sentences when describing devastation or loss. Let the story's heartbeat shape the style. If you need a push, you can even prompt ChatGPT to help you generate action scenes or emotional monologues on the fly. It's your secret weapon to stay moving when your own brain gets tired.

And don't forget to build in breaks. Even if you're writing at a frantic pace, you'll need time to breathe, reset, and let your mind process what's happening in the story. Take a walk, drink water, stare out a window—let your own body mirror the rhythm of survival that your characters are experiencing.

At the end of the day, you're going to have a full draft of a disaster story that didn't exist when you woke up that morning. That's an incredible feeling. It might be rough. It might be raw. But it will be real. And you'll be able to refine it later. For now, the goal is survival. Just like your characters are trying to make it through the collapse, you're trying to make it to the end of the story. And when you do, you'll have proven something important—not just about writing, but about yourself.

You're a survivor. You're a storyteller. And the world you create in a day might just be the one someone else remembers forever.

Starting with the End: Visualizing the Aftermath

When you start a disaster story, it's tempting to immediately dive into chaos. Fire, floods, explosions, sirens blaring—that's the adrenaline rush most writers crave when they picture disaster fiction. But if you really want to write a story that hits hard, lingers, and matters, you have to start by asking yourself one quiet but essential question: *what does the world look like after it's all over?* The aftermath is where the real weight of a disaster lives. It's not in the moment of impact; it's in the silence after. It's in the ruins, the empty homes, the memories that refuse to fade. It's the bruised but still beating heart of survival. When you know what that ending looks like before you even write your first sentence, your entire story has a purpose, a gravity that pulls the reader—and yourself—through every scene.

Visualizing the aftermath means you have to decide what shape your world is in when the dust settles. Is the city half underwater? Are there only a few survivors staggering through ash? Is the entire world eerily quiet, communication cut off, no planes in the sky, no cars on the roads? Is there a new leader rising from the chaos—or has everyone scattered into isolated tribes, fighting for scraps? When you create this image clearly in your mind, you're doing more than setting a scene. You're defining the emotional destination of your story. Are you aiming for despair, resilience, rebirth, something bittersweet, or something terrifying? The emotional texture of your ending will ripple backward through the whole story, shaping every decision you make along the way.

A strong disaster story ending usually captures a simple but profound human truth. It might be that survival has a cost. That love can endure even when the world falls apart. That nature is indifferent to human suffering. That society is more fragile than we think. That hope stubbornly sprouts from ruins. Whatever emotional truth you choose, it should saturate your final scenes like rain soaking into broken concrete. You're not writing just for spectacle; you're writing for meaning. And meaning comes from how the disaster changes people, not just how it destroys things.

Another reason for starting with the end in mind is because it keeps your plot tight and purposeful. Disaster fiction can easily spiral into endless scenes of chaos if you're not careful. Cars crash, buildings collapse, people scream, and before you know it, the story feels like one long, noisy mess. But if you already know the ending, you can make every scene a step toward that inevitable conclusion. Every choice your protagonist makes, every piece of destruction they witness, every new character they meet, is part of the journey to that final image. Writing this way creates a natural sense of tension and momentum. It feels like the story is falling downhill toward a cliff you can't look away from.

Visualizing the aftermath also forces you to think about what your characters have lost—and what they might still have. Loss is at the core of every good disaster story. It might be the loss of a home, a loved one, a way of life, a belief system. It might be the loss of innocence, the loss of faith in humanity, or the loss of hope. But sometimes, survivors find something too. A new sense of purpose. A deeper understanding of themselves. A reconnection with others. A determination to rebuild. When you know what your protagonist will have gained or lost by the final page, you can make sure every earlier moment points toward that evolution. This is how you create character arcs that feel natural and satisfying instead of forced.

When you're creating your disaster aftermath, think about the physical world too. What does it look like? Smell like? Sound like? A flooded city has a different feel from a scorched wasteland. A frozen landscape after a sudden ice age has a different atmosphere from a city crumbled by earthquakes. Bring that sensory detail into your ending and you'll leave readers with a lasting, vivid impression. Readers may not remember every plot twist you throw at them, but they will remember the way the empty streets glowed under a blood-red sunset. They will remember the way your characters trudged across a cracked bridge hanging over nothing. These are the images that stick in the mind and soul.

Starting with the end doesn't mean you have to lock every detail in stone. Sometimes, the story surprises you as you write, and that's part of the fun. But having a strong vision of the emotional and physical state of the world after the disaster gives you a compass. Even if you take a few unexpected detours, you'll still know where you're headed. And if you're using ChatGPT to help with brainstorming or scene generation, you can be much more precise with your prompts. Instead of asking for "chaotic scenes during a hurricane," you can ask for "a final moment where the protagonist sees their destroyed childhood home and finds their old, soaked diary still intact." That level of specificity gives your AI assistant a much better sense of what you're aiming for, which saves you time and keeps your momentum strong.

There's also a huge emotional advantage to starting with the aftermath. It puts you in the right mindset. Instead of writing with the gleeful destruction of a Michael Bay movie, you write with the aching heart of someone who knows what's about to be lost. Your scenes of action and chaos will feel different when you're carrying that emotional weight with you. They won't just be explosions and noise; they'll be the last moments of normal life shattering. They'll be the last laugh before the silence. Writing with that sense of impending loss gives your story depth and poignancy, even in its wildest scenes.

Sometimes the most powerful aftermaths are quiet ones. One survivor planting seeds in a burned field. A small group lighting candles in an abandoned subway station. A single radio transmission crackling into the darkness. Other times, they're brutal: mass graves, empty cities, desperate people turning against each other. The tone depends on the story you want to tell. But either way, the ending needs to feel like it *means* something. Readers should be left with a feeling that the journey mattered, that the characters' struggles mattered, that even amid destruction, there was something worth fighting for—or worth mourning.

And the beauty of disaster fiction is that the "aftermath" can be both an end and a beginning. Maybe your story ends with the first green sprout pushing up through cracked pavement. Maybe it ends with the first plane flying overhead in months, signaling that civilization is coming back. Maybe it ends with your protagonist walking away from the ruins, carrying only memories. The final scene doesn't have to close every question. But it should satisfy the emotional journey you promised at the start.

When you write knowing where you're going, every sentence feels more urgent. Every scene feels like it matters. And when you finally reach the last line, it won't just be an ending—it will be a culmination, an echo of every beat that came before it. Readers will feel the weight of the journey in their bones.

So before you dive into describing collapsing skyscrapers or frantic evacuations, take a quiet moment. Close your eyes. Picture the ruins. Picture who's standing there. Picture what they've lost—and what tiny, stubborn ember of hope they still carry. Picture the world they'll have to rebuild, or the one they'll have to wander through alone. Start with the end. Start with the silence after the storm. And from that silence, build your story.

Reverse Engineering Your Disaster Plot

Once you have a vivid picture of your disaster story's aftermath, it's time to reverse-engineer everything that leads to it. Think of it like walking backward through the ruins, asking yourself at every step, how did this happen? What decisions, what failures, what accidents led to this point? Reverse engineering your disaster plot means starting at the end and unraveling the story piece by piece until you find your way back to the beginning. It's one of the most powerful techniques you can use, especially when writing quickly, because it turns the overwhelming chaos of plotting into a clear sequence of cause and effect.

Most writers are trained to think forward: what happens next, what happens next, what happens next. But disaster stories benefit when you flip that around. Instead of trying to build momentum blindly, you already know where your momentum needs to go. You have an emotional target. Now your job is to build the chain of events that makes that emotional target feel inevitable. It's a little like setting up a row of dominoes—not randomly, but with careful, deliberate spacing so that when you tip the first one, the whole story falls perfectly into place.

Start by asking what your protagonist looks like at the end. Who have they become? Are they broken, hardened, reborn, lost? Have they lost everything, or have they salvaged something precious from the destruction? Once you know that emotional state, you can start figuring out what experiences they needed to go through to get there. If your survivor is clinging to hope at the end, maybe earlier they had to see hope almost die. If they're isolated at the end, maybe earlier they had to watch their community fall apart. If they're filled with guilt, maybe earlier they had to make a decision that sacrificed others for survival. Plotting backward from the emotional outcome ensures your story has a real arc instead of just a series of random disaster scenes.

Next, think about the physical state of the world at the end. If the city is flooded and abandoned, how did that happen? Was there a government cover-up about the severity of the hurricane? Did the evacuation plans fail? Were the levees too old and weak? Did panic spread faster than help could arrive? Building your plot in reverse means tracing the failure points. You get to show not just the disaster itself but all the little human mistakes, blind spots, and betrayals that made it worse. Disaster stories aren't just about bad luck; they're about the cracks that were already there before the final blow hit.

As you work backward, keep asking yourself "why" and "how." Why did the protagonist end up alone? How did the fire spread so fast? Why were the rescue teams too late? How did the disease mutate out of control? Every answer you come up with becomes a new scene, a new layer of tension, a new twist. And because you're building from the ending, every choice you make feeds the emotional and thematic core of the story instead of pulling away from it. Your story stops being a random collection of events and starts being a tightly woven inevitability.

This method also helps you avoid one of the biggest problems in disaster fiction: pacing that flatlines. If you plot forward without a clear end goal, you can accidentally create a story where all the big action happens too early, leaving the second half to limp along without tension. But if you reverse-engineer, you naturally shape the rise and fall of the narrative. You know when to escalate the stakes. You know when the protagonist needs to face their darkest hour. You know when a temporary victory needs to collapse into a bigger defeat. You build the rhythm intentionally, like a composer building to a final crescendo.

Let's say your ending image is a woman standing alone at the edge of a flooded city, holding the only surviving photograph of her family. To reverse-engineer that, you might decide she was part of a group at the start—a neighborhood evacuation team trying to help each other. Maybe in the middle of the story, a betrayal splits the group apart. Maybe she tries to save someone she loves and fails. Maybe a series of mistakes—trusting the wrong people, believing the worst was over—gradually strip everything away from her until she's the last one left. Each beat flows logically into the next because you're constantly asking: how do we get from hope to devastation?

Working backward also lets you embed foreshadowing effortlessly. If you know the ending is isolation and loss, you can plant seeds early—lines of dialogue, small decisions, symbolic images—that hint at the outcome without giving it away. When readers reach the final scenes, they'll feel the payoff of those earlier moments even if they didn't consciously notice them at the time. Foreshadowing built from the ending backward feels organic, not forced, because you're planting it with knowledge of where the story must land.

And if you're using ChatGPT to help you brainstorm or fill in scenes, reverse engineering makes your prompts sharper and more effective. Instead of asking for generic disaster ideas, you can ask for specific moments that bridge emotional and physical shifts. You can prompt for "a scene where a rescue attempt fails disastrously because of a bad radio transmission," or "a confrontation between two survivors over dwindling supplies that leads to a permanent fracture." ChatGPT can become your scene generator, your conflict builder, your pacing assistant—all guided by your crystal-clear vision of the ending.

Another bonus of reverse engineering your disaster plot is that it keeps the protagonist's emotional journey front and center. Disaster fiction can sometimes get lost in spectacle, with characters becoming tiny figures overwhelmed by explosions and floods. But if you build from the emotional end first, you're always pulling the story back to the character. Every collapse matters because it hits *them*. Every betrayal hurts because it costs *them*. Every moment of courage shines because it comes from *them*. Your protagonist becomes the lens through which the reader experiences the disaster, and that personal connection is what makes readers care about more than just the falling buildings.

Of course, you can leave room for discovery. You might find new emotional beats or surprising twists as you write, and that's part of the creative magic. But having the broad strokes of the ending and major turning points in place gives you freedom to explore without getting lost. It's like knowing you're hiking toward a mountain peak—you can take different paths, but you always know which direction to head.

When you reverse-engineer well, writing a disaster story becomes less about guessing what should happen next and more about unveiling what *must* happen next. It becomes less about inventing scenes out of thin air and more about pulling them out of the logical consequences of your world and your characters. It makes your storytelling feel natural, inevitable, powerful. And when you're racing the clock to write a complete disaster narrative in one day, that kind of clarity is priceless.

So before you start writing in a frantic rush of falling debris and panicked screams, take a breath. Picture your final scene again. Walk backward through the rubble. Find the trail of choices, failures, triumphs, and heartbreaks that led there. Build your story backward until it stretches like a tightrope from beginning to end, humming with tension and possibility. Then, when you sit down to write forward, it will feel like you're tracing fire through a fuse you already carefully laid down. It will feel inevitable. It will feel alive. And your readers, whether they realize it or not, will feel it too.

Finding the Perfect Catastrophe: Natural vs. Man-Made Disasters

Every disaster story starts with a bang—or a tremor, or a warning siren, or a strange silence falling over the world. Before you can get into writing scenes of survival, betrayal, courage, or heartbreak, you need to choose your engine: the disaster itself. The kind of catastrophe you pick isn't just a backdrop; it shapes the entire emotional DNA of the story. It decides what your characters will face, how they'll react, and what parts of human nature get pushed to the surface. Picking the right disaster isn't about finding the flashiest or deadliest one. It's about finding the catastrophe that fits the kind of emotional journey you want to tell.

The first big decision to make is whether your disaster is natural or man-made. It might seem like a small choice, but it actually changes everything. Natural disasters—hurricanes, earthquakes, floods, wildfires, tsunamis—come with a very specific emotional texture. They feel indifferent. Impersonal. A hurricane doesn't hate you. An earthquake isn't out to get you. Nature simply moves, and you just happen to be in the way. This makes stories about natural disasters deeply existential. They force your characters to confront their own fragility, their own insignificance. Survival becomes a quiet, humbling act of endurance rather than a battle against an evil force. It's man versus nature, but really, it's man versus the limits of human control.

When you pick a natural disaster, you're often writing a story where your characters have to find meaning in chaos that has no meaning. They might blame themselves for not evacuating sooner. They might rage at the sky or the sea. But in the end, there's no villain to defeat. There's only survival, adaptation, and resilience. The drama comes from how people turn toward each other—or against each other—when the natural world strips away the illusions of safety.

On the other hand, man-made disasters bring a different emotional current. Explosions, nuclear meltdowns, viral outbreaks caused by human error, cyberattacks that crash infrastructure, chemical spills that poison whole towns—these stories carry a heavy load of blame, guilt, and betrayal. Someone made a mistake. Someone cut corners. Someone lied. In man-made disasters, your characters aren't just fighting to survive; they're often fighting to understand why it happened, who's responsible, and whether justice or revenge is even possible.

Choosing a man-made disaster often creates sharper interpersonal conflict. The survivors aren't just at the mercy of forces beyond their control—they're angry. They have grudges. They're suspicious of each other. Maybe someone in their group caused the disaster without realizing it. Maybe help isn't coming because someone high up decided to save themselves first. There's a layer of moral rot underneath the physical destruction, and it colors every interaction. Man-made disaster stories can be deeply political, psychological, and personal. They can feel like horror stories where the monster is human weakness, greed, or arrogance.

Sometimes, of course, the line blurs. A hurricane made worse by climate change. A wildfire started by a neglected power line. A viral outbreak made deadlier by bureaucratic failure. Blended disasters—part natural, part man-made—offer rich ground for complex stories. They let you explore both the helplessness of facing nature's fury and the rage of knowing human choices made it worse. These are the stories where your protagonist might struggle not just to survive the physical danger but to grapple with betrayal, guilt, and a shattered trust in the systems meant to protect them.

When you're choosing your catastrophe, think about the emotional tone you want your story to have. Natural disasters tend to produce stories that are more about endurance, community, grief, and rebirth. They lend themselves to quieter, more introspective endings. Man-made disasters often drive stories full of suspicion, bitterness, and moral reckoning. They lend themselves to bitter ironies, revenge arcs, or hard-won justice. Blended disasters give you a full palette to paint with, letting you shift between awe, rage, sorrow, and hope.

Also, consider the scale of the disaster. A global pandemic obviously has a different feeling than a small-town chemical spill. A city-wide blackout feels different from a nuclear winter. The bigger the disaster, the more likely your story will have themes of societal collapse, leadership failure, and civilization in free fall. The smaller the disaster, the more likely you'll be telling a tight, character-driven story about personal survival and relationships under pressure. There's no right or wrong scale—it depends on whether you want to zoom in close on one family huddling together or pull back to show nations falling apart.

Another factor to think about is immediacy. Some disasters strike like lightning—a tornado, an earthquake, an explosion. Others unfold slowly but unstoppably—a drought, a pandemic, a nuclear meltdown. Fast disasters force quick reactions and split-second decisions. They're great for stories packed with frantic action, improvisation, and raw panic. Slow disasters give you time to show the psychological decay, the simmering tensions, the gradual erosion of hope. They're perfect for stories that build dread and despair step by step until the final collapse.

Ask yourself, too, what kind of setting excites you. A raging wildfire in a remote forest. A city slowly flooding after days of relentless rain. A quarantined hospital during the outbreak of a new plague. A crumbling space station after a catastrophic software failure. Different disasters naturally fit different environments. The more you can connect your disaster to a vivid, sensory-rich setting, the more immersive and gripping your story will feel. Setting isn't just background—it's the atmosphere that gets into your characters' lungs, burns their skin, freezes their hands. The disaster and the setting should feel like they belong together.

One more thing: make sure you personally feel something about the disaster you choose. If you're fascinated by earthquakes, if you're terrified of pandemics, if you've always been haunted by images of tsunamis, trust that instinct. The emotional charge you bring to the disaster will infect the writing. Readers can feel when a writer is genuinely invested. Your fear, awe, anger, sorrow—they will bleed onto the page and make the story come alive.

Choosing the perfect catastrophe is about more than just the spectacle. It's about matching the disaster to the emotional journey you want to take your characters—and your readers—on. Whether it's a sudden explosion, a slow suffocation, a merciless fire, or a hidden betrayal, the right disaster becomes more than just an event. It becomes the crucible that reveals who your characters really are. It becomes the test that shows what they'll fight for, what they'll sacrifice, and whether, in the end, they can still find a way to survive—not just physically, but emotionally.

When you pick the right catastrophe, every scene feels sharper. Every decision feels heavier. Every victory feels harder won. And when your readers finally reach the end, they'll feel like they've survived something too. They'll remember not just the disaster, but the heartbeat of humanity that carried them through it.

So take a moment. Picture the world you want to break. Listen for the rumble under the earth, the crackle of flames, the whine of sirens, the low hum of something going terribly, terribly wrong. Choose your disaster. Own it. And get ready to tell a story that will leave readers breathless, haunted, and, somehow, a little bit hopeful.

Apocalypse Now: Exploring End-of-the-World Scenarios

There's disaster, and then there's *apocalypse*. A disaster story might wreck a town, ruin a region, even shake a nation, but the world itself survives. The system wobbles but doesn't fall. Life goes on for most people, even if it changes forever for the characters in your story. But when you step into apocalypse territory, you're not just setting fire to a house—you're pulling the whole world down around it. An apocalyptic story doesn't just describe damage. It redefines life itself. Survival becomes not a temporary state, but the only state. Normal is dead. Rules are gone. Humanity itself is up for grabs.

When you're exploring end-of-the-world scenarios for your story, the stakes shift dramatically. You're no longer writing about isolated tragedy. You're writing about extinction, rebirth, reinvention. Your characters aren't just trying to make it through the night. They're trying to find meaning in a reality where everything they grew up believing has crumbled. Apocalypse stories are about survival, but even more than that, they're about transformation—whether that transformation is physical, social, emotional, or spiritual.

Choosing an apocalypse means choosing how much to destroy and how much to leave behind. It's about deciding what the world looks like when the dust clears, and what kinds of lives are even possible afterward. Is it a world where a lucky few huddle underground while the surface burns? Is it a wandering nomad landscape of scavengers and survivors? Is it a rigid society clinging to strict new rules in a desperate bid to rebuild order? Or is it a free-for-all, where anarchy rules and trust is the rarest commodity?

First, you have to choose your apocalypse event. The classic options still work for a reason. Nuclear war, pandemic, climate catastrophe, asteroid impact, ecological collapse, rogue AI takeover—each one brings its own flavor of destruction. Nuclear war gives you radiation wastelands, poisoned water, and ruined cities. Pandemics give you empty streets, quarantine zones, a creeping invisible death. Climate disasters create drowned coastlines, desertification, storms that reshape continents. Asteroids wipe the slate clean in an instant, and maybe the story picks up generations later, in a rebuilt world that barely remembers what came before.

Then there are the slower apocalypses, the ones that don't come from a single blast or outbreak but from a slow erosion of the systems that keep society together. Economic collapse that triggers mass famine. Political collapse that leads to widespread civil wars. Environmental degradation that quietly makes parts of the planet unlivable, inch by inch. These slow apocalypses can be even more terrifying because they feel so real, so plausible. They feel like they could happen tomorrow—or maybe are already happening.

One of the most important things to remember when building an apocalyptic story is that it's not just about what's gone. It's about what's left. No matter how shattered the world is, some things survive. People survive. Hope survives. Greed survives. Love survives. Violence survives. Memory survives. What you choose to let linger in the ruins tells the reader what kind of story you're really telling. Is it a story of final collapse, or of stubborn rebirth? Is it a warning, or a prayer?

Apocalypse stories give you incredible freedom to reshape society. Without governments, economies, or laws as we know them, you can invent new systems. Maybe cities are ruled by warlords who hoard clean water. Maybe survivors form tight-knit clans that live by strict honor codes. Maybe science and technology are revered like ancient magic because so few people remember how they actually work. Or maybe it's even darker—maybe people devolve into pure survival mode, turning against each other, abandoning morality in the name of staying alive.

The psychological weight of apocalypse stories is heavier, too. It's not just the terror of the initial collapse. It's the long, grinding despair of daily survival. Characters have to wrestle with what survival means when it's stripped of comfort, community, and hope. Do they survive just to see another miserable day? Or can they find—or create—some new reason to keep going? Some apocalypse stories are ultimately about rediscovering meaning in a meaningless world. Others are about the triumph of cruelty and cynicism. Others are about the slow rebuilding of something better, brick by painful brick.

You also have a choice about how much of the old world still lingers. In some stories, like *The Road* by Cormac McCarthy, civilization is utterly smashed—nothing recognizable remains. In others, like *Station Eleven* by Emily St. John Mandel, fragments of the old world persist in memory, artifacts, rituals. The echoes of the lost world can be a haunting counterpoint to the new reality your characters live in. They can mourn it. They can try to recreate it. They can reject it. How your characters relate to the past gives your story emotional depth.

Tone is another huge decision in apocalyptic writing. Is your apocalypse grim, brutal, and merciless? Is it dreamy, surreal, a slow drift into oblivion? Is it hopeful, showing humanity's resilience? Are there flashes of beauty amid the decay? Is it a world where a dying planet still manages to throw up a few desperate flowers? Your tone colors everything—how characters speak, how they act, how they treat each other, what moments you focus on. Two apocalypse stories can have the same surface events—cities falling, food vanishing, lawlessness spreading—but feel completely different depending on the emotional lens you choose.

And let's not forget scale. Is the apocalypse total, or partial? Maybe one continent collapses while another holds on. Maybe humanity survives in isolated pockets, connected only by dangerous journeys through wastelands. Maybe the apocalypse isn't complete—maybe it's still unfolding, and your characters are caught in the middle, watching civilization decay in real time. Partial apocalypses open up room for stories about contrast—between the dying and the surviving, the chaos and the order, the forgotten and the remembered.

If you're using ChatGPT to brainstorm your apocalypse scenario, you can be as broad or specific as you like. You can prompt for general world-building ideas—"describe a post-climate-collapse America"—or for specific moments—"generate a scene where a wandering survivor finds an abandoned library filled with relics of the old world." The more you anchor your prompts in emotional goals (grief, awe, terror, hope), the more vivid and useful the outputs will be.

It's also important to think about the personal apocalypse within the global one. The end of the world isn't just something that happens "out there." It happens inside your characters too. The loss of a child. The betrayal by a friend. The crumbling of faith. The realization that they are no longer who they used to be. These personal disasters make the larger catastrophe hit harder because readers experience it through human eyes, not just through images of broken skylines and empty streets.

When you write an apocalyptic story, you're stepping into a deep tradition that stretches back thousands of years. Every culture has its end-of-the-world myths—floods, fires, battles between gods, final winters. We've always been fascinated by how it all might end. And just as often, we've been fascinated by what comes after the end. Your disaster story can be bleak, but it can also be beautiful. It can mourn the lost world while dreaming of a better one. It can rage against human folly or celebrate human endurance. The apocalypse is not just an ending; it's a canvas. It's a chance to tear down everything and ask, *what will you build instead?*

So don't be afraid to go big. Don't be afraid to end everything. Collapse the buildings. Dry up the rivers. Blot out the sun if you have to. But after the world ends, show us something that matters. Show us a spark in the ashes. Show us the stubborn beating heart of survival, still fighting, still dreaming, still alive.

Brainstorming the Big Event with ChatGPT's Help

Now that you've thought about disasters and apocalypses, you're probably feeling the creative pressure building. You know you want to blow something up, wipe something out, or tear something down. But what exactly? What's the Big Event that sets your story into motion? What tips the first domino and sends your characters scrambling for survival? That's where brainstorming comes in—and that's where ChatGPT becomes one of the best creative tools you'll ever use.

One of the biggest mistakes writers make when trying to create a disaster story quickly is overthinking the initial event. They feel like they have to come up with something totally original, something no one's ever seen before. But the truth is, originality isn't about inventing an entirely new kind of earthquake or virus or societal collapse. It's about taking a familiar disaster and layering it with unique characters, perspectives, emotions, and consequences. The Big Event doesn't have to be something the world's never heard of. It just has to matter deeply to the people experiencing it.

When you're brainstorming your Big Event, the first thing to understand is that it's a launchpad, not the whole story. The flood, the fire, the outbreak—that's just the opening salvo. What you build on top of it is where the magic happens. So instead of trying to invent the craziest disaster possible, focus on creating an event that feels real, urgent, and full of storytelling possibilities. And that's where ChatGPT can help you move faster and think wider than you might on your own.

Start by prompting simple ideas. Ask ChatGPT for a list of disaster events if you're stuck. You can be as broad or specific as you want. Maybe you ask for "twenty unique natural disaster scenarios" or "ten futuristic man-made catastrophes that could collapse a city." Let the AI throw a bunch of ideas at you without worrying about whether they're perfect. You're brainstorming, not committing. Sometimes seeing a bad idea is what jolts you into thinking of a good one. Sometimes a half-baked suggestion plants the seed for something brilliant.

Once you have a few general disaster ideas, start adding layers. Ask ChatGPT to imagine what would happen next. If you pick a mega-earthquake, ask it to describe how the local government fails to respond. If you pick a solar flare that knocks out power globally, ask what happens after a month without electricity. You're not just brainstorming events—you're brainstorming consequences. The best Big Events aren't static. They evolve, they spiral, they trigger chain reactions. The initial disaster should be like lighting a fuse that burns hotter and faster with every chapter.

You can also prompt ChatGPT for character-driven ideas around the event. For example, instead of just focusing on a virus outbreak, ask for "a personal story of a nurse who becomes trapped in a quarantined hospital during a sudden viral epidemic." Or if you're writing about a flood, ask for "the story of a father trying to get his children to safety across a city submerged by rising waters." The disaster creates the world, but the human story gives it soul. Combining an event with a specific, emotional character struggle turns a news headline into a gripping narrative.

Another powerful use of ChatGPT is to brainstorm "what went wrong" moments. Most disaster stories aren't about the disaster itself; they're about how human mistakes make it worse. Ask for ways evacuation plans fail. Ask for ideas about how panic spreads faster than the danger. Ask for ways people react badly under pressure. A disaster event feels bigger and scarier when it's clear that human error, arrogance, fear, or selfishness has made survival even harder.

If you're feeling ambitious, you can even layer multiple disasters together—but be careful. It's easy to overload your story if you try to cram too many catastrophic events into one narrative. The trick is to make sure each layer logically follows from the previous one. A massive earthquake might rupture a nuclear power plant. A global pandemic might cause supply chain collapses that trigger famines and riots. You don't just want random bad things happening; you want a believable, horrifying chain of cause and effect.

When brainstorming with ChatGPT, don't be afraid to go weird. Sometimes the most memorable disaster stories have an unusual twist. Maybe it's not just a volcano eruption—it's a volcano that releases a mysterious ancient virus frozen in the ice. Maybe it's not just a solar flare—it's a solar flare that awakens long-dormant AI systems buried in old government facilities. Let yourself play. The brainstorming phase isn't about setting limits. It's about seeing how many wild possibilities you can put on the table.

You can also brainstorm based on the setting you want to explore. If you know you want to set your story in the Arctic, brainstorm disasters that would fit there. If you know you want to set your story on a crumbling space station, brainstorm events that could turn an isolated satellite into a deathtrap. The setting and the disaster should feel like they belong to each other. ChatGPT can help you brainstorm these tailored disaster scenarios quickly, giving you more time to pick the one that really sparks your imagination.

And don't forget to brainstorm emotional beats alongside the physical disaster. Ask for "five moments where characters must make heartbreaking choices during a flood" or "three ways a group could betray each other during a pandemic lockdown." The Big Event might be the hook that draws readers in, but it's the emotional stakes that make them stay. Disaster is just the beginning. What matters most is how people change, what they fight for, and what they lose.

One of the best parts of using ChatGPT for disaster brainstorming is how fast you can generate material. In the time it would take you to second-guess one idea on your own, you can generate twenty possibilities. Not all of them will be winners, but you only need one great spark to start your fire. You're not looking for a perfectly polished plot at this stage—you're looking for raw energy. The Big Event should make you feel something immediately. Fear. Excitement. Curiosity. Grief. If it doesn't move you, it won't move your readers either.

Once you have a disaster idea that makes your heart race a little, lock it in. Commit to it for this story. You can always explore other ideas later, but part of writing fast is not letting yourself drown in endless "what if" questions. Trust your instincts. Trust the emotional pull. The story wants to be told. Your job is to grab that Big Event and start building the human drama that will carry it from first page to last.

The Big Event isn't the end of brainstorming, of course. It's just the beginning. After this, you'll brainstorm the characters, the first scenes, the turning points, the climax. But everything grows from that initial disaster. Choose one. Own it. Build a world around it. And get ready—because the real writing is about to begin.

The Butterfly Effect: How a Small Spark Ignites a Disaster

When most people imagine a disaster story, they picture the big moment—the skyscraper falling, the dam breaking, the firestorm rolling across the hills. But what's often more powerful, more chilling, and far more real, is the tiny spark that sets it all off. The small, seemingly insignificant moment that, if it had gone just a little differently, might have averted the entire catastrophe. In disaster storytelling, this is called the Butterfly Effect—the idea that small causes can have massive, world-altering consequences. And if you understand how to use it, you can turn a good disaster story into a great one.

The Butterfly Effect gets its name from the famous metaphor that a butterfly flapping its wings in Brazil might ultimately set off a tornado in Texas. It's the idea that complex systems—like weather, societies, or economies—are so sensitive that tiny changes at the beginning can trigger huge outcomes later on. In disaster fiction, it means that your Big Event doesn't have to start with an explosion. It can start with a missed warning. A bad decision. A simple mistake. And from that small moment, everything unravels.

When you think about your disaster story, ask yourself: what's the tiny thing that goes wrong first? Maybe it's a technician skipping a maintenance check on a dam. Maybe it's a scientist ignoring a strange test result. Maybe it's a politician downplaying an early warning. Maybe it's a single person deciding not to evacuate because they think it's just another false alarm. Small actions—or inactions—can build tension in ways that big, obvious moments can't. Readers feel a creeping dread because they recognize how fragile the world really is. They realize how easily it could happen to them.

One of the most powerful ways to use the Butterfly Effect in your story is to show the human side of the spark. Make it relatable. Maybe the technician skipped the maintenance check because his daughter was sick and he rushed home. Maybe the politician downplayed the warning because they were terrified of causing public panic. Maybe the scientist ignored the test result because it would have meant blowing up years of careful research. If you show that the initial mistake wasn't made out of malice, but out of fear, love, pride, or exhaustion, your readers will feel a gut-punch when the disaster unfolds. They'll understand how small, human flaws can cascade into unstoppable destruction.

You can also use the Butterfly Effect structurally. Instead of dropping readers into chaos immediately, you can start with ordinary life—showing the small decisions stacking up, unnoticed. A missed phone call. A computer glitch. A truck carrying chemicals taking a wrong turn. Readers will start to pick up on the little signs that something's wrong before the characters do. That slow-build suspense is incredibly effective in disaster fiction. It makes the moment the disaster finally strikes feel both shocking and inevitable.

Another way to build this into your story is by showing characters dismissing early signs. In real life, people are incredibly good at convincing themselves that everything is fine. The strange news reports. The weather patterns that don't make sense. The unusual illness spreading faster than expected. People want to believe that things will stay normal. In your story, show that denial. Show people rationalizing away the early warnings. Then, when the disaster hits, it feels all the more tragic because you can see how close they were to preventing it if only they had listened, if only they had acted sooner.

If you're using ChatGPT to help brainstorm these small sparks, try prompting for minor, human-scale mistakes that could lead to bigger disasters. You can ask for "ten small errors that could lead to a dam collapse" or "five overlooked warnings before a pandemic outbreak." This will help you layer your story with tiny moments of tension before the big catastrophe arrives. And layering is key. One small mistake probably isn't enough to destroy a city. But five small mistakes, building on each other, can be absolutely catastrophic.

One of the other great things about using the Butterfly Effect is that it lets you keep surprising your readers. Disaster stories can sometimes fall into predictable patterns—big threat, big reaction, big survival moment. But if you build your plot around small, cascading failures, your story becomes less predictable. Maybe a character thinks they've fixed one small problem, only to realize it's triggered an even bigger one. Maybe a survivor's attempt to help someone unintentionally causes a new collapse. Every action becomes fraught with potential consequences, keeping readers on edge.

The Butterfly Effect also makes your world feel more interconnected. A disaster isn't just one thing going wrong. It's a hundred little things failing in sequence. The power outage that shuts down emergency communication. The traffic jam that blocks evacuation routes. The misinformation that causes people to stay when they should flee. When you build these layers, your disaster feels massive without having to invent bigger and bigger explosions. The collapse feels organic, inevitable, and terrifyingly plausible.

And don't underestimate the emotional weight of these small sparks. When your characters realize that the apocalypse they're living through started with something so tiny, it adds a layer of tragic irony. Maybe the protagonist discovers that if they had made one different choice—called someone back, sent one extra warning, double-checked one system—they might have saved lives. Maybe they carry that guilt with them. Maybe they find a way to forgive themselves. Either way, it makes their journey richer and more heartbreaking.

Sometimes the Butterfly Effect can even be literal in your story. Maybe your characters piece together the chain of failures after the disaster. Maybe a key moment late in the story is realizing what tiny thing started it all—and that realization changes how they view survival. Maybe they decide to rebuild differently. Maybe they realize that some things are truly beyond human control. Or maybe they vow to never repeat the mistakes that led to the fall. Knowing the origin of the collapse gives your story a feeling of closure, even if the world can never go back to the way it was.

When you write the Butterfly Effect into your disaster story, you create a deep, resonant feeling of tragedy and inevitability. You show that the end of the world didn't come from one evil villain twirling a moustache. It came from ordinary people, doing ordinary things, with unintended consequences. It came from fear, pride, laziness, denial—small human flaws that, together, tipped the world over the edge.

Readers feel that. They recognize it. It makes the story scarier because it feels so real. It makes the characters' struggles more heartbreaking because it could have been different. And it makes the moments of survival more meaningful because they're fighting against a collapse that was seeded long before the first wall cracked or the first siren sounded.

So as you build your disaster story, don't just think about the explosion at the end. Think about the butterfly at the beginning. Think about the small moment, the overlooked detail, the dismissed warning, the missed opportunity. Plant it early. Let it flap its wings. Let the disaster grow naturally from that tiny, almost invisible moment. And when your readers finally stand with your characters amid the ruins, they'll feel the full weight of everything that was lost—and everything that might still be saved.

The Hero's Journey in a Collapsing World

If there's one storytelling structure that survives almost every disaster, it's the Hero's Journey. Even when the world is falling apart—maybe *especially* when it's falling apart—the human heart craves stories of growth, change, challenge, and triumph. The Hero's Journey isn't just for fantasy or adventure stories. It fits disaster fiction perfectly because a world-ending event naturally pushes ordinary people into extraordinary transformations. When everything familiar is stripped away, the question becomes: who will you become? That's the essence of the Hero's Journey, and that's why it's so powerful inside a collapsing world.

Let's start by remembering what the Hero's Journey really is at its core. It's not about slaying dragons or finding magic swords. It's about facing the unknown, being tested, failing, learning, changing, and ultimately becoming something more. In a disaster story, the unknown isn't a mystical land—it's the new, dangerous, broken world that appears the moment the disaster hits. And the tests aren't mythical—they're brutal, physical, emotional, and moral challenges that determine who survives and who doesn't, and more importantly, who grows and who crumbles.

Your disaster story's hero doesn't need to be a traditional "hero" at all. In fact, the best disaster protagonists often start as ordinary people. A schoolteacher. A delivery driver. A nurse. A teenager. Someone who didn't wake up that morning expecting to be thrown into chaos. That ordinariness makes their journey more relatable. It makes readers root for them because we can see ourselves in them. The Hero's Journey in disaster fiction is about survival, but it's also about transformation—about becoming someone who *deserves* to survive.

In the classic Hero's Journey, the story begins in the Ordinary World. For your disaster story, this is life before everything falls apart. Even if the cracks are already showing, life still has its routines, its illusions of stability. Maybe your protagonist is dealing with mundane problems: work stress, family issues, personal regrets. The point is, they're not ready for what's coming. And they don't know yet that they're going to have to change or be destroyed.

The next stage is the Call to Adventure—the moment when the disaster strikes, or the warning signs become undeniable. This could be a siren, a news report, the ground starting to shake, the first wave of illness hitting the hospital. Suddenly, the world tilts, and the protagonist is forced to choose: ignore the danger and cling to the old world, or step into the chaos and fight to survive. Some characters refuse the call at first, clinging to denial, but the best disaster stories show that refusal isn't an option for long. The disaster doesn't wait politely for people to be ready.

Meeting the Mentor is a stage that translates beautifully into disaster fiction. In traditional stories, the mentor might be a wizard or a wise elder. In your disaster story, it might be a seasoned firefighter, a survivalist neighbor, an old doctor who's seen too much, or even a wise child who understands the new rules faster than the adults. Mentors in disaster stories might not even survive long—but their lessons live on, shaping how the protagonist grows.

Crossing the First Threshold happens when your character steps fully into the new world. This could be evacuating their home, venturing into a flooded city, leaving the false safety of a shelter that's about to collapse. It's the point of no return. After this, there's no going back to normal. There's only forward, into danger and change.

Tests, Allies, and Enemies is where disaster stories shine. Every survival decision is a test. Every new person encountered could be an ally—or a threat. In the ruins of the old world, trust becomes precious and betrayal becomes lethal. Characters are constantly forced to evaluate others and themselves. They might find unexpected allies: the neighbor they barely knew, the stranger who turns out to have a good heart, the enemy who isn't as cruel as they first seemed. And they might discover that the real enemy isn't the disaster itself—it's fear, greed, selfishness, despair.

The Approach to the Inmost Cave in disaster fiction is often a moment of reflection or confrontation with a deeper fear. Maybe it's when the protagonist realizes they can't save everyone. Maybe it's when they face the death of a loved one. Maybe it's when they have to decide whether to sacrifice others to survive. This is a turning point—not a physical battle, but a psychological one. It's where the protagonist must confront the reality of what they're willing to do to live.

The Ordeal is the climactic moment of highest danger and tension. In a disaster story, this could be a final escape attempt, a last stand against looters, a desperate search for a lost family member before the next catastrophe hits. It's the moment when death feels most certain. And it's the moment when the protagonist either breaks—or breaks through.

Reward, in disaster stories, isn't always treasure or triumph. Sometimes it's something small but profound: finding a safe place to rest, reuniting with someone thought lost, reclaiming a sense of humanity, forgiveness, or hope. The world may still be broken, but the protagonist has earned something real.

The Road Back often involves a new challenge or a new disaster. Maybe the place they thought was safe isn't. Maybe survival demands another terrible decision. Maybe the final escape isn't easy. In disaster fiction, the collapse keeps pushing, testing whether the character's transformation was real or just a survival mask.

The Resurrection is the final, deepest test. The protagonist must use everything they've learned. They must face death one more time—and this time, who they have become matters more than what they have. Courage, compassion, strength, resilience—the real survival traits—are proven here. It's not just about living. It's about living *as someone better.*

And finally, the Return with the Elixir. Your protagonist emerges from the disaster changed. They might return to a surviving community and become a leader. They might walk alone into the wilderness, carrying hard-won wisdom. They might simply sit down among the ruins, at peace with what's been lost and what's been saved. Whatever form it takes, the journey is complete. The old self is gone. A new self remains.

When you weave the Hero's Journey into your disaster story, you're not just writing about external survival. You're writing about internal rebirth. You're giving readers more than explosions and destruction—you're giving them a reason to care, a reason to hope, a reason to believe that even when the world falls apart, people can rise higher than they ever thought possible.

You don't have to follow every step of the Hero's Journey perfectly. You can skip, bend, twist, and improvise. Disaster fiction is messy, and that's part of its beauty. But keeping the emotional shape of the Hero's Journey in your mind will help you craft a story that feels powerful and satisfying, even amid chaos.

In the end, disaster doesn't just destroy—it reveals. And through that revelation, your hero is born.

Defining Your Protagonist: Survivors, Saviours, and Sinners

In any disaster story, the world falls apart. Buildings collapse, fires rage, societies crumble. But the real story—the one readers care about—is what happens to the people caught inside that collapse. And at the center of it all is your protagonist. When you're writing a disaster story, your main character isn't just someone who reacts to the world ending. They embody the emotional journey of the story itself. They're the human pulse inside the chaos. Choosing the right kind of protagonist means deciding how you want readers to experience the disaster—and what you want them to feel when they reach the final page.

Disaster fiction naturally sorts protagonists into three broad archetypes: survivors, saviors, and sinners. Each one offers a different lens through which to view collapse and survival. Each one pulls your story in a different emotional direction. And the fun part is, you don't have to pick just one archetype. You can mix them. You can let your character start as one and evolve into another. But knowing these basic types gives you a powerful starting point for building a character that fits the heart of your disaster narrative.

Let's start with survivors. The survivor protagonist is the most common and the most instinctively relatable. Their goal is simple: stay alive. They don't necessarily want to save the world. They don't necessarily want to lead others. They just want to make it through the next hour, the next day, the next catastrophe. Survivor characters are often ordinary people thrown into extraordinary circumstances. They have no special training, no secret weapons. What they have is grit, stubbornness, adaptability. They make mistakes. They panic. They lose hope sometimes. But they keep going. And in doing so, they capture something deeply human: the will to live, even when everything seems lost.

Writing a survivor protagonist means digging into emotional endurance. How do they cope when they realize no one is coming to save them? How do they deal with guilt if others don't make it? How do they change when survival demands hard, ugly choices? The best survivor stories aren't just about dodging falling debris—they're about finding a reason to keep breathing when it would be so much easier to give up. They're about transformation through suffering and perseverance. They're about the small, stubborn victories that feel bigger than any explosion.

Then there are the saviours. Saviours aren't content to survive. They have a mission. Maybe it's saving their family. Maybe it's leading a group of survivors to safety. Maybe it's protecting a city or rebuilding a broken world. Saviours carry a different kind of emotional weight. They take responsibility—not just for themselves, but for others. And that responsibility can be both noble and crushing. In disaster fiction, saviours are the ones organizing rescue efforts, risking their lives to pull strangers from rubble, making the terrible decisions about who gets a seat on the last helicopter and who doesn't.

Writing a saviour protagonist means exploring leadership under pressure. It means dealing with moral compromise, because no saviour can save everyone. It means exploring guilt, pride, anger, hope. Sometimes the saviour succeeds—but at what cost? Sometimes the saviour fails—and has to live with that failure. Saviours are compelling because they embody the human urge to protect, to rebuild, to believe that even when the world ends, something can still be saved.

And then there are the sinners. Disaster fiction is the perfect stage for flawed, selfish, desperate protagonists. Not every main character has to be noble. Some of the most fascinating disaster stories center on characters who lie, cheat, hoard, or abandon others in order to survive. These sinner protagonists might start off looking like villains—or at least cowards—but great disaster fiction gives them depth. Maybe they hoard supplies because they watched their family die of starvation once. Maybe they leave others behind because they're terrified of feeling helpless again. Maybe they're selfish until they're forced to confront what that selfishness costs.

Writing a sinner protagonist means leaning into moral ambiguity. It means making readers uncomfortable sometimes. It means challenging readers to ask themselves, what would *I* do? Would I be better? Would I be worse? And sinner characters offer huge potential for growth. A sinner can become a savior. A coward can become a hero. A selfish survivor can discover unexpected courage. Or they can fall even further and become the true antagonist of the story. The arc is wide open.

Of course, real people—and great characters—are rarely just one thing. A survivor might have moments of selfishness. A saviour might snap and abandon their group. A sinner might risk everything for a stranger at the last moment. These shifts create emotional complexity. They make your protagonist feel alive, unpredictable, painfully real. Disaster strips away the masks people wear. It reveals the raw, messy truth underneath. Your protagonist's journey is about how they respond to that revelation.

Another important factor when defining your disaster protagonist is motivation. Survival is a basic instinct, but layered motivations make for deeper stories. What *specifically* drives your character? Are they trying to get back to a child stranded across town? Are they trying to redeem themselves for a past mistake? Are they trying to protect a secret that, if revealed, could doom others? Are they just trying to keep a small group of strangers alive because nobody else will? The stronger and more personal the motivation, the more gripping the story becomes.

You also want to think about internal conflict. In disaster fiction, the external conflict is obvious—the world is ending. But the internal conflict is what really makes a story sing. A survivor might wrestle with fear and hopelessness. A saviour might wrestle with guilt and impossible choices. A sinner might wrestle with shame and redemption. These internal battles mirror the external collapse, creating resonance and emotional depth.

And don't forget vulnerability. Readers don't fall in love with perfection. They fall in love with characters who bleed, who cry, who make mistakes and get back up again. Your protagonist doesn't need to be fearless. They don't need to be a genius strategist. They just need to *feel*. Fear. Grief. Love. Regret. Rage. Hope. Vulnerability connects readers to characters faster and deeper than any amount of clever plotting.

If you're using ChatGPT to help shape your protagonist, you can prompt for ideas like "describe a reluctant survivor protagonist who slowly becomes a leader" or "describe a morally ambiguous character trying to survive a city under siege." You can also ask for character flaw ideas that would create tension during a disaster—fear of crowds, distrust of authority, a need for control, guilt over a past failure. Layering these traits into your protagonist makes their journey richer and more unpredictable.

The disaster itself can also shape your protagonist. In a flood, maybe your protagonist is someone with a deep fear of drowning. In a pandemic, maybe they're a germaphobe struggling with extreme isolation. In a warzone, maybe they're a pacifist forced to pick up a weapon. The disaster forces the protagonist to confront their deepest fears and contradictions. That collision—between who they were and who the world demands they become—is where your best scenes will come from.

Ultimately, defining your disaster protagonist comes down to one question: what part of humanity are you putting under the microscope? Endurance? Sacrifice? Betrayal? Hope? Fear? Whatever you want to explore, your protagonist will be the living, breathing vehicle for it. They will stumble through the ruins, carry the emotional weight, and give readers someone to cheer for, weep for, or even rage at.

In the end, the collapsing world isn't the real heart of your disaster story. The protagonist is. Through their eyes, readers will feel every aftershock, every betrayal, every fragile flicker of hope. Through their journey, readers will believe that even when everything burns, even when everything crumbles, something human and true can survive.

Crafting a Worthy Antagonist: Nature, People, or Fate

In most stories, the antagonist is easy to spot. It's the villain in the dark cloak, the rival scheming in the background, the monster lurking in the shadows. But disaster stories flip that dynamic. The enemy isn't always a person. Sometimes it's nature itself. Sometimes it's the slow grind of fate. Sometimes it's the people who were supposed to help—and sometimes it's the darkness inside the characters you trusted most. When you're writing a disaster story, crafting a worthy antagonist means thinking bigger, deeper, and sometimes crueler than a single villain could ever be.

One of the first questions to ask yourself is simple: what kind of story are you telling? If your disaster is purely natural—an earthquake, a tsunami, a wildfire—then nature itself becomes the antagonist. Not in the cartoonish sense of "the evil hurricane," but in the existential sense of a world that is terrifyingly indifferent to human survival. Nature doesn't hate your characters. It doesn't even notice them. It just moves, and crushes, and burns. Writing nature as an antagonist means making your characters feel small, vulnerable, and humbled. They can't reason with a tornado. They can't plead with a virus. They can only adapt, fight, endure—or fall.

When nature is your antagonist, the conflict becomes man versus the elements, but also man versus himself. Your characters will rage at the sky, scream into the winds, curse the earth for shaking—but deep down they'll know that there's no one to blame. That helplessness can be incredibly powerful. It forces your characters to find strength within themselves rather than triumphing over a traditional enemy. Survival becomes an act of defiance, a way of shouting, "I am still here," into a universe that doesn't care.

But maybe your disaster is made worse by people. Maybe it's a man-made catastrophe: a pandemic spread by negligence, a power grid collapse caused by corruption, a flood caused by a greedy developer cutting corners. In that case, people become the antagonists—either specific individuals or broken systems. The politician who ignores evacuation warnings. The corporation that lies about structural damage. The looters who prey on the weak when the lights go out. When people are the enemy, your story takes on a sharper edge. It's not just about surviving the elements—it's about surviving betrayal, greed, fear, and cruelty.

Writing human antagonists in a disaster story gives you room for incredible emotional tension. It's not enough that your characters are facing a collapsing bridge or a raging inferno—they're also facing the horrifying reality that other people might choose to save themselves at any cost. That a neighbor might steal their supplies. That a leader might abandon them. That trust might be the most dangerous gamble of all. These kinds of antagonists aren't just external threats—they force your characters to question their own values, to decide whether survival is worth the price of losing their humanity.

And then there's fate. Sometimes, in the best disaster stories, the real antagonist is the slow, grinding inevitability of collapse. It's the realization that no matter what your characters do, no matter how hard they fight, the world they knew is gone. Fate isn't a villain you can punch. It's not a fire you can put out or a virus you can outrun. It's the crushing weight of reality. The way you write fate as an antagonist is by showing your characters' hopes slowly slipping away. The evacuation that doesn't come. The rescue team that fails. The safety plan that falls apart because nobody can hold back the flood.

Fate as an antagonist turns your story into a battle against despair. It asks the hardest questions: If you know you're doomed, do you still fight? If you know you can't save everyone, do you still try? If hope itself becomes a liability, what do you hold onto? Stories where fate is the true enemy tend to be heavier, more philosophical, sometimes bleaker—but they can also be the most beautiful. Because when a character stands up against inevitable defeat, even knowing they might lose, that's heroism at its purest.

Sometimes you'll combine these antagonistic forces. Nature might start the disaster, but people make it worse. A virus wipes out half the city, and then gangs form in the lawless ruins. An earthquake breaks the infrastructure, but government corruption leaves survivors stranded without aid. Fate weaves through it all, the slow, relentless pressure squeezing your characters to their breaking points. The interplay between these different kinds of antagonists makes the story richer, more unpredictable, more real.

If you're using ChatGPT to brainstorm your antagonist forces, try prompting for different layers of conflict. You could ask for "ways survivors might turn against each other after a flood" or "systemic failures that worsen a pandemic." You can also prompt for nature-based challenges, like "what complications could survivors face after a major earthquake." Building multiple threats keeps your disaster story tense and dynamic. If nature doesn't get them, maybe people will. If people don't, maybe despair will.

One of the most important things to remember when crafting your disaster antagonist—whatever form it takes—is that it must feel believable. Readers will suspend a lot of disbelief when it comes to giant explosions or massive floods, but they won't forgive a fake-feeling human reaction. If you have human antagonists, make sure their actions come from understandable motivations: fear, desperation, greed, love twisted into something ugly. If you have nature as the antagonist, make sure it behaves consistently with the rules you set. If fate is the enemy, make sure the collapse feels grounded and inevitable, not random or lazy.

Another powerful tip: let the antagonist forces evolve over the course of the story. Maybe at first the biggest threat is the storm. But after the storm passes, the real danger becomes human conflict over scarce resources. Or maybe the disaster was triggered by a single event, but every failed rescue attempt, every bad decision, every selfish act deepens the catastrophe. Let the antagonist forces shift and mutate, just like real disasters do. It keeps the tension high and forces your characters to adapt or die.

You can also personify the antagonist if you want to give readers a clear face to hate. Maybe it's a corrupt official hoarding supplies. Maybe it's a ruthless gang leader taking control of a refugee camp. Maybe it's a cold, calculating scientist who unleashed something they thought they could control. Having a personal villain can give your story a sharper emotional focus, but remember: even if you have a human villain, the environment and fate are still massive, looming threats in the background. They don't go away just because there's a bad guy to fight. At the heart of it, the antagonist in a disaster story isn't just something for your characters to battle. It's a force that reveals who they really are. It strips away the comfortable layers of civilization and shows the raw, pulsing truth underneath. It forces choices that matter. Will they save themselves at any cost? Will they risk everything for a stranger? Will they cling to hope, or sink into despair?

When you build a worthy antagonist—whether it's nature, people, fate, or some terrible fusion of all three—you're not just writing obstacles. You're writing the emotional machinery that will test your characters, shape your story's pacing, and ultimately define the meaning of survival in your collapsing world. And the best part is, when the world fights back with everything it's got, when the hurricane howls and the mobs close in and the slow crush of inevitability tightens its grip, your protagonist's victory—even a small one—will feel that much bigger. That much harder earned. That much more real.

The collapse is coming. The enemy is rising. Now it's time to find out what your characters are really made of.

Building a Cast of Survivors: Who Makes It, Who Doesn't

A disaster story with only one character feels a little like a city with only one building left standing. It might be powerful for a moment, but it's the variety of people, their choices, their conflicts, their failures, and their triumphs that turn your crumbling world into something that feels real. Building a cast of survivors isn't about stuffing your story with dozens of characters who all blend together. It's about carefully choosing people who represent different ways humans react to disaster—and different ways they might rise or fall under pressure.

When you start designing your cast, it's useful to think about diversity—not just in surface traits like age, gender, or background (though those matter too)—but in mindset, skills, fears, and moral codes. Disasters are great equalizers. They throw together people who would never normally meet. The CEO and the janitor. The soldier and the poet. The mother and the loner. Forced proximity creates natural tension and drama. Your survivors should clash, bond, betray, and redeem themselves based on who they are deep down, not just on what the world expects of them.

Think about different roles people naturally fall into during a crisis. Some will step up as leaders—whether they're ready for it or not. Some will freeze, waiting for someone else to tell them what to do. Some will look for opportunities to take advantage of others. Some will collapse under the pressure. Some will find strengths they didn't know they had. A strong survivor cast shows all these reactions, and watching them play off each other gives your story emotional depth and dynamic momentum.

Not every survivor has to be a hero. In fact, it's better if they're not. Flawed survivors are more interesting because they create internal and external conflict. Maybe there's a character who's brave but reckless, endangering others with impulsive choices. Maybe there's one who's smart but selfish, hoarding supplies. Maybe there's one who's gentle but naïve, putting the group at risk by trusting the wrong person. These imperfections create natural points of tension—and give your characters room to grow (or fail) as the story progresses.

It's also smart to think about what skills your survivors bring to the table—and how those skills create both strengths and weaknesses. The ex-military guy might know how to navigate danger but struggle to work with others peacefully. The engineer might be able to rig up survival systems but panic when forced into leadership. The medic might be the heart of the group, holding people together emotionally, but carry the burden of guilt when they can't save everyone. Disaster fiction thrives on characters who are useful but vulnerable, capable but haunted.

Another thing to consider when building your cast is relationships. Some survivors should have pre-existing bonds: spouses, siblings, friends, co-workers. Others should be total strangers. The mix creates layers. Pre-existing bonds offer built-in emotional stakes—how far will you go to save the person you love? What happens when you fail? Total strangers force characters to build trust—or decide whether to trust at all. And that question of trust is pure gasoline for a disaster story's fire.

When deciding "who makes it, who doesn't," the most important thing to remember is that survival shouldn't feel random. Readers don't want to feel like you're rolling dice behind the scenes. Every death (or survival) should feel earned emotionally, even if it's shocking. If a character dies, it should either reflect a flaw (they couldn't adapt, they made a selfish choice) or reinforce a theme (sacrifice, fate, the cruelty of chance). If a character survives, it should reflect growth, resilience, or a cost paid earlier in the story.

Don't be afraid to kill off important characters if it serves the story. In a disaster narrative, real stakes mean real losses. Readers need to believe that no one is completely safe—not even the people they love most. But at the same time, don't kill characters just for shock value. Every death should push the story forward, impact the other characters, and deepen the emotional landscape. A good character death leaves scars on the survivors—and those scars shape who they become.

On the flip side, be careful about plot armor. If a character survives impossible odds too many times without cost readers will start to feel disconnected. Survival should cost something: physically, emotionally, spiritually. The survivors who limp across the finish line should be changed, marked, and scarred by everything they've been through. Disaster doesn't leave people untouched. It leaves them different—sometimes better, sometimes worse, but always different.

As you build your survivor cast, think about arcs. Not just for your protagonist, but for the supporting characters too. Maybe the coward learns to stand and fight. Maybe the selfish one sacrifices themselves for the group. Maybe the leader collapses under the burden and someone unexpected rises in their place. Every character doesn't need a huge transformation, but those small personal arcs make the story richer and more memorable.

It's also powerful to mirror the disaster's arc through your survivors. If the world starts relatively intact and falls apart, show relationships doing the same. Show characters who trust each other at first but fracture under pressure. Show alliances breaking. Show betrayals hurting worse than physical injuries. Conversely, if your world starts chaotic and moves toward rebuilding, show characters learning to trust, to hope, to lead. Use your survivors' journeys to reflect the larger collapse—or the larger rebirth—happening around them.

If you're using ChatGPT to help brainstorm survivor casts, you can prompt for ideas like "five flawed survivors trapped in a flooded city" or "three strangers and their hidden secrets during a pandemic lockdown." You can also prompt for group dynamics: "a team where distrust grows after a rescue mission goes wrong." This helps you quickly generate interesting combinations of personalities, skills, and tensions that will bring your survivor cast to life.

One trick that works beautifully in disaster fiction is the unexpected survivor. Readers often assume the strongest, bravest, most physically capable character will make it. Subverting that expectation can create powerful emotional moments. Maybe it's the quiet kid who knew how to stay unnoticed. Maybe it's the frail old woman who refuses to quit. Maybe it's the criminal who, against all odds, finds redemption. Survival isn't always about strength. It's often about adaptability, resilience, and heart—and readers feel those victories more deeply.

Another technique is the mirror character. Pair your protagonist with a survivor who represents what they could become if they give in to fear or cruelty. Maybe your protagonist struggles with selfishness, and they meet someone who has completely surrendered to it. Maybe they wrestle with despair and find someone who's already broken. These mirror characters give your protagonist something tangible to fight against—not just outside threats, but the darkness inside themselves. In the end, your survivor cast isn't just background noise for the main character's journey. They're part of the world you're creating. They shape the emotional landscape. They create bonds, friction, sacrifice, betrayal, hope. Every survivor who lives, every survivor who dies, every survivor who changes—they all tell a piece of the larger story about how humanity responds when the walls come crashing down.

When you build your cast carefully, with love and ruthlessness, your disaster story stops being just about destruction. It becomes a story about people. About fear and courage. About loss and love. About the small, stubborn hope that survives even when the world doesn't. Because in the end, it's not the explosions readers remember. It's the faces of the survivors walking out of the rubble, changed forever—and somehow, still moving forward.

Setting the Stage: Cities, Suburbs, Wilderness, Oceans, and Space

When you're writing a disaster story, the setting isn't just a backdrop—it's an active part of the drama. The environment shapes the story almost as much as the disaster itself. A fire in a forest tells a different story than a fire in a skyscraper. A virus outbreak feels different if it spreads through an isolated village compared to a packed megacity. Oceans swallow things differently than deserts do. Space offers a whole different level of terror. Choosing your setting isn't just about where the action happens. It's about deciding what kind of emotional atmosphere you want, what challenges your characters face, and what survival even looks like in your world.

Cities are the classic disaster setting for a reason. They're packed with people, infrastructure, ambition, noise, and movement. When disaster strikes a city, the consequences are immediate and overwhelming. Skyscrapers become death traps. Subways flood. Streets clog with panicked crowds. Resources vanish fast. Cities offer incredible scale for chaos—there's something about seeing a whole skyline go dark that hits differently than seeing a single house burn. But cities also offer opportunities for layered storytelling. You can write about the people trapped in penthouses, the ones in the underground shelters, the ones trying to navigate clogged freeways or collapsed bridges. A city falling apart is a hundred small stories intersecting—and each story gives you a different angle on survival.

Suburbs, on the other hand, offer a slower kind of collapse. In a suburban disaster, there's more space, more isolation. Neighbors might band together—or turn against each other. Help is slower to arrive, and sometimes doesn't arrive at all. Suburbs give you a setting where disaster creeps in rather than crashing down all at once. Power outages, food shortages, communications going dark—it feels like the slow boiling of a frog. One day the mail stops coming. Then the grocery store shelves are empty. Then the neighbors' house is dark. Suburban disaster stories often feel more intimate, more psychological. The world doesn't end with a bang—it unravels quietly, house by house, street by street.

And then there's the wilderness. Mountains, forests, deserts, tundras—the natural world is beautiful, but it's also merciless. Setting a disaster story in the wilderness strips away the safety net almost immediately. No emergency services. No stores. No hospitals. If something goes wrong, you either fix it yourself or die. Wilderness settings naturally emphasize human vulnerability and smallness. Nature doesn't even have to be actively hostile for survival to be brutal. A fall. A storm. A simple wrong turn. Wilderness disaster stories often have a primal, almost mythic quality. They're about the raw, direct relationship between humans and an uncaring world. They ask questions like: How long can you last on just your wits and will? What do you do when your only company is silence?

Oceans are their own special kind of nightmare. A disaster story set on the water—whether it's a cruise ship, a fishing boat, an oil rig, or a tiny raft—traps your characters in an environment that's both vast and claustrophobic. There's nowhere to run. No safe ground to reach. The ocean itself becomes an endless, living threat. Storms. Rogue waves. Sharks. Isolation. Dehydration. Mutiny. Fear. Everything feels amplified when there's only water in every direction. Oceans make survival stories feel desperate, almost hallucinatory. They tap into deep fears of being lost, alone, insignificant against a force that doesn't even notice your existence. And writing an ocean-based disaster forces you to think differently about pacing and tension. Time becomes an enemy. Supplies run out. Morale crumbles. Horizons stay empty.

And then, of course, there's space—the final, terrifying frontier. Disaster in space is about as pure and unforgiving as it gets. One wrong move, one cracked seal, one malfunction, and death is immediate and absolute. Space settings take all the isolation and danger of the ocean and crank it up to eleven. There's no breathable air. There's no gravity to help or hinder. There's no outside world you can call for help. Space disaster stories often feel colder, sharper, more existential. They're not just about survival—they're about sanity, about the human spirit reaching for survival in a place where humanity was never meant to exist. Writing disaster in space lets you explore loneliness, existential dread, and the triumph or collapse of hope in an environment that doesn't just kill you—it erases you.

When you pick your setting, you're also picking the kind of sensory experience your readers will live through. Cities smell like smoke and metal and spilled gasoline. Suburbs smell like overgrown lawns and rotting garbage. Wilderness smells like pine and damp earth—or dry dust and baking sand. Oceans smell like salt and rot and fear. Space smells like nothing, but the silence will be deafening. Think about what your setting sounds like, feels like underfoot, looks like when the sun rises or when the disaster cuts the power. These sensory details ground your readers in the story and make the disaster feel real.

Setting also controls the logistics of survival. In a city, your characters might have access to supplies—but face massive competition and danger from other survivors. In a suburb, they might be better stocked but more isolated, vulnerable to both nature and human threats. In the wilderness, survival might depend on skills like hunting, shelter-building, and navigation. On the ocean, survival is a matter of conserving water, avoiding exposure, and staying afloat. In space, survival is a race against oxygen, radiation, and psychological collapse. Each setting demands different skills, different fears, different kinds of courage.

Another thing to think about is how your setting transforms over time. A city after an earthquake doesn't just stay static. Fires spread. Buildings collapse. Streets flood. Suburbs after a pandemic start to rot and crumble. Wilderness after a blizzard changes hour by hour, beautiful and deadly. Oceans after a storm become fields of wreckage. Space stations after catastrophic failure start to fall apart, systems shutting down one by one. Show your setting evolving. Let it become another character—an antagonist or an ally, depending on the moment.

If you're using ChatGPT to brainstorm settings, you can prompt for specific ideas like "describe a city in the immediate aftermath of a Category 5 hurricane" or "describe a drifting space station slowly losing power." You can also ask for layered challenges tied to the setting: "obstacles survivors face in a flooded suburban neighborhood" or "dangers lurking in a post-wildfire mountain range." Layered settings give your story texture and momentum, as new dangers emerge naturally from the environment itself.

One more tip: don't be afraid to twist the setting a little. Maybe the city isn't completely destroyed—it's partly functional, but only for the ruthless and powerful. Maybe the wilderness is haunted by old survival myths that turn into psychological horror. Maybe the ocean your survivors float on isn't deserted after all. Maybe the space station your characters are trapped in isn't as abandoned as it seems. Your setting isn't just a physical space—it's an emotional and thematic engine. Use it to deepen your characters' journeys and keep your readers guessing.

In the end, setting the stage in a disaster story is about building a world that tests your characters in every possible way. It's about creating an environment that's not just hostile, but alive—changing, reacting, pushing back. It's about putting your characters in a place where survival is not guaranteed and hope is something they have to fight for, inch by inch, breath by breath.

Because in disaster fiction, the world isn't just falling apart. It's remaking itself. And the question your setting asks—loudly, mercilessly, endlessly—is simple:

Who will endure, and what will they become?

Creating Atmosphere: The Smell of Smoke, the Roar of Collapse

If the setting is the skeleton of your disaster story, the atmosphere is the blood, the heartbeat, the breath. It's what makes the reader feel like they're really standing in the ruins, breathing the smoke, hearing the distant sirens, feeling the sticky sweat of fear on their skin. Atmosphere isn't just decoration. It's an emotional experience. It's how you turn a scene from something readers understand with their brains into something they *feel* in their bodies. And in disaster fiction, creating atmosphere is everything.

When disaster strikes in real life, the first thing people remember later often isn't just what they saw—it's what they smelled, heard, and felt. They remember the acrid stink of burning plastic. They remember the deep, sickening groan of a building starting to fall. They remember the strange, metallic taste in the air after a blast. Those details stay burned into memory because they bypass our logical brains and hit us straight in the gut. That's what you want to do with your writing: bypass analysis and punch your readers right in their senses.

Start with smell. It's the most primal of all senses and one of the most evocative. In a disaster story, smell can be a constant background character. Smoke, ash, blood, sewage, saltwater, burnt rubber, mildew, rot—these smells tell the reader what kind of danger the characters are in even before you spell it out. A character waking up to the sharp smell of smoke knows before opening their eyes that something is terribly wrong. A survivor gagging on the stench of flooded streets knows instinctively that the water is not safe. Don't be shy about describing smells in your story. A single sentence about the way the air thickens with the stink of burning wires can make a disaster scene leap off the page.

Next, think about sound. In a disaster, silence is almost never truly silent. There's the constant background noise—the pop and hiss of distant fires, the low groan of stressed metal, the sporadic wail of sirens—or the eerie absence of sound where there should be life. Sound creates tension before anything visible happens. A low rumble might hint at an aftershock. A sudden crack might mean a floor giving way. In disaster fiction, sound often acts like an early warning system, and you can use it to keep readers on edge. Short, punchy sentences mimic the sharpness of sudden noises. Long, droning descriptions can recreate the hypnotic, maddening endlessness of a catastrophe dragging on.

Don't forget texture—the way things feel underfoot or against the skin. The gritty sting of ash in the eyes. The slick, treacherous feel of wet marble during a flood. The dry cracking of lips and skin during a drought. The oppressive weight of a heavy emergency blanket thrown over shock-numbed shoulders. Texture roots your characters in their physical world. It reminds readers that survival isn't just about big moments. It's about the constant abrasion of discomfort, danger, and fear grinding them down.

Temperature is another powerful tool. Disaster often messes with the environment in extreme ways. Fires create unbearable heat. Snowstorms create bitter, deadly cold. Storms leave everything clammy and chilled. Heatwaves sap strength and willpower. Let your readers *feel* what your characters feel. Make them sweat. Make them shiver. Make them desperate to find shade, shelter, or fire. Temperature adds invisible pressure to every scene, tightening the screw on your characters' endurance.

Light—or the lack of it—can shape atmosphere more powerfully than almost anything else. In a disaster, darkness becomes a living threat. A city after a blackout isn't just dim—it's alive with invisible dangers. A tunnel after a collapse isn't just shadowy—it's claustrophobic, almost suffocating. Even daylight can turn sinister under the right conditions: blood-red skies during a wildfire, a sun that bakes the ground to cracking during a drought. Think about how the quality of light changes during your disaster. Blinding flashes. Guttering firelight. The cold, washed-out colors of emergency floodlights. Light tells the reader how safe or unsafe the world feels without needing a single word of exposition.

Movement is another overlooked aspect of atmosphere. Disasters rarely stand still. Smoke billows. Floodwaters rise. Debris shifts. Crowds surge and scatter. Animals flee or fall silent. Buildings shudder before they fall. The landscape of a disaster is constantly changing, and that movement can create powerful visual and emotional momentum. Let readers feel the instability of the world. Let them feel how every second brings a new danger, a new loss, a new horror.

And then there's the emotional atmosphere—the thick, invisible weight of fear, panic, grief, hope, or despair that fills the air like a storm cloud. Disaster brings out extremes in people, and those emotions can seep into every line of your story. A scene set among panicking crowds feels different from one set in the aftermath, when only numb survivors remain. A moment of stolen joy—a found family member, a patch of blue sky—can shine brighter than anything else because it stands against the background of ruin. Emotional atmosphere isn't something you tell the reader about directly. It's something you create by choosing the right details, the right rhythms, the right balance between chaos and silence.

When you're using ChatGPT to brainstorm atmosphere, you can prompt for highly specific sensory descriptions. Ask for "sensory details during a citywide blackout after an earthquake" or "describe the atmosphere in a flooded subway tunnel." Ask for "sounds and smells in a town after a chemical spill." The more specific your prompts, the richer the sensory palette you'll get to weave into your story.

One trick you can use when creating atmosphere is to focus on how your protagonist experiences it personally. Maybe the protagonist's ears ring after an explosion, muting the world for a few terrible moments. Maybe the smoke stings their throat so badly they can barely scream for help. Maybe their hands shake uncontrollably from cold or terror. By filtering the sensory world through your protagonist's body and emotions, you make the disaster intimate instead of distant. Readers don't just *see* the collapse. They *feel* it.

Another technique is contrast. Use brief moments of unnatural calm to heighten the terror. The way the wind dies just before the tornado touches down. The eerie silence after the first bomb falls. The sudden stillness of a street where a crowd fled minutes ago. These pauses make the next explosion of chaos even more powerful. They also give readers—and characters—a moment to breathe, to hope, to despair.

And don't forget rhythm. Disaster scenes should feel different to read depending on what's happening. During a collapse or a fire or a flood surge, your sentences should get shorter, punchier, faster—mirroring racing heartbeats and chaotic decisions. In the aftermath, your sentences can stretch out again, slow and heavy, mirroring exhaustion and shock. Rhythm shapes atmosphere almost invisibly, but it's one of the most effective tools you have to control how your readers experience the story moment by moment.

In the end, atmosphere is about immersing the reader so completely that they forget they're reading. They're *there.* They're choking on smoke, slipping on shattered glass, blinking against burning light, shivering under blood-red skies. They're hearing the city groan like a dying animal, feeling the ground tremble, tasting fear and dust.

The world you're building isn't just collapsing in front of their eyes. It's collapsing *around* them. Inside them.

That's the real magic of creating atmosphere. It turns disaster from spectacle into experience—and that's what readers will remember long after they close the book.

Writing Emergency Services Characters with Authenticity

When a disaster strikes, the first people everyone expects to see are the emergency services. Firefighters, paramedics, police officers, search and rescue teams, doctors, nurses, even volunteer first responders—they are the thin, fragile line standing between survival and chaos. If you're writing a disaster story and you want it to feel real, getting these characters right matters a lot. Done well, emergency services characters bring urgency, heartbreak, hope, and even tragedy to your story. Done poorly, they feel like stereotypes—cardboard cutouts barking orders or rushing around without depth. Authenticity makes all the difference.

First, understand that emergency services personnel are trained for disaster, but they're still human. They carry skills, sure. Knowledge, discipline, procedures. But under that training is the same raw fear, doubt, exhaustion, and anger that any person would feel in a catastrophe. Real emergency workers aren't superheroes. They make mistakes. They get overwhelmed. They have bad days. What sets them apart isn't that they're fearless. It's that they act anyway, even when they're terrified. That courage under fire is what makes them so compelling to write—and to read.

A big part of writing these characters authentically is showing the limits of what they can do. In real disasters, emergency services get overwhelmed quickly. Supplies run out. Communications break down. Hospitals overflow. Fires spread faster than they can be fought. In those moments, the best-trained people in the world have to triage: who can be saved, and who can't. That's a brutal reality emergency responders live with—and it shapes them. Writing those hard choices with sensitivity gives your story depth. It's not just about running into burning buildings. It's about living with the faces you couldn't reach in time.

Another important thing to remember is that emergency services are a team effort. No single paramedic saves everyone. No firefighter handles an entire inferno alone. No police officer controls a panicking crowd by themselves. Teams work in brutal conditions with limited information, relying on training, instincts, and each other. If you're writing a medic trying to save someone trapped under rubble, remember they're probably calling for backup, coordinating with firefighters, fighting exhaustion after hours of non-stop work. These aren't solo action heroes. They're members of a battered, relentless army trying to hold the line.

Hierarchy matters too. In real disaster response, there's a chain of command. Officers give orders. Medics triage under protocols. Fire captains decide which building gets saved and which one burns because the resources simply aren't there to do both. These decisions aren't made randomly or emotionally—they're made based on training, experience, and brutal math. Showing that structure, and showing how it strains and sometimes cracks under pressure, adds another layer of realism to your story.

Procedures matter, but they aren't foolproof. A paramedic knows how to treat burns, but what happens when they run out of bandages? A firefighter knows how to rescue people from a collapsed structure, but what happens when aftershocks keep hitting? A cop knows how to control a crowd, but what happens when panic spreads faster than reason? Disaster pushes procedures beyond their limits—and your emergency services characters have to improvise, adapt, or sometimes watch helplessly. Showing the tension between protocol and improvisation makes your story feel alive and real.

When you're writing dialogue for these characters, remember that emergency workers often develop a very specific tone—direct, sometimes dry, sometimes darkly humorous. They don't have time for long speeches. They're used to giving and receiving orders fast. In moments of downtime, gallows humor often surfaces—not because they don't care, but because humor is a shield against trauma. Let your characters use clipped phrases when things are falling apart. Let them bark orders or crack a joke no one laughs at. It's part of surviving the unbearable.

Also, don't forget the emotional toll. Emergency services personnel are trained to stay calm under pressure—but they're not emotionless. When the crisis finally breaks, when the fire is out or the survivors are counted, that's often when they collapse. That's when the tears come, or the anger explodes, or the guilt crushes them. Showing that emotional release—even briefly—can be one of the most powerful moments in your disaster story. It reminds readers that heroism isn't just about bravery in the moment. It's about carrying the scars afterward.

Another layer you can add is the way public perception affects emergency workers. In the early stages of a disaster, they're often hailed as heroes. But when things get worse, when not everyone can be saved, blame starts flying. Survivors accuse them of not doing enough. Officials throw them under the bus. The media twists the story. Writing about this shift in how emergency responders are seen—from saviors to scapegoats—adds realism and complexity to your narrative.

And then there are the personal stakes. Many emergency workers live in the same communities they serve. In a disaster, they're not just saving strangers—they're trying to save their own families too. What happens when a firefighter has to choose between rescuing a stranger or searching for their missing child? What happens when a nurse has to triage her neighbors? Personal connections make every decision harder, every failure heavier. They humanize the characters and deepen the emotional punch of the story.

If you're using ChatGPT to help with brainstorming or writing emergency services characters, you can prompt for things like "describe the mindset of a paramedic in a disaster zone" or "generate dialogue for a firefighter trapped during a building collapse." You can also ask for procedural details like "how a search and rescue team operates after an earthquake" or "standard triage procedures in a mass casualty event." Layering real details into your scenes grounds your fiction and makes the extraordinary feel believable.

One more important tip: remember that not every emergency worker fits the same mold. Some are idealists, driven by a deep need to help. Some are adrenaline junkies. Some are veterans carrying old scars. Some are rookies in way over their heads. Some have secret fears they hide behind bravado. Some will rise under pressure; others will break. Let them be individuals, not just uniforms. Give them quirks, regrets, secret hopes, bad habits. Make them human first, hero second.

In the end, writing emergency services characters authentically is about respect—not just for the reality of the job, but for the emotional cost. It's about showing the courage and the cracks. It's about showing that heroism isn't shiny or clean. It's bloodied hands digging through rubble. It's sleepless eyes watching the floodwaters rise. It's broken voices giving bad news, steady hands pulling one more person from the wreckage.

In your disaster story, these characters aren't just there to save others. They are part of the disaster too. Part of the struggle. Part of the heartbreak. And when written well, they will stay with your readers long after the fires have burned out and the waters have receded.

Because real heroes don't walk away untouched.

They walk away carrying the weight of everyone they couldn't save.

Exploring Government Response and Breakdown

Disasters don't just smash buildings and flood streets. They smash systems. The bigger the disaster, the more pressure it puts on the structures people normally depend on to keep life orderly: the hospitals, the police departments, the fire stations, the emergency management agencies, and the political leaders behind them. In a disaster story, showing the government's response—and especially its breakdown—is one of the fastest ways to escalate the feeling of helplessness, panic, and chaos. It's not just the physical world collapsing. It's the safety net shredding, leaving your characters dangling over the void.

When a real disaster hits, government agencies move into action. Plans kick in. Emergency broadcasts go out. Shelters open. Roads are blocked off. Evacuations are ordered. The first stages of a response are often filled with a frantic, strained kind of hope. People want to believe the system will save them. That help is on the way. That the authorities know what they're doing. In your disaster story, you can reflect this early stage—show people tuning into radios, refreshing news apps, waiting for the National Guard to show up. Show the small, stubborn hope that the big machine will keep grinding forward even when the ground itself crumbles.

But disaster always pushes the system further than it's designed to go. First responders can only do so much. Stockpiled supplies run out. Roads become impassable. Communication networks crash. Leaders make bad decisions—or get paralyzed by indecision. The sheer scale of need overwhelms the best intentions and the best plans. When you write the government breakdown into your story, you show readers not just the physical destruction but the collapse of trust. It's not just that the buildings are falling—it's that the safety nets people believed in their whole lives are snapping.

One of the most chilling moments you can write is when characters realize that help isn't coming. Maybe they're waiting at an evacuation point, staring at the sky for helicopters that never arrive. Maybe they see emergency workers retreating because the situation is too dangerous. Maybe they hear rumors—maybe true, maybe not—that the government has decided to abandon certain areas, certain people. That moment, when the belief in the system crumbles, changes everything. Suddenly survival isn't about waiting for rescue. It's about saving yourself.

Government breakdown can happen at all levels. Maybe the local response fails first. The mayor orders evacuations too late. The city's emergency plans are outdated or ignored. First responders are overwhelmed. Then the state-level systems crumble. The highways are jammed. The shelters are full. The National Guard is stretched thin. Then the federal systems start to show cracks. Relief funds are mismanaged. Critical supplies get stuck in bureaucracy. Political leaders start blaming each other instead of leading. The bigger the disaster, the more the failures pile up. And every time the system fails, the survivors fall deeper into chaos.

Corruption makes it even worse. In some disaster stories, government breakdown isn't just about incompetence—it's about greed, selfishness, and betrayal. Officials steal supplies. Leaders abandon their posts. Powerful people protect themselves while ordinary citizens are left to drown, burn, starve, or fight for scraps. Writing this kind of breakdown taps into real-world fears and anger. It shows how disasters don't just destroy cities—they expose the rot that was already there, hidden under the surface.

At the same time, not every failure has to be malicious. Sometimes the system collapses simply because it wasn't built to survive this kind of strain. Leaders can be overwhelmed. Emergency plans can be based on outdated assumptions. Supplies can run out because no one ever truly believed they would be needed. Showing well-meaning people failing under pressure makes your story feel more complex and real. It's not always about villains. Sometimes it's about systems that were never as strong as people thought they were.

You can also explore how different communities are treated differently during a disaster. In real life, wealthier, more connected neighborhoods often get help faster. Poorer areas, marginalized communities, rural towns—they get left behind. Writing these inequalities into your disaster story adds another layer of realism and emotional weight. Who gets rescued first? Who gets forgotten? How does that injustice shape the survivors' view of the world—and of themselves?

If you're using ChatGPT to brainstorm this part of your story, you can prompt for ideas like "examples of government failures during a flood disaster" or "how a slow government response worsens a pandemic." You can also prompt for historical examples—disasters like Hurricane Katrina, the COVID-19 pandemic, or wildfires in Australia and California are full of real-world moments where government systems were stretched to the breaking point or beyond. Studying those examples can give you inspiration for scenes that feel chillingly plausible.

Government breakdown doesn't have to happen all at once. It can erode slowly over the course of your story. First the evacuation plans fall apart. Then the communications fail. Then the supplies stop coming. Then the leadership vanishes. Layering the collapse like that creates rising tension and a growing sense of dread. Every small failure sets up the next bigger one, until finally there's nothing left to hold onto except personal courage, luck, and the willingness to keep moving.

Another powerful layer is how different characters respond to the collapse. Some might cling stubbornly to the belief that help is still coming, even when all signs say otherwise. Some might fall into despair. Some might try to become leaders themselves, creating new rules, new structures, even small communities trying to survive without the old systems. Disaster doesn't just destroy—it remakes. Showing how characters react to the vacuum of authority gives your story emotional energy and keeps readers invested in what happens next.

You can also create moral dilemmas around the breakdown. What happens when a group of survivors has to decide whether to stay at a designated evacuation center that seems increasingly abandoned—or risk heading out into unknown dangers? What happens when a character realizes the official orders are wrong, dangerous, even fatal? Do they follow orders anyway? Rebel? Run? These moments test loyalty, morality, and self-preservation in ways that pure action scenes never could.

And don't forget the emotional gut punch of realizing that not all breakdowns are permanent. Maybe help does finally arrive—but it's too late for some. Maybe supplies are dropped—but chaos and distrust keep survivors from getting them. Maybe a new order tries to rise—but it's harsher, crueler, built on fear instead of hope. Sometimes survival means adapting not just to a lack of government—but to a new kind of government that isn't interested in saving everyone.

In the end, exploring government response and breakdown in your disaster story isn't about cynicism for its own sake. It's about truth. Systems are fragile. Trust is fragile. When the ground shakes and the floodwaters rise and the sirens fade, what's left isn't the neatly printed emergency plan. It's people. It's the human spirit, raw and battered, choosing to survive—or not.

By showing the collapse of government systems, you set the stage for everything that follows. The chaos. The betrayal. The unexpected acts of heroism. The desperate, stubborn will to endure. When the big machine fails, the small, personal stories take over—and those are the stories your readers will never forget.

Writing First Responders: Firefighters, Paramedics, Police

When disaster strikes, the first ones into the fire, into the flood, into the chaos, are the first responders. Firefighters, paramedics, police officers—they are the ones who don't have the luxury of running away. Their job, their calling, demands that they move toward the danger. In a disaster story, writing first responders authentically brings an immediate pulse of realism, tension, and heartbreak. These aren't superheroes. These are trained people doing their best, often with crumbling resources, limited information, and personal fear sitting heavy on their backs. Getting them right gives your story emotional weight that's hard to fake.

The first thing to understand is that first responders are human first, responders second. They feel fear. They feel helplessness. They make mistakes. Training kicks in when adrenaline hits, but training doesn't erase emotion—it just gives them something to hold onto when instinct says run. Writing them authentically means showing both their competence and their humanity. It's the firefighter who knows exactly how to enter a burning building but still hesitates when they hear a child's cry. It's the paramedic who treats injuries with steady hands but can't stop thinking about their own family caught somewhere in the same disaster. It's the police officer who maintains crowd control until the moment they realize the radio's gone dead and backup isn't coming.

Firefighters are often the face of disaster response, and for good reason. They deal not just with fires but with collapsed buildings, chemical spills, trapped survivors, and emergency rescues. In a disaster, firefighters are usually among the first ones called—and often the last ones to leave. Writing firefighter characters means understanding their mindset: tactical, practical, focused. They think in terms of risk, time, and survival. They assess danger in seconds. They prioritize life over property. They know when a building is too dangerous to enter and when it's worth the gamble. But that doesn't make the decisions easier. The emotional burden of knowing they couldn't save everyone eats at them, even if they followed every protocol perfectly.

When you're writing firefighter scenes, don't fall into the Hollywood trap of invincible heroes charging through explosions untouched. Firefighting is brutal, exhausting, and terrifying. Visibility is often zero. The heat can melt metal and turn gear into an oven. Breathing is labored even with air tanks. Equipment is heavy and cumbersome. Every second counts, and bad luck—or a bad decision—can turn a rescue into a tragedy. Show your firefighter characters making hard choices: which part of the building to search first, when to pull back, when to push forward. Show them wrestling with exhaustion, fear, and guilt.

Paramedics bring a different kind of intensity. Their battlefield isn't fire—it's the human body breaking down under stress, injury, or illness. In a disaster, paramedics are stretched thinner than almost anyone else. They triage patients, deciding who gets treatment now, who can wait, and who is too far gone to save. Those choices are brutal, and they have to be made fast. Writing paramedic characters means showing that split-second calculus. The pressure of knowing that every second lost might cost a life. The frustration of knowing they don't have enough supplies, enough stretchers, enough ambulances. The quiet, stubborn act of treating one more wound, starting one more IV, saying one more prayer that maybe, somehow, this one will make it.

Paramedics often carry deep emotional scars. They see death up close, far more often than the general public. They see it in all its messy, ugly reality. A paramedic in a disaster isn't just patching up injuries—they're trying to create tiny pockets of hope in a world that feels like it's falling apart. Some use dark humor to cope. Some go numb. Some burn out quietly. Writing paramedics well means showing the emotional cost behind the quick hands and steady voices.

Police officers in disaster fiction are complicated. They are often tasked with impossible jobs—maintaining order in a world where the normal rules no longer apply. Directing evacuations. Controlling panicked crowds. Preventing looting. Making snap decisions about safety and violence. And because they carry authority, they often become lightning rods for fear, anger, and resentment from the public. Writing police officers authentically means recognizing that they aren't just enforcers. They're human beings trying to walk a line between protecting people and following orders—and sometimes those two things come into direct conflict.

Some officers rise to the occasion with compassion, bravery, and fairness. Others crumble under the pressure, misuse their power, or break under the strain. Disaster doesn't create character flaws, but it exposes them brutally. Show the internal struggles. The rookie who freezes. The veteran who bends the rules to save lives. The officer who clings too tightly to procedure because it's the only thing keeping their world together. Show them making hard calls when there are no good answers.

If you're using ChatGPT to help build first responder characters, you can prompt for details like "common emotional struggles of firefighters after major disasters" or "triage protocols for paramedics in mass casualty events." You can also ask for dialogue samples under pressure: "how a paramedic reassures a patient trapped under rubble" or "how a police officer negotiates with a panicking crowd at an evacuation point." These details, layered into your story, create authenticity that readers will feel, even if they don't consciously notice.

Another powerful trick when writing first responders is to show what happens *after* the immediate crisis. The moment when the fire's out but the building's a ruin. The moment when the triage line is empty but the stretchers aren't moving anymore. The moment when the crowd disperses but the damage is permanent. Those moments of silence, reflection, grief, and exhaustion reveal character more deeply than any action scene ever could.

It's also important to show the personal stakes. First responders often live in the communities they serve. In a disaster, they might be rescuing neighbors, friends, even family. That emotional entanglement complicates everything. A firefighter who recognizes the car crushed under rubble. A paramedic treating a child they know from the local playground. A cop evacuating a school their own kids attend. Disaster personalizes everything, and for first responders, the line between professional and personal survival can blur dangerously fast.

Another layer to explore is how first responders handle leadership and failure. In many disaster stories, natural leaders emerge—not necessarily the ones with rank, but the ones who can keep moving, keep deciding, keep caring even when it feels pointless. Other times, leadership crumbles. Bad orders are given. Good orders are ignored. People break under pressure. Showing both the heroic and the broken sides of leadership inside emergency services makes your story feel raw and real.

And don't forget about the civilians watching them. To ordinary survivors, first responders often look like hope incarnate—until they don't. Until the trucks stop arriving. Until the ambulances are too full. Until the officers stop answering questions. That shift—from awe to disillusionment—is heartbreaking, and when you write it well, it echoes the larger collapse of faith in institutions that disaster always brings.

In the end, writing first responders authentically is about honoring the complexity of what they do. It's about showing not just the heroism but the cracks. The choices that leave scars. The bravery that isn't fearless, but conscious and stubborn. The loyalty that holds teams together when everything else is falling apart. Because when the world burns, floods, shakes, or falls silent, it's the first responders who step forward—not because they're invincible, but because they're needed.

And they carry the cost with them, long after the sirens fade.

When Help Fails: Society's Rapid Decline

At the beginning of most disasters, people believe someone will come to save them. It's built into us. We expect the fire trucks, the ambulances, the helicopters, the government announcements. We expect order to snap back into place after the first shock. But what happens when the help fails? When no one comes—or when they come too late? In disaster stories, the moment help fails is the moment the real collapse begins. It's not just buildings falling anymore. It's society itself cracking open. And what comes pouring out is not always pretty.

The early stages of disaster feel chaotic, but there's often still a strange kind of hope humming underneath. Survivors gather at evacuation points. They follow emergency instructions. They wait for the system to catch up. But systems have limits, and disaster strips them away fast. Supplies run out. Communications break down. Leadership falters. And when people realize that no cavalry is coming, the emotional terrain shifts dramatically. Fear stops being temporary. It hardens into something desperate, something dangerous. That's the moment when society's polite rules—the invisible social contracts that hold everyday life together—start to tear apart.

In your disaster story, showing this moment of realization is crucial. It's a pivot point, emotionally and structurally. Maybe it's a mother sitting in a packed shelter when the power goes out—and no one comes to fix it. Maybe it's a group of survivors standing on a flooded rooftop, watching the rescue helicopters turn away. Maybe it's a character scrolling through a dead phone, realizing that no one's even broadcasting anymore. These moments don't need a lot of fireworks. Sometimes the most chilling thing is the silence. The absence. The dawning knowledge that they're on their own.

Once help fails, survival becomes improvisation. Resources that used to be abundant—clean water, food, medicine, gasoline—become precious currency. At first, people share. They cooperate. They form quick alliances. But as scarcity sharpens, fear sharpens too. Suspicion creeps in. Groups splinter. Some people hoard. Some steal. Some decide that survival justifies anything. Writing this shift means showing how easily fear corrodes trust, how quickly kindness can erode when hunger gnaws and safety vanishes.

Laws stop mattering. Not because people consciously reject them, but because the enforcement mechanisms behind them collapse. If there are no police to respond, no courts to judge, no prisons to hold, then law becomes a whisper against the roaring wind of survival. In your story, that breakdown might happen gradually, like a slow slide into darkness—or it might snap in an instant, triggered by one act of violence that no one can afford to punish or forgive.

Authority figures lose their power too. Leaders, once respected, become irrelevant—or worse, become targets. A mayor who failed to evacuate a city becomes a scapegoat. A police captain who can't guarantee protection becomes a liability. A shelter manager who can't feed the crowd becomes the focus of fury. Leadership shifts from official titles to whoever can protect, provide, or dominate. Sometimes new leaders rise—charismatic survivors who organize defenses, scavenging runs, water rationing. Sometimes it's the strong who seize control by force. Writing these new power structures gives your disaster world a living, evolving feeling—and sets up conflicts that drive your story forward.

Economies collapse too. Money loses meaning when stores are gutted and supply chains are dead. What matters now is what people can eat, drink, burn, or use to survive. Barter systems pop up. A can of beans becomes more valuable than a wallet full of cash. Antibiotics are worth more than gold. Writing this shift makes your world feel authentic. Show characters bargaining, fighting, stealing—not for luxuries, but for survival essentials. Every transaction becomes a test of character. Every deal carries a cost.

Morality becomes slippery. Actions that would have been unthinkable days before become survival strategies. Theft. Violence. Abandonment. Even murder. In your story, you can show characters wrestling with these choices—or embracing them. Maybe a character starts off idealistic, refusing to steal from others, but later faces a moment where stealing means their child lives. Maybe a character clings to their moral code until it gets someone they love killed—and then they break. Disaster fiction at its best digs into these moral fractures and lets them bleed.

But society's rapid decline isn't all darkness. Strange new communities sometimes form in the ashes. Groups of survivors band together to protect each other. New rules get made. New codes of honor emerge. Not everyone descends into savagery. Some people rise, finding strength and compassion they never knew they had. Writing these flickers of rebuilding makes the destruction hit harder, because it shows that even amid the collapse, humanity isn't completely dead. Hope, though battered and bloodied, still refuses to die.

One thing that speeds up society's decline is misinformation. In a disaster, rumors spread faster than fire. People panic over fake evacuation routes, phantom rescue efforts, imagined threats. Fear breeds conspiracy theories. Trust dies. In your story, showing how information warps and shatters in the chaos makes the collapse feel even more believable. Maybe characters make deadly decisions based on a rumor. Maybe a group falls apart because they believe a lie. Maybe a character realizes too late that the rescue they waited for was never coming at all.

Another factor that accelerates collapse is resource bottlenecks. If survivors are trapped in one area—an island cut off by flooding, a neighborhood isolated by downed bridges, a city quarantined by disease—the pressure intensifies fast. Starvation, disease, violence, despair—all magnify when there's nowhere to go and no supplies to replace what's lost. Setting up bottlenecks like this in your story creates natural pressure cookers of tension and forces characters into brutal decisions.

If you're using ChatGPT to brainstorm society's collapse scenes, you can prompt for things like "describe the progression from order to chaos after a city-wide blackout" or "examples of new laws that might emerge in a collapsed neighborhood." You can also ask for examples of barter economies, power struggles, or breakdowns in communication systems. Using real-world dynamics makes your fictional collapse feel sharp and uncomfortably plausible.

One writing trick when showing society's rapid decline is to show characters clinging to little rituals even after the big structures fall. Maybe someone keeps dressing in a work uniform even though there's no more work. Maybe someone keeps waiting for a daily news broadcast that never comes. Maybe someone sets up a "store" trading goods with no real currency, pretending it's business as usual. These small, sad attempts to keep normalcy alive reveal just how hard people fight to pretend everything isn't lost—even when deep down, they know it is.

And finally, remember that collapse doesn't happen evenly. Some areas fall faster than others. Some communities manage to hold together longer. Some places recover only to fall again later. Disaster fiction that captures this uneven collapse feels richer, more layered, more believable. Maybe one block becomes a war zone while another becomes a fragile safe haven. Maybe survivors stumble into a town that looks untouched—only to find the real collapse hidden under the surface.

In the end, society's rapid decline isn't just about violence and hunger and fear. It's about identity. People have to figure out who they are when the world they knew is gone. Are they protectors or predators? Builders or destroyers? Survivors or something darker?

The moment help fails is the moment the masks come off.

And what's underneath—the beautiful, the terrible, the hopeful, the broken—that's the real story your disaster narrative gets to tell.

Family Dynamics during Crisis: The Ultimate Test

When disaster strikes, everything gets tested—but nothing gets tested more brutally than family. In the everyday world, families argue, forgive, love, fight, drift apart, come back together. All of that unfolds over years, decades, sometimes lifetimes. But when the world collapses in an instant, all those dynamics get compressed. Everything bubbles to the surface fast. Every old wound is torn open. Every bond is stressed until it either holds firm or snaps. Writing family dynamics during crisis means diving into the deepest parts of your characters' emotional lives and asking the hardest questions about loyalty, sacrifice, resentment, and love.

In a disaster, the first instinct for most people is simple: get to their family. Find them. Protect them. Save them. That primal drive gives your story an emotional motor that's far more powerful than just "survive because I want to live." Survival becomes about something bigger—something sacred. It becomes about saving the people who are part of your identity, the people who define you, the people you feel responsible for. That urgency can make your protagonist's actions reckless, noble, foolish, heroic. It can drive them to push past limits they didn't know they had—or to make fatal mistakes.

But disaster doesn't just strengthen family bonds. It exposes the cracks already there. Maybe the father who seemed so reliable crumbles under pressure. Maybe the siblings who always fought find themselves united by desperation. Maybe the mother who seemed gentle and weak turns out to be the fiercest survivor of them all. Crisis rewrites family roles. The protector might become the protected. The black sheep might become the leader. The favorite might fall apart. Writing these shifts gives your story emotional authenticity and raw power.

Think about the stresses disaster puts on a family: physical danger, exhaustion, hunger, fear, grief. Add the moral dilemmas: if supplies are limited, who gets the last of the food? If someone's hurt and slowing the group down, do you carry them—or leave them behind to save others? Disaster turns love into a battlefield where every decision cuts deep. Your characters don't stop loving each other. They love harder, more desperately. But that love starts colliding with survival in ways that hurt.

One of the strongest emotional arcs you can write is a family struggling with blame. Maybe a character believes another family member caused their situation—ignored evacuation orders, made a bad decision, stayed behind when they should have run. Maybe guilt weighs heavily: a brother who feels responsible for not saving his sister, a mother haunted by the belief she chose the wrong child to protect first. Disaster doesn't wipe these feelings away. It magnifies them. A story where family members must forgive each other in order to survive can be just as gripping as any fight against nature or other survivors.

Don't forget that family dynamics are deeply shaped by history. Old resentments don't magically vanish because a building collapsed or a firestorm swept through town. If two brothers were already barely speaking before the earthquake, they're not going to suddenly become best friends because they're stuck together. If a parent was abusive, if a child was rebellious, if trust was already frayed, the disaster will poke at those scars, not heal them. Writing these layers into your story makes every conversation, every decision, every act of loyalty or betrayal more meaningful.

At the same time, crisis can also create opportunities for healing. Sometimes it takes the end of the world to say the things people never had the courage to say before. Regrets surface. Apologies are offered—sometimes too late, sometimes just in time. A father tells his son he's proud. A sister forgives a brother. A mother admits she was wrong.

These moments of emotional honesty, set against the background of destruction, burn brighter because they're rare and hard-won.

If you're using ChatGPT to brainstorm family dynamics, you can prompt for ideas like "how an estranged father and daughter might reconnect during a flood" or "tensions between siblings during a city evacuation." You can also prompt for conflict points like "deciding who eats when supplies are low" or "choosing whether to save a family member versus a group of strangers." Family creates natural, built-in tension because the stakes aren't just physical survival—they're emotional survival too.

Another powerful layer to explore is generational differences. How do parents and children react differently to disaster? Maybe the older generation wants to cling to routines, traditions, old ideas of safety. Maybe the younger generation adapts faster, letting go of the old world more easily—but resenting the older generation for dragging their feet. Maybe parents hide the truth of how bad things are from children to protect them—or maybe children end up protecting their parents. These dynamics create rich emotional conflict and opportunities for growth on all sides.

It's also worth thinking about how different family structures survive. A traditional nuclear family is just one option. Maybe your story focuses on a single parent and child. Maybe it's an extended family all crammed into one house. Maybe it's a found family—a group of friends or strangers who become a family through shared hardship. Found families are a classic disaster story element because they show that family isn't just about blood. It's about choice. About trust built in fire. About bonds forged in collapse.

Conflict within families can escalate dangerously in crisis conditions. Stress pushes people to the edge. A minor disagreement over food or direction can spiral into screaming matches, physical fights, even permanent rifts. Show these blow-ups happening fast and messy. One minute they're arguing over which way to go; the next minute they're dredging up twenty years of buried resentment. In the heat of disaster, everything surfaces.

And sometimes, families fail. Sometimes the bonds break. A parent sacrifices one child to save another. A sibling leaves the group behind in a moment of panic. A child chooses to save a friend over a parent. Writing these moments isn't about cruelty for shock value. It's about truth. Survival costs something. Sometimes it costs the people we love most. Sometimes it costs the illusions we had about what love really means.

But if you balance it right, family dynamics during disaster also give you a place to show hope. Loyalty that doesn't crack. Sacrifices that aren't bitter but beautiful. Forgiveness that comes not from weakness, but from strength. In a world falling apart, a family that stays together—through rage, grief, betrayal, terror—becomes a symbol of what's worth fighting for. It becomes the heart of your story.

Family is messy even in the best of times. In disaster, it becomes explosive. But inside that explosion are the most powerful emotions you can tap into as a writer: love, loyalty, fear, guilt, forgiveness, rage, sacrifice, redemption. Every choice matters more. Every argument cuts deeper. Every hug, every whispered "I'm sorry," every desperate attempt to protect what's left of the people you love—it all matters.

Because in the end, when the fires burn out, when the waters recede, when the buildings are dust, what matters most isn't what's lost.

It's who's still standing beside you.

It's who you fought for—and who fought for you.

Friendship and Betrayal at the End of the World

Disaster stories aren't just about surviving falling buildings, rising waters, raging fires, or empty cities. They're also about surviving each other. When the world falls apart, friendships become lifelines—or landmines. Bonds between people can save lives, give hope, and offer moments of grace in the darkness. But they can also crack under pressure, twist into rivalry, or snap into betrayal. Writing friendship and betrayal at the end of the world taps into the deepest parts of human nature, where loyalty and survival instincts wrestle inside the same battered heart.

Friendship during a disaster feels different than friendship in normal life. It's not about grabbing coffee together or trading jokes. It's about trust when trust might kill you. It's about leaning on someone when you barely have the strength to stand. It's about making yourself vulnerable when vulnerability could get you hurt—or worse. In the middle of chaos, friends aren't just social companions. They are safety nets. They are backup plans. They are the difference between collapsing alone and stumbling forward together.

Writing these friendships means focusing on how disaster accelerates intimacy. Two people who would have been casual acquaintances in the normal world might become inseparable under pressure. A stranger who helps carry an injured friend through a flood can become family overnight. Shared danger forges fast, deep connections—but it also tests them brutally. Disaster doesn't give friendships years to slowly develop trust. It gives them minutes. Hours. A handful of life-or-death moments. And in those moments, true character emerges.

One of the best ways to write realistic disaster friendships is to show how survival pressures shape them. Sometimes friends grow closer because they rely on each other completely. They become each other's anchor, each other's sanity check, each other's reason to keep going. Sometimes, though, survival drives wedges between friends. Maybe one is more ruthless than the other. Maybe one makes a decision that gets others hurt. Maybe one cracks under the pressure, becoming a liability instead of an asset. These fractures are painful because they feel so personal—and because readers will have seen the bond build before it broke.

Betrayal in a disaster story cuts even deeper than betrayal in a normal story. When the stakes are survival, when trust literally means life or death, betrayal isn't just personal—it's existential. It's someone choosing their own life over yours. It's someone deciding that your friendship isn't worth the risk. And it can happen fast. One moment, they're sharing their last can of food with you. The next, they're locking you out to die while they take the only working vehicle. The betrayal doesn't have to be grand or dramatic. Sometimes it's as small—and as devastating—as someone looking away when you need them most.

Writing betrayal well means understanding the motivations behind it. Rarely does someone betray a friend in disaster fiction just for the fun of it. Usually, it's fear, desperation, or terrible logic. Maybe they believe they have no other choice. Maybe they convince themselves it's for the greater good. Maybe they crack under the weight of survival instincts. Showing the betrayer's human side—showing the internal struggle, the guilt, the cowardice, the rationalizations—makes the betrayal hurt more, feel more real. Readers hate shallow villains, but they fear friends who break under pressure because that feels uncomfortably close to home.

One of the hardest but most powerful arcs you can write is a character who is betrayed—and still finds a way to forgive. Forgiveness in disaster fiction isn't soft. It's a hard, bloody, stubborn act of choosing not to let betrayal define you. Maybe the character who was betrayed has to work alongside the betrayer again because survival demands it. Maybe they have to risk trusting someone else, even when every instinct screams not to. Maybe they never forgive—and that choice scars them permanently, hardening them against any future human connection. Either way, betrayal changes people. It should ripple through the rest of your story, shaping every choice your characters make going forward.

If you're using ChatGPT to brainstorm friendship and betrayal arcs, you can prompt for ideas like "describe how two best friends drift apart during a survival situation" or "examples of betrayal between survivors in a disaster setting." You can also ask for specific emotional beats: "moments when distrust turns into open conflict" or "scenes where former friends have to work together despite betrayal." Layering these emotional shifts into your disaster story makes it feel more raw, more human.

Another layer you can add is betrayal that isn't personal—but feels that way. Maybe supplies are limited, and a friend has to choose who gets the last dose of medicine. Maybe the friend chooses their younger sibling over your protagonist. Logically, it makes sense—but emotionally, it feels like a knife in the gut. In disaster fiction, betrayal doesn't always come from malice. Sometimes it comes from impossible choices. Sometimes good people hurt each other because the situation leaves them no other way.

You can also explore the tension between loyalty and pragmatism. One character might insist on sticking together no matter what. Another might argue that loyalty is a death sentence—that only the strong, the fast, the ruthless will survive. These philosophical differences can create rifts between friends even before any direct betrayal happens. Survival isn't just a test of strength. It's a test of ideals. Watching those ideals clash—and break—can create some of the most intense emotional drama in your story.

And don't forget that friendship can save lives too. In the darkest moments, when despair threatens to choke your characters, it might be the memory of a friend's sacrifice, or a friend's stubborn loyalty, that keeps them moving forward. Disaster strips away comfort, safety, civility—but it doesn't always strip away humanity. Friendship, even battered and bloodied, can survive. And sometimes, it's the only thing that does.

Another way to heighten the emotional stakes is to use layered relationships. Maybe two friends have a complicated past. Maybe one has always carried a secret resentment. Maybe there's a buried love that never had a chance to bloom. Disaster pulls all those buried emotions to the surface. In the middle of running from fire or fighting off looters or scavenging for food, the personal still matters. The heart still aches. The old wounds still bleed.

When writing betrayal, pace it carefully. A sudden, shocking betrayal can work if you've seeded just enough foreshadowing—the hints of selfishness, the flickers of fear, the moments of hesitation. But a slow betrayal, one that unfolds piece by piece, can be even more devastating. Show a character lying once. Hoarding supplies once. Looking the other way once. Each small choice adds up until the final, undeniable break. Readers will feel every step of the fall, every missed chance to stop it, and it will hit that much harder when the betrayal comes.

In the end, friendship and betrayal at the end of the world are about what we hold onto when everything else is gone. They're about what survival costs—and what's worth fighting for even when the fight seems hopeless. They're about the terrible beauty of trust, and the even more terrible consequences when that trust shatters.

Because when the ground cracks and the sky burns and the sirens fade, sometimes the last thing you have left isn't a weapon, a shelter, or a plan.

Sometimes the last thing you have left is a hand reaching for yours—or a hand letting go.

And in that moment, everything changes.

Survival vs. Morality: Hard Choices in Hard Times

One of the hardest things disaster stories force characters—and readers—to face is the brutal clash between survival and morality. It's easy to believe in right and wrong when life is comfortable, when there's time to think, when resources are plentiful. But when the world collapses and survival becomes a daily gamble, morality doesn't vanish—it gets heavy. It becomes a burden that might get you killed. And in the darkest moments, characters have to ask themselves: what am I willing to do to stay alive? And more terrifyingly, what am I willing to become?

In a survival setting, hard choices come fast and without warning. It might be a question of whether to steal supplies from another group. Whether to leave behind the injured because they'll slow everyone down. Whether to kill someone threatening your group—or risk everyone's lives trying to find another way. In those moments, the line between right and wrong blurs. The instincts for survival crash into the ideals people once thought were absolute. And the disaster story becomes something deeper: a mirror, reflecting who we are when everything else is stripped away.

When you're writing survival vs. morality dilemmas, the first thing to remember is that no choice should feel easy. If a choice feels simple, it's probably not a real crisis. Real survival dilemmas hurt no matter what your character chooses. They're situations where every path costs something precious—safety, dignity, loyalty, humanity. Maybe a character chooses survival and has to live with what they did. Maybe they choose morality and lose something—or someone—they can never get back. Either way, the consequences should echo through the rest of the story, shaping their journey.

One of the classic survival dilemmas is resource theft. In the early days of a disaster, when supplies start to vanish, characters may face situations where they have to choose: take food, medicine, or water from others—or risk dying. Maybe the supplies belong to strangers. Maybe they belong to another struggling group. Maybe they belong to a child. Writing this choice forces your character to confront what survival means when it's bought with someone else's suffering. And how your character feels about their decision—whether they justify it, regret it, harden because of it—becomes a core part of their arc.

Another brutal choice comes with triage. In a situation where you can't save everyone—who do you choose? The strongest? The most vulnerable? The ones you love? Disaster doesn't care about fairness, and neither do the hard choices it forces. Writing triage moments forces your characters into heartbreaking moral territory. It asks them—and your readers—to face the fact that saving one life might mean sacrificing another. And once that choice is made, there's no undoing it.

Violence is another moral minefield in disaster fiction. When survival is on the line, the instinct to defend yourself or your group can clash with the ideals of peace, mercy, or restraint. Maybe your character believes in nonviolence—but is forced to kill to protect a loved one. Maybe they cross a line they swore they never would—and discover they can't cross back. Writing violence with moral complexity means showing that it's never just physical. It leaves emotional scars, questions, fears that linger long after the body count fades.

Then there's betrayal for survival. What happens when a character lies, abandons, or even sacrifices others to save themselves or their family? Writing betrayal isn't just about the moment it happens—it's about the emotional aftershocks. Maybe the character justifies it at first. Maybe guilt eats at them. Maybe they become colder, harder, convinced that survival demands it. Or maybe the betrayal haunts them until they reach a breaking point. Either way, survival at the cost of loyalty creates cracks that run through the entire story.

If you're using ChatGPT to brainstorm survival versus morality conflicts, you can prompt for situations like "scenarios where a survivor must choose between saving one person or many" or "examples of moral compromises during an apocalypse." You can also brainstorm character reactions: "how a character might rationalize stealing food from children" or "how guilt might manifest after abandoning a friend." Building layered emotional fallout from these decisions gives your disaster story a raw, aching authenticity.

A powerful structure to use in your story is escalation. Early on, the choices might be smaller: take extra rations when no one is looking, lie about the severity of an injury to avoid being left behind. But as the disaster drags on and pressures mount, the choices grow darker: abandon the injured, steal from friends, kill to protect supplies. Each decision pushes the characters—and readers—closer to the edge. By the climax of your story, your characters should be standing at a moral cliff they never thought they would approach, let alone cross.

Another dynamic to explore is division within survivor groups. Not everyone will agree on where the line between survival and morality should be drawn. Some characters will argue that survival is everything—that morality is a luxury no one can afford anymore. Others will cling to their ethics even as the world burns. These debates, these schisms, create tension, drama, and heartbreak. Maybe groups split. Maybe betrayals happen not because of hatred, but because of moral differences that become too deep to bridge.

And don't shy away from characters who regret their survival choices—or who don't. Some survivors harden, justifying every terrible thing they did. Others crumble under the weight of guilt. Some lose their sense of self entirely, becoming something monstrous to stay alive. Others find a way to survive without losing who they are, though it costs them dearly. Disaster fiction thrives on this range of human responses. No two people break—or endure—the same way.

One of the hardest, most powerful emotional questions you can ask in your disaster story is this: who deserves to survive? It's not a comfortable question. It has no easy answer. And that's exactly why it hits so hard. Maybe the strongest aren't the kindest. Maybe the bravest aren't the ones who make it. Maybe survival has nothing to do with worthiness at all—and everything to do with chance, ruthlessness, or pure blind luck. Writing characters who wrestle with this question adds emotional gravity to every decision, every sacrifice, every moment of despair or hope.

And sometimes, survival and morality can align. Sometimes, doing the right thing doesn't cost your life—it saves it. Sometimes protecting others, acting with compassion, building trust, becomes the difference between surviving alone and surviving together. These rare victories, these moments where morality and survival coexist, shine even brighter against the brutal backdrop of disaster. They remind readers—and characters—that even in the worst circumstances, humanity isn't doomed to devour itself.

In the end, survival versus morality isn't a simple choice your characters make once. It's a grinding, endless tension that follows them through every scene, every decision, every sleepless night. It's the slow erosion—or fierce protection—of their soul. It's the whispered doubt that haunts their dreams. It's the hard, necessary truths they can't unlearn.

Because in the ruins of the old world, survival is no longer just about breathing.

It's about deciding what part of yourself is worth saving—and what part you're willing to lose forever.

The Importance of Small Moments amidst the Catastrophe

When you think of disaster stories, it's easy to picture the big moments first. The explosion that tears the city apart. The massive wave swallowing the coastline. The power going out and the long darkness that follows. These are the fireworks of the narrative—the spectacle that captures attention. But the real heart of a disaster story, the part that stays with readers long after the last building has fallen, is the small moments. The quiet ones. The human ones. The ones that whisper instead of scream.

Disaster strips life down to its bare bones, but what gives a survival story its soul isn't just who lives and who dies. It's what tiny pieces of normalcy or humanity survive along with them. A child sharing a bruised apple with a stranger. Two exhausted people laughing at a stupid joke as the city smolders around them. Someone singing quietly in the dark to remind themselves they're still alive. These small moments are what make the chaos meaningful. Without them, a disaster story is just noise. With them, it becomes unforgettable.

One of the reasons small moments matter so much is because they create contrast. When everything is loud and fast and deadly, a single soft breath, a shared glance, a moment of kindness feels massive. It hits harder because it shouldn't even exist in a world so broken. When you slow down to show these moments, you make the disaster bigger, not smaller. You remind readers what's at stake—what could be lost, what might still be saved.

Writing small moments isn't about slowing the story down just to pad word count. It's about deepening the emotional stakes. A character sewing a ripped jacket by candlelight while bombs fall in the distance. A survivor brushing dust off a battered family photo before moving on. A rescue worker scribbling a note to a missing loved one they hope is still alive. These small actions tell us more about who your characters are than a hundred action scenes ever could.

Small moments also build connection between characters—and between the characters and the reader. When two people share a laugh, or a memory, or a cigarette while waiting for the next disaster to strike, they're not just surviving. They're living, however briefly. They're claiming a little piece of humanity in a world that wants to strip it away. Readers feel these moments in their gut because they mirror what we all crave when things fall apart: touch, voice, comfort, remembrance.

If you're using ChatGPT to help brainstorm small moments, try prompting for ideas like "quiet scenes of hope between survivors during a flood" or "personal rituals characters might cling to during an apocalypse." You can also ask for emotional beats like "ways characters show love or loyalty without words" or "small acts of kindness that change a survivor's fate." These scenes won't be flashy, but they'll be the ones your readers carry with them long after they've finished the last chapter.

Small moments often hold the seeds of character arcs, too. A soldier who's hardened by loss might slowly open up again because a child shares their only piece of candy. A loner who believed they didn't need anyone might risk their life to save a friend because of one kind conversation. A leader staggering under the weight of command might keep going because someone quietly ties their battered bootlaces for them without being asked. In disaster fiction, survival is physical, but it's also emotional. Small moments help your characters survive themselves.

One way to structure small moments is to treat them like lifelines scattered through the story. After every major trauma—every escape, every fight, every loss—drop in a quiet scene. A moment where the characters breathe, remember, connect. Let them mourn. Let them dream. Let them hope, even if it's foolish. These beats don't break the tension—they sharpen it. They remind the reader what's precious, which makes the next threat even more terrifying.

Another powerful use of small moments is to anchor characters to their lost world. In a collapsing city, a character might stop to fix a crooked picture frame on a crumbling wall. In a flooded suburb, a survivor might wade into a drowned house just to retrieve a beloved book. In a starving village, a grandmother might insist on setting the table properly even when there's almost no food left. These gestures don't change the outcome of the disaster—but they change how readers experience it. They show that even as the world falls, people still carry fragments of who they were before. And sometimes, that's enough to keep them fighting.

Small moments also offer opportunities for thematic resonance. If your disaster story is about hope in the face of despair, your small moments can be tiny acts of defiance against hopelessness—a character planting seeds in a ruined garden, a couple getting married in the ashes of their hometown. If your story is about moral compromise, your small moments might be the last flickers of decency—a soldier refusing to loot a corpse, a thief sharing stolen food with a stranger. Themes are big ideas, but small moments make them live and breathe.

And don't underestimate the power of sensory detail in small moments. The rough feel of a wool blanket. The bitter sweetness of cold, gritty chocolate. The sound of rain tapping on a collapsed roof. The smell of smoke layered with the sharper tang of blood. These details pull readers deeper into the story without needing long paragraphs of exposition. A single vivid, human moment can paint a world more completely than pages of description.

Another way to use small moments is to show the gradual change in your world and characters. Early in the story, survivors might still flinch when they hear sirens or mourn when they see abandoned homes. Later, they might walk past without noticing. The moment they stop seeing—or stop caring—can be devastating to readers, even if it's just a single sentence. A small moment like that can say volumes about how much has been lost, both outside and inside.

If you want to really tear at readers' hearts, layer hope and heartbreak into the same moment. A child carefully saving a candy bar for their missing parent. A couple carving their names into a ruined bridge before parting ways forever. A survivor tucking a photo into a crack in a wall, believing they'll come back someday. Hope and loss mixed together make small moments hurt more—but they also make them beautiful.

And finally, small moments prepare readers for the end of the story. When everything climaxes—the final escape, the final collapse, the final confrontation—the small moments you've woven throughout your disaster narrative will give those climactic scenes emotional weight. It won't just be buildings falling or people dying. It'll be everything those characters dreamed of, clung to, lost, and fought for. It'll be all the little human things that mattered more than survival alone.

Because in the end, disaster stories aren't really about the disasters.

They're about the tiny acts of humanity that survive even after the world ends.

The smile in the darkness.

The hand offered to a stranger.

The stubborn refusal to forget what it means to be alive.

Weaving Themes of Hope, Loss, and Resilience

When you strip disaster stories down to their core, you'll almost always find the same three powerful forces at work: hope, loss, and resilience. They're the emotional currents running under every collapsed building, every flooded street, every desperate decision. Hope keeps characters moving forward when it would be easier to give up. Loss gives their struggles meaning and stakes. And resilience is the thread that ties it all together—the stubborn, battered human spirit that refuses to quit even when everything else falls away.

Weaving these themes into your disaster story isn't about giving speeches or hammering readers over the head with Big Important Messages. It's about layering them into the choices your characters make, the way they react to triumph and tragedy, the way they speak, act, and dream even when the world crumbles around them. Done right, these themes don't just make your story more emotional—they make it unforgettable.

Let's start with hope. In a disaster story, hope isn't naïve. It's not the blind optimism of someone who doesn't understand how bad things really are. True hope is forged in darkness. It's the voice that says, *just one more step,* even when there's no reason left to believe the next step will matter. Writing hope means showing characters choosing to believe in survival, in reunion, in rebuilding, even when logic screams that they shouldn't.

Hope can take a thousand forms. A mother promising her child that they'll see the sun again. A leader refusing to abandon a broken-down shelter full of survivors. A wounded firefighter crawling back into the flames because someone might still be alive in there. Hope isn't loud in disaster fiction. It's quiet, stubborn, sometimes even bitter. It's not about ignoring the horror—it's about choosing to fight anyway.

Layering hope into your story means planting seeds everywhere. The small gestures. The stolen moments of laughter. The handmade signs saying "Help is Coming" in broken cities. The decision to bury the dead with care instead of leaving them behind. It's in the way characters treat each other, protect each other, believe in each other when there's no good reason left to. Hope makes the devastation hit harder, not softer, because it reminds us what's being fought for.

Now let's talk about loss. Loss is the heartbeat of disaster fiction. It's not just about losing people—though that's often the most gut-wrenching form. It's also about losing homes, routines, identities, dreams. It's about the slow, brutal stripping away of everything your characters thought was permanent. And it's not clean or neat. Loss in disaster fiction is messy, raw, unresolved. Sometimes there's no closure. Sometimes a character doesn't even know if their loved one is dead or alive. That uncertainty can be even more devastating than confirmed loss.

Writing loss authentically means letting it linger. It's not a single tearful scene and then moving on. It's a weight characters carry into every new moment. It's seeing a child pick up a broken toy and not know why they're crying. It's watching a leader who once rallied dozens now sit alone, staring at the ruins of a failed evacuation. It's a mother setting an extra place at an empty table because she can't break the habit yet. Loss shapes your characters' actions, their relationships, their resilience—or their collapse.

When writing about loss, resist the urge to tidy it up too soon. Let characters mourn badly. Let them rage, deny, fall apart. Let them lash out or withdraw. Real grief isn't pretty, and in the brutal honesty of disaster fiction, it shouldn't be. And sometimes, the deepest loss isn't even about death. Sometimes it's the loss of trust, the loss of faith, the loss of the version of yourself you thought you were before everything fell apart.

And then there's resilience—the rough, scarred core that keeps survivors moving when hope flickers and loss bites deep. Resilience isn't about being untouched by disaster. It's about being broken and still crawling forward. It's about grieving and still reaching out to help someone else. It's about facing the ashes and still planting seeds.

Writing resilience means showing characters at their lowest—and then showing them choose to stand up anyway. It's the soldier who can barely walk but lifts another to their feet. It's the nurse who bandages one more wound after burying a friend. It's the teenager who finds a way to make the broken-down truck run just long enough to get everyone out of the city. Resilience is sweaty, painful, bone-deep. It's not flashy. It's stubborn.

One of the most powerful ways to weave these themes together is to let them overlap. Hope feeds resilience. Loss tests resilience. Resilience rekindles hope. They're not separate threads running side by side—they're tangled up in every decision, every conversation, every breath your characters take. In one scene, a character might be driven by pure hope. In another, they might be fueled by grief and anger. In another, they might have nothing left but a hollow, automatic resilience. This constant shifting mirrors real emotional survival and makes your story feel alive.

If you're using ChatGPT to help brainstorm, you can prompt for things like "small acts of resilience during a flood" or "ways characters cling to hope during an epidemic" or "scenes showing the emotional impact of loss during an evacuation." You can also ask for thematic arcs: "how a character could regain hope after losing everything" or "how resilience can fail and be rebuilt after betrayal." Building these emotional beats into your structure gives your disaster story a pulse that readers can feel under every collapsed wall and broken promise.

Another trick is to echo these themes visually and symbolically. A single flower blooming in a scorched city. A lone candle burning in a flooded church. A handwritten sign on a highway that simply says *Still Here.* Symbols like these give your themes visual weight without needing exposition. They stick in readers' minds, haunting and hopeful at the same time.

You can also mirror your themes in your character arcs. Maybe your protagonist starts the story hardened and cynical but rediscovers hope through others. Maybe another character begins hopeful but loses their way under the weight of grief. Maybe a minor character who seems weak at first shows incredible resilience when it matters most. Let hope, loss, and resilience not just exist around your characters—but transform them.

And finally, remember that these themes don't require happy endings. A disaster story can end in tragedy and still be about hope. It can end in survival and still be soaked in grief. It can end with characters battered and broken and still be a story of resilience. What matters is that the emotional journey feels true—that readers walk away feeling that even in the worst moments, even when the world ends, the core of what makes us human can survive.

Because disaster stories aren't just about how things fall apart.

They're about how people hold on—sometimes to hope, sometimes to love, sometimes just to the stubborn, beautiful will to go on breathing, one more minute, one more hour, one more day.

Fear as a Character: Using Dread to Power Your Story

When you're writing a disaster story, fear isn't just something your characters feel—it's a force that moves through the entire narrative like a living thing. Fear is more than a reaction. It becomes its own character, its own presence. It shapes decisions. It twists relationships. It changes people in ways even they don't recognize. If you treat fear not just as a symptom of disaster but as a driving, breathing element in your story, you'll create a much deeper and more gripping emotional experience for your readers.

Fear in disaster fiction isn't always loud. It's not always people screaming and running. More often, it's slow. It's sticky. It's the weight pressing down on every breath. It's the silence after the sirens stop. It's the long moments when nothing happens—but could, at any second. The best disaster stories don't just show explosions and collapses; they create a constant, simmering dread that makes every ordinary moment feel like standing on a ticking bomb.

One of the most effective ways to write fear as a character is to layer it into the environment. Maybe the city is too quiet after the hurricane, every footstep echoing too loud. Maybe the air smells wrong after the chemical spill, and nobody knows what that smell means yet. Maybe the rumble of distant thunder sounds just enough like shelling to make everyone flinch. When readers feel fear through setting, it gets under their skin without needing long descriptions of what characters are feeling. They *know* something's wrong because the world tells them so.

Fear also lives inside your characters—and it should never be simple. People don't all react to fear the same way. Some freeze. Some lash out. Some make jokes. Some get angry. Some go numb. If every character reacts the same way to fear, your story will feel flat and fake. But if you show the wide, messy spectrum of fear responses, you make your disaster world feel real. One character might become hyper-focused and efficient. Another might deny the danger completely until it's too late. Another might break down, or worse, become dangerous to others out of panic.

If you're using ChatGPT to help brainstorm, you can prompt for ideas like "different fear responses in a survival situation" or "how fear changes group dynamics during a disaster." You can also brainstorm specific sensory details: "how a character might experience fear physically during an earthquake" or "how fear changes behavior during an evacuation." These details make the emotion tangible rather than abstract.

One trick for making fear feel alive in your disaster story is to escalate it slowly. Start with discomfort—something small, like noticing the water pressure is dropping or seeing a line at the gas station stretch around the block. Let it build into anxiety—hearing about evacuations, seeing the grocery shelves empty. Let it sharpen into panic—sirens, smoke, gridlock, violence. And finally, let it sink into dread—the realization that no help is coming, that survival depends entirely on what you do next. Fear that evolves feels more real, because it mirrors how people actually experience it in stages, not all at once.

Another powerful tool is **anticipatory fear**—the fear of what might happen, even if it hasn't yet. In many disaster stories, the scariest moments are the ones where nothing is happening yet, but everyone knows it's about to. The evacuation order that hasn't been given but hangs in the air. The creaking dam that hasn't burst yet. The cough that might mean infection. Anticipatory fear keeps characters—and readers—on edge, watching, waiting, imagining. It makes every safe moment feel temporary, every breath feel borrowed.

Silence plays a huge role in this. Let the quiet stretch sometimes. Let characters sit with their fear instead of always running or fighting. A family sitting in a boarded-up house, listening to the storm tear the world apart outside. A survivor holding their breath in a flooded subway, waiting for a distant noise they can't identify. In those silences, fear grows enormous, pressing against the characters' minds and bodies until it almost feels like another presence in the room.

Fear also changes relationships. Under pressure, trust becomes fragile. Paranoia blooms. Old grudges surface. Decisions that would be simple under normal conditions become impossible. Writing how fear poisons friendships, families, teams, and communities adds emotional complexity to your story. Maybe two characters who trusted each other completely now hesitate. Maybe a leader who seemed steady starts to second-guess themselves and lose their followers. Maybe a survivor's love for their family turns possessive and dangerous, driven by fear of losing them.

And don't forget that fear can be manipulated. In collapsed societies, fear becomes a weapon. Leaders can use it to control people. Thieves can use it to intimidate. Groups can turn on each other because someone whispered the right lie at the right time. Writing about how fear spreads, how it's used, how it shapes decisions and systems, turns your disaster story into something bigger than just a personal survival narrative—it becomes a study of human nature under stress.

Sometimes, fear becomes so big that it turns characters into the very thing they were afraid of. A man afraid of losing his family becomes violent and drives them away. A leader afraid of losing control becomes a dictator. Fear reshapes people. It strips away civility, sometimes exposing hidden strength—but sometimes revealing ugly truths people never wanted to see. Tracking how fear changes your characters over time gives your story emotional momentum. It's not just about surviving the environment anymore. It's about surviving yourself.

One of the most haunting emotional beats you can hit is when characters stop feeling fear. That deadened, hollow acceptance of death is often more chilling than screams. A teenager staring blankly at the city burning. A mother calmly packing her child's things even though she knows they won't make it. A rescuer walking into danger without hesitation because they've given up hope of surviving. The absence of fear at the wrong moment tells readers that the character has been pushed beyond human limits—and it's devastating to witness.

Ultimately, writing fear as a character in your disaster story means making sure it's always present—not just when the bombs fall or the floodwaters rise, but in the quiet, aching spaces in between. It means showing how fear changes people, how it tests love, how it shatters communities, how it can even—sometimes—be overcome. Not erased. Not forgotten. But faced. Endured. Survived.

Because disaster stories aren't just about what collapses outside.

They're about the battles fought inside—the trembling hands reaching for another, the quiet breaths in the dark, the refusal to let fear become the only thing that survives.

Pacing a Disaster Story for Maximum Tension

Pacing in a disaster story is everything. Get it wrong, and your readers feel lost or bored. Get it right, and you can pull them through your story with white knuckles, shallow breaths, and a pounding heart. A disaster narrative thrives on tension, and tension lives and dies by pacing. You need to know when to push, when to hold back, when to sprint, and when to let everyone catch their breath—just enough to make the next collapse hit even harder.

When people think of pacing in a disaster story, they often imagine it's all go-go-go from page one. But constant action is actually the death of tension. If everything is loud and urgent all the time, nothing feels urgent anymore. Disaster pacing works best when you alternate between pressure and release—moments of frantic action followed by uneasy stillness, like the eye of a hurricane before the other side hits. That ebb and flow keeps readers hooked, leaning forward, dreading what comes next.

The beginning of your disaster story sets the rhythm for everything that follows. Early on, you want to build a low, rising hum of tension rather than dropping readers straight into chaos. Give them small cracks in the ordinary world first: the missed news report about a brewing storm, the quiet empty shelves in the supermarket, the distant sound of sirens nobody quite knows how to interpret. These early clues are your way of tightening the strings without snapping them yet. Readers should feel something's wrong even if they can't yet say what.

Then, when the disaster strikes—*really* strikes—you hit hard. Short, sharp scenes. Rapid developments. Escalating stakes. This is your first sprint. Readers should barely have time to process before the next threat hits. The pacing here should mimic the characters' experience: breathless, disoriented, reactive. Use shorter paragraphs. Break dialogue into fragments. Let the structure of your sentences reflect the chaos of the world collapsing around them.

But—and this is key—after the initial chaos, you need a pause. Not a peaceful break. An uneasy one. This is when your survivors regroup, count their losses, realize how bad things really are. Slowing the pace here doesn't kill the tension—it deepens it. Readers know the worst isn't over. They know the disaster world is just beginning to unfold. The quiet moments between disasters are often when fear really sinks in.

From there, your pacing should work like a heartbeat—steady rises and sudden spikes. A survivor scouting for supplies might encounter no immediate threat—but every shadow feels dangerous, every creak of floorboards could be the start of a collapse. A conversation about strategy can suddenly explode into an argument, a betrayal, a panic. Movement through the story world—through flooded streets, broken cities, burned forests—should feel like moving through a minefield: slow, deliberate, and tense.

One smart trick is to vary the types of tension. Physical tension comes from threats like aftershocks, fires, disease outbreaks. Emotional tension comes from distrust, fear, grief, moral choices. Strategic tension comes from characters planning something risky and readers wondering if it will blow up in their faces. Mixing these types of tension means you're not just repeating the same kind of scene over and over—you're layering different kinds of pressure until readers feel as trapped as your characters do.

If you're using ChatGPT to brainstorm pacing ideas, you can prompt for things like "ways to escalate tension in a disaster story without using action scenes" or "quiet scenes that still build dread between major disaster events." You can also generate scene lists that alternate between physical danger and emotional fallout, giving you a natural rise-and-fall structure to work with.

Another thing to think about is escalation. In a good disaster story, the situation should keep getting worse. Even when characters solve a problem—find shelter, secure supplies, reunite with loved ones—the victory should either come with a price or open the door to a bigger problem. Maybe the shelter is already occupied by desperate strangers. Maybe the supplies are contaminated. Maybe the loved ones bring news that makes everything more complicated. Disaster fiction is about surviving today only to face something even harder tomorrow. The tension should ratchet up with each new development.

And remember: even hope should be risky. A moment of hope—a rescue helicopter spotted on the horizon, a working radio found in the wreckage—should make readers nervous, not relaxed. Will the helicopter land safely? Will the radio call for help—or alert enemies? Hope should offer relief *and* dread at the same time. That emotional complexity keeps your pacing tight because readers never know if the next beat will be triumph or tragedy.

Another important pacing tool is time pressure. Deadlines ramp up tension naturally. Maybe the storm will make the bridge impassable by nightfall. Maybe the disease spreads faster once the temperature drops. Maybe the evacuation convoy leaves at dawn, whether you're on it or not. Time ticking down forces characters into decisions they're not ready to make, into risks they wouldn't normally take. It creates urgency without needing to add more explosions or violence.

You can also use geography to control pacing. Moving through the disaster world should feel dangerous and exhausting. A trip across town might take hours because streets are blocked, bridges are out, or hostile survivors control key checkpoints. Characters should constantly be navigating both the physical collapse and the human chaos layered over it. Setting physical milestones—cross the river, reach the safe zone, get to the tower before dark—gives your story natural beats where tension spikes and pacing tightens.

Pacing isn't just about speeding up or slowing down scenes, either. It's about emotional pacing, too. After a major death or a betrayal or a loss, don't rush past it. Let it sink in. Let the weight settle. Readers need space to grieve or rage alongside your characters. Then, once that emotion has had time to breathe, hit them again with the next danger. It's this emotional whiplash—the swing between fear and sorrow and fleeting hope—that keeps readers emotionally hooked.

If you want your story to hit even harder, use repetition—but carefully. A character hearing the same emergency broadcast over and over as they move through different ruined spaces. The sound of sirens fading in and out at random intervals. A haunting lullaby someone hums in multiple key scenes. These repeated elements create a sense of inescapability, that the disaster isn't just around your characters—it's inside their heads now, coloring everything they do.

One more tip: think about the endgame. Disaster stories often build to either an escape or a final stand. As you approach the climax, your pacing should tighten. Fewer breaks. Shorter scenes. Less time for debate. Decisions come faster. Consequences hit harder. Readers should feel the characters—and the story itself—racing toward a point of no return. Whether it ends in survival, death, or something messier, the final chapters should feel breathless, inevitable, cathartic. In the end, pacing a disaster story for maximum tension is about understanding the emotional journey as much as the physical one. It's about pulling readers into the collapse, making them feel every uncertain step, every rising panic, every impossible choice.

It's about never letting them feel completely safe—even when the sky is briefly clear. Because disaster isn't just the moment when the world falls apart. It's the long, aching suspense of not knowing what—or who—will survive.

Building Rising Stakes: When Things Go From Bad to Worse

One thing that makes disaster stories so compelling is how they keep turning the screws. Just when the characters think they've hit rock bottom, the ground gives way beneath them again. Disaster fiction is all about escalation—about taking a bad situation and making it worse, then worse again, until survival feels almost impossible. And if you build the rising stakes carefully, your readers won't be able to look away. They'll be trapped with your characters, holding their breath, needing to know how much more they can take before they break—or break through.

Rising stakes don't mean just throwing bigger explosions or louder disasters onto the page. It means deepening the personal, emotional, and survival consequences every step of the way. It's not just that the earthquake hit—it's that the aftershocks are trapping the characters further and further underground. It's not just that the virus is spreading—it's that a character's own brother might be infected and hiding it. Escalation works best when it's not only external, but internal. When the danger outside mirrors and feeds the tension inside.

One of the first keys to building rising stakes is to start with a clear first goal. Maybe it's reaching a shelter, finding a missing family member, escaping the city. Give the characters a target—and give readers a reason to hope they'll get there. Then, once that target feels almost within reach, throw a wrench into the plan. The shelter is full. The family member is already gone. The escape route is blocked. The goalposts move, and now the stakes aren't just survival—they're adaptation under crushing disappointment.

Another powerful method is **compounding problems**. In real disasters, it's rarely just one thing going wrong. An earthquake doesn't just knock down buildings—it ruptures gas lines, triggers fires, cuts off water supplies. In your story, let each new challenge create a ripple of secondary challenges. Characters finally find a working car—but the roads are jammed with abandoned vehicles. They find an abandoned house to rest in—but it's already claimed by desperate survivors. Every victory opens a new problem, forcing constant adjustment, constant risk.

You also want to escalate personal stakes along with physical ones. It's not just that survival gets harder—it's that the choices get crueller. Early in the story, a character might have to scavenge for food. Later, they might have to choose whether to share it with a wounded stranger—or protect their family's dwindling supplies. Early on, loyalty might seem obvious. Later, when tensions rise and betrayal lurks, trust becomes lethal. As the disaster grinds on, the emotional cost of survival should get heavier and heavier.

If you're using ChatGPT to brainstorm escalating stakes, you can prompt for things like "unexpected complications during an evacuation" or "moral dilemmas survivors might face as resources run out." You can also build escalating personal conflicts: "how a friendship might fracture under disaster pressure" or "how leadership struggles could escalate into violence." Layering these personal escalations onto the physical collapse gives your story real emotional traction.

Another key to escalating stakes is time pressure. The longer characters wait, the worse things get. Disease spreads. Riots break out. Supplies dwindle. Weather worsens. Time becomes an enemy just as deadly as the disaster itself. Adding ticking clocks—deadlines for evacuation, limits on supplies, approaching storms—forces characters to make decisions faster and with less information, increasing the risk of failure and the intensity of every choice.

And don't underestimate the power of hope to raise stakes too. A glimpse of rescue—a flare in the distance, a helicopter spotted overhead—raises emotional stakes enormously. Readers want the characters to make it. They hope for a break in the chaos. So when that rescue fails or is ripped away, it hits ten times harder. False hope isn't cruel storytelling—it's good storytelling, because it invests readers even more deeply in the characters' fight to survive.

One smart technique is **ratcheting escalation**—small problems that spiral into big ones through characters' understandable but flawed choices. Maybe they delay leaving because they're waiting for someone. Maybe they split up to cover more ground. Maybe they take a shortcut to save time. Each decision seems reasonable in the moment, but leads to disaster later. This technique keeps your story grounded in character agency rather than pure bad luck, which makes the rising stakes feel earned rather than arbitrary.

Another critical layer is **worsening group dynamics**. As fear and desperation build, the bonds between survivors strain and sometimes snap. Group decisions become battlegrounds. Leaders are questioned or overthrown. Alliances fray. Violence or abandonment becomes a real threat inside the group, not just from outside forces. Internal collapse mirrors external collapse, amplifying tension and making every step forward feel like a powder keg ready to explode.

As you escalate stakes, think also about **changing the kind of threat** your characters face. Early threats might be environmental—fires, floods, earthquakes. Later threats might be human—other survivors, rogue militias, broken authority structures. And later still, the greatest threat might come from inside your own characters—their own fear, despair, guilt, or rage. Shifting the nature of the danger keeps the story fresh and unpredictable.

Pacing matters a lot here too. If you escalate too fast, readers get overwhelmed and disconnected. If you escalate too slowly, they get bored. Aim for a rising curve—a few moments to breathe and gather strength after each major blow, just long enough for hope or plans to start building, before the next hammer falls. That rise-and-fall rhythm keeps the tension dynamic and constantly climbing without exhausting the audience.

Symbolism can also reinforce rising stakes beautifully. Maybe the landscape itself changes over the course of the story—more burned-out cars, more abandoned homes, fewer signs of life. Maybe the weather worsens, skies darken, water becomes scarcer. Maybe characters lose mementos or rituals that connected them to their old lives. Physical signs of decay mirror the emotional and societal breakdown happening inside your story.

And always remember: escalation doesn't have to mean bigger explosions. Sometimes the worst escalation is a quiet, horrifying realization. That the safe zone is a lie. That the infection can't be stopped. That there's no way home. Psychological escalation can be even more devastating than physical destruction if you ground it in characters readers care about.

In the final acts of your story, escalation should push your characters to their breaking points. Survival should no longer be just about enduring—it should demand sacrifice, transformation, or loss. Maybe a character must betray their own values to save others. Maybe they lose someone they swore to protect. Maybe they have to choose between survival and humanity. Escalation forces choices that define who your characters truly are.

By the end, readers should feel that the stakes couldn't possibly get higher—not just because the world is broken, but because the characters' hearts are laid bare. Survival isn't just about dodging danger anymore.

It's about facing the terrible cost of everything they've lost, everything they've done, and everything they still dare to hope for.

Because disaster stories aren't about how things fall apart.

They're about how people keep moving, even when it feels like there's nothing left to move toward.

How to Write Your Disaster in Waves

Disasters don't usually hit once and then politely stop. They come in waves. In the real world, it's rarely the initial event that destroys everything—it's the endless chain reaction afterward. The earthquake triggers aftershocks. The flood brings disease. The blackout leads to fires, looting, violence. In a disaster story, writing the event in waves instead of one big hit creates a much richer, more dynamic narrative. It makes survival a journey, not a single escape. It turns the story into a rising, pounding tide that wears your characters down, tests them again and again, and forces them to change with each new blow.

When you write your disaster in waves, you tap into a much more realistic emotional rhythm. In real crises, the first impact brings panic—but then comes a false calm. People breathe, regroup, start thinking they made it through the worst. And that's exactly when the next wave hits, harder, smarter, crueler. Using this natural emotional cycle lets you control pacing, tension, and character development at a deeper level than just stacking random bad events together.

The first wave in your story should feel overwhelming but survivable. It's the earthquake that levels part of the city but leaves shelters standing. It's the initial virus outbreak before the mutation. It's the first flood surge that forces evacuation but leaves high ground untouched. This wave introduces your characters to survival—but also gives them hope. They start making plans. They believe there's a way out. They think if they can just handle this one crisis, they'll be okay. Readers breathe with them. Hope rises.

That's when you hit them with the second wave.

The second wave takes what they thought they understood and smashes it. Maybe the aftershocks bring down the shelters. Maybe the virus mutates into something deadlier. Maybe a second, stronger surge floods the last high ground. The second wave forces characters to abandon old plans, reassess old assumptions, and realize that survival isn't going to be about enduring a single moment of terror—it's going to be about adapting again and again. The emotional impact here is huge. You move readers from adrenaline to dread. You show them that hope is fragile—and survival is a moving target.

The third wave, if you use it, is the one that breaks them—or nearly does. By now, the characters are exhausted. Supplies are low. Trust is fraying. Injuries are accumulating. Hopes have been betrayed. This wave doesn't just test their bodies—it tests their spirit. Maybe it's not a physical wave at all. Maybe it's a betrayal inside the group. Maybe it's a moral collapse. Maybe it's the simple, devastating realization that rescue isn't coming after all. This wave strips your characters down to their core, forcing them to face who they really are when there's no safety net left.

Writing in waves also gives your story a natural **rise and fall** in tension. After each wave, there's a brief lull—time to breathe, regroup, hope, mourn, or scheme. Those lulls are where you deepen character development. Who hardens? Who falls apart? Who rises as a leader? Who fractures under the strain? Then, just as they start to find their feet, the next wave crashes down. It's not random cruelty—it's the natural shape of survival under relentless conditions.

If you're using ChatGPT to brainstorm wave ideas, you can prompt for things like "secondary disasters after a major earthquake" or "how a flood could worsen after a dam breaks." You can also ask for emotional impacts: "how survivors' morale shifts after multiple disasters" or "ways trust within a survivor group might erode after repeated catastrophes." These layered ideas help you design disasters that feel organic, escalating, and terrifying.

Another way to structure waves is **different kinds of disasters** stacked together. Maybe the initial wave is a hurricane. The second wave is mass flooding and contaminated water. The third wave is disease spreading through overcrowded shelters. Each disaster naturally follows from the last, creating a chain reaction that feels inevitable but still shocking. This approach keeps your world feeling alive and dangerous long after the initial chaos.

Character reactions should evolve with each wave. Early on, they might have quick plans, clear goals. After the second or third wave, decision-making gets messier. Fear creeps in. Trust erodes. Desperation leaks into their choices. Writing characters adjusting—or failing to adjust—to the changing disaster landscape makes the story more emotionally authentic and keeps readers emotionally tied to the journey.

Symbolism can also reinforce the idea of waves. Maybe the physical landscape gets more broken with each strike—buildings leaning more precariously, streets submerged, neighborhoods abandoned. Maybe personal items are lost wave by wave—a backpack, a photo album, a family heirloom—until the characters are literally stripped down to survival and memory. These small visual details show the rising cost without needing a ton of exposition.

The idea of "writing in waves" also lets you explore **hope differently**. Hope isn't a steady candle in disaster fiction. It's a flickering flame, flaring up with each survival, guttering out with each new collapse. Every time a character makes it through a wave, they hope a little more—but also fear a little more, because they've learned the next wave could be even worse. Hope and dread grow side by side, creating richer emotional tension.

You can also weaponize the pauses between waves. Survivors might think the worst is over. They might let their guard down. They might start celebrating small victories. When the next wave hits, the betrayal of that fragile safety makes the impact even sharper. Readers, too, will feel that sting—the emotional whiplash of almost believing things were getting better before the hammer falls again.

When you think about your overall story arc, designing your disaster in waves also helps you pace your climax naturally. The final wave—the big one, the breaking point—should feel earned. By then, readers have been through so much with your characters that they understand, viscerally, how high the stakes are. Whether the characters survive or fail depends not just on luck, but on everything they've learned, endured, and chosen across all the earlier waves.

It's important, too, that not every character survives every wave. Loss should accumulate. Costs should rise. Group dynamics should shift. Maybe a strong character is lost early, throwing the others into disarray. Maybe a minor character survives against all odds, symbolizing resilience. Maybe betrayals, deaths, and moral failures build with each new blow, until survivors are defined as much by who they've lost as by what they've endured.

And not every wave needs to be physically bigger. Psychological waves—loss of hope, collapse of leadership, inner group betrayals—can be even more devastating than external threats. Readers expect the city to crumble. They don't always expect the loyal friend to turn their back or the strong leader to lose faith. Hitting your characters from the inside and the outside at once makes survival feel like a true, almost impossible act.

In the end, writing your disaster in waves isn't just about prolonging the action. It's about turning survival into a brutal, beautiful marathon rather than a sprint. It's about showing how humans adapt, crumble, fight, and rebuild in cycles, just like the disasters that hammer at them.

It's about teaching your characters—and your readers—that survival isn't a finish line you cross.

It's a battle fought over and over, one wave at a time.

Moments of Silence: Letting the Story Breathe

When you're writing a disaster story, it's tempting to think you need to keep your foot slammed down on the gas the whole time. More action, more chaos, more destruction. And while disaster fiction thrives on tension and urgency, the truth is that constant noise eventually numbs the reader. If you never let the story breathe, none of the tension lands the way you want it to. The trick to writing a truly powerful disaster story isn't just in the explosions and collapses. It's in the silences in between—the spaces where fear, grief, hope, and humanity have room to rise up and take center stage.

Moments of silence are where readers—and characters—catch up with the emotional cost of what's happening. When everything is moving at a breakneck pace, survival is instinctual. There's no time to think, no time to mourn, no time to feel. But when the dust settles, even for a little while, that's when the real weight of the disaster starts to hit. That's when characters realize what they've lost, what they still have, and how much further they have to go. Without those quiet beats, the whole story risks feeling hollow—like a series of disconnected dangers without meaning.

Think about real disasters. Survivors don't just sprint from one collapsed building to another. They sit in broken streets, heads in their hands. They stare at the sky because they don't know what else to do. They whisper final prayers. They cling to each other in the dark. These silences aren't breaks from the story. They *are* the story. They're the emotional glue that holds the chaos together, that makes readers care not just about what happens next, but about who it happens to.

Writing silence isn't about writing nothing happening. It's about shifting the focus inward, from external survival to internal survival. Maybe two characters sit in an abandoned bus and share a memory. Maybe a lone survivor takes a moment to bury someone properly, even though danger is everywhere. Maybe the group watches the sunrise after a night of terror, too exhausted to speak. These scenes aren't filler. They are the heartbeats of your story—the proof that your characters are still human, still fighting for more than just their next breath.

If you're using ChatGPT to brainstorm, you can prompt for things like "quiet scenes that deepen character bonds in a disaster setting" or "ways survivors might emotionally process loss after a major catastrophe." You can also look for sensory-focused prompts: "what a survivor hears and feels while waiting for help in a destroyed city." These sensory details ground your moments of silence, making them vivid and alive without needing action to carry them.

Another powerful use of silence is building **anticipation and dread**. A devastated city block where the only sound is a distant creaking beam. A flooded street where no birds sing, no engines hum, no voices call out. Silence in these moments doesn't relax the reader—it tightens the tension. It signals that something is wrong, that danger might strike at any second. Silence becomes not a break from fear, but a sharpening of it. Used right, a moment of quiet can be more terrifying than the loudest explosion.

Moments of silence also offer a place for reflection and decision-making. In the chaos, characters react. In the silence, they choose. Who do they trust? What do they believe is still worth fighting for? Do they keep moving forward—or give up? These choices, made in stolen moments of stillness, shape the arcs of your characters and give the story emotional momentum that no amount of action could ever replace.

One trick is to think about **visual storytelling** during your silent moments. Let the setting speak. A burned playground. A toppled clock tower frozen at the moment of impact. A makeshift memorial of candles flickering in the ruins. These images tell readers everything they need to know about grief, loss, and hope without a single word spoken. Disaster fiction is at its strongest when it trusts the world itself to carry the emotional weight alongside the characters.

And don't be afraid of stillness in dialogue, too. Sometimes the most powerful conversations are the ones where what's *not* said matters more than what is. A shared look. A half-finished sentence. A hand reaching out and being squeezed back. Dialogue in quiet scenes can be sparse, fragmented, raw. Let characters struggle to find words—or realize there are no words left. Those moments are the ones readers remember long after the action scenes blur together.

If you really want to twist the emotional knife, pair a moment of silence with a small act of normalcy. Someone brushing dust off a book and sitting down to read, even though the world is ending. Someone whittling a toy for a lost child. Someone fixing their hair before a long, dangerous march. These tiny rebellions against despair shine brighter when set against the shattered world—and they remind readers that survival isn't just about breathing. It's about staying human.

Another important thing to consider is **timing**. Silence shouldn't come randomly. It should feel earned. After a frantic escape, a death, a betrayal—*then* you let the silence fall. Let the characters (and readers) feel the full impact of what just happened. It's like the echo after a thunderclap: it's not the sound itself that stays with you, but the ringing absence that follows.

Moments of silence also create natural pivot points in your story. After a major loss, a character might change direction—deciding to find their family, to seek revenge, to give up or to double down. After a brush with death, they might rethink their priorities. Quiet scenes give you space to show these shifts believably, rather than rushing through them in the middle of chaos. Readers need to see not just what your characters do—but why they do it.

Silence can also be used to reflect on **themes**. If your disaster story deals with resilience, the quiet moments are where resilience is tested. If it's about loss, these moments are where grief lives. If it's about hope, these moments are where hope flickers stubbornly into life. You don't have to spell it out. Let the mood, the setting, the silence itself carry the emotional message.

And sometimes—sometimes—you can let a scene *just breathe*. No big revelations. No sudden attacks. No new disasters. Just characters sitting with the weight of what they've survived so far, knowing there's more to come. Those breaths make everything else feel real. Without them, your story risks feeling like just a sprint from one danger to the next. With them, your story feels like a real world full of real people fighting battles both outside and inside.

Because survival isn't just about running faster or fighting harder.

It's about finding the strength to sit with fear, grief, and hope—and keep breathing anyway.

Even when the world outside has fallen silent.

Timing the Big Twists and Turns

A disaster story thrives on tension, but tension without surprise gets stale fast. To keep readers truly gripped, you need twists and turns—those sharp pivots where everything the characters believed, planned for, or hoped is suddenly flipped upside down. But it's not just about having twists. It's about *timing* them. Throw a twist too soon, and it feels rushed. Too late, and readers might already have guessed it—or worse, stopped caring. When you time your twists just right, though, you create unforgettable jolts of emotion that send ripples through the entire story.

The first thing to understand about twists in disaster fiction is that they aren't always about shocking the reader. They're about shocking the characters—and making that shock *matter*. A twist in a disaster story doesn't just pull the rug out from under them. It redefines what survival even means. It changes goals, alliances, resources, risks. It forces a pivot not just in plot, but in emotion. That's why a well-timed twist feels like a punch to the chest—not because it's clever, but because it changes everything at the worst possible moment.

The early sections of a disaster story are usually about survival basics: escaping the immediate danger, finding shelter, securing supplies, locating missing loved ones. Twists here need to be more about complicating survival rather than redefining it. Maybe the shelter the group reaches is already overrun. Maybe a trusted ally reveals they're infected. Maybe the disaster isn't over—an aftershock, a second wave, a new threat emerges. Early twists should escalate problems without completely disorienting the reader. You're setting traps now, but you're not ready to spring the biggest ones yet.

The middle of the story is where the biggest turns start to hit. This is the point where characters feel like they have a plan—or at least a fragile grip on their situation. They believe if they can just hold out a little longer, or get to a specific destination, they'll be okay. This is where you time a major twist that guts that hope. Maybe the safe zone has fallen. Maybe the rescue mission was a lie. Maybe the enemy isn't the disaster anymore—it's other survivors. This kind of mid-story twist shakes the entire foundation, forcing characters to change strategies, change alliances, even change who they are.

If you're using ChatGPT to brainstorm twists, you can prompt for things like "unexpected betrayals during a survival mission" or "how a safe haven might secretly be dangerous." You can also ask for environmental turns: "how a disaster might evolve into a second, deadlier threat." Generating several possibilities lets you pick twists that feel organic to your world and your characters, rather than random surprises thrown in just to shock.

One key to timing your big twists is to watch the emotional energy of your story. Readers can only handle so much straight suffering or straight triumph before it flattens out. Twists work best when they hit after a high point—right after a victory, a reunion, a successful plan. That's when readers are emotionally vulnerable. That's when they—and your characters—aren't braced for more pain. And when the fall comes, it feels devastatingly real.

Another technique is **foreshadowing without promising**. You want readers to feel like, in hindsight, they *could* have seen the twist coming—but you don't want them to actually predict it. Drop small hints. A line of dialogue that sounds harmless at first but carries deeper meaning later. A strange detail that seems like background until it becomes crucial. A gut feeling a character ignores. These little signals build subconscious tension, setting readers up for the twist without giving the game away.

Sometimes the biggest twists come not from betrayal or failure, but from internal shifts. Maybe a character breaks a moral code they swore to uphold. Maybe the leader loses faith and deserts the group. Maybe someone who seemed fragile turns ruthless. Timing these emotional twists is just as important as timing external plot twists. Ideally, emotional twists should align with the moments when survival becomes hardest—forcing characters to reveal parts of themselves even they didn't know existed.

Twists can also deepen existing problems rather than introducing totally new ones. Maybe a small injury early on—ignored because there's no time to deal with it—turns septic and endangers the entire group's escape. Maybe a lie told for a good reason earlier finally explodes into a full-blown betrayal. These kinds of turns feel satisfying because they grow naturally from seeds planted earlier, making your story feel tightly woven and inevitable.

Another pacing trick is **mini-twists**—small surprises that keep readers off balance without blowing up the whole story structure. Maybe a trusted guide reveals they've been lost the whole time. Maybe the river they needed to cross has dried up—or turned toxic. These smaller twists keep the tension sharp between bigger story pivots, so readers stay alert and invested without getting exhausted.

As you move toward the climax, your twists should feel bigger, riskier, and more personal. Early on, twists change plans. Later, twists change lives. Maybe the protagonist has to face that saving everyone isn't possible. Maybe the disaster was human-made, not natural. Maybe the person they fought to protect chooses to leave them behind. These twists aren't just about surviving anymore—they're about redefining what survival even means.

Timing the final twist—or the series of final twists—is crucial. You want it close enough to the end that it slams home hard, but not so close that readers don't have time to feel its emotional impact. After the final big twist, you need enough space to show the fallout. Let characters react. Let choices be made. Let the cost of survival, and the scars it leaves, fully settle.

If your disaster story ends with a twist that shifts the entire meaning of what's come before, that's powerful—but risky. Make sure the groundwork has been laid. Readers will forgive heartbreak. They will not forgive feeling tricked. A final twist should feel shocking *and* inevitable. Like a door they didn't know was there—but realize now they've been walking toward the whole time.

One last tip: don't be afraid of **emotional reversals** as twists. The discovery of unexpected kindness. A sacrifice by a selfish character. A reunion that was thought impossible. Disaster stories are brutal—but they're also about survival, resilience, and sometimes, redemption. The most powerful twist might not be one that breaks the characters, but one that saves them when no one, not even they, believed it was still possible.

In the end, timing your big twists and turns isn't about outsmarting your readers.

It's about outsmarting your characters—just enough to show them (and your audience) that survival isn't about clinging to the old plan.

It's about adapting, enduring, and facing the brutal truth that nothing—not even hope—is safe in a world that's falling apart.

Designing Scenes of Chaos and Stillness

When you're writing a disaster story, one of the most powerful tools you have is contrast. Readers expect chaos, of course—collapsing buildings, fires raging, people screaming, confusion thick enough to choke on. But what really makes a disaster story breathe, what makes it *feel* real and devastating, is the way you balance that chaos with stillness. The crashing and the silence. The sprinting and the stunned standing still. Designing scenes where both live side-by-side gives your story emotional shape and texture that pure action could never achieve.

Chaos is easy to imagine. It's the pounding of feet over broken ground, the crack of distant gunfire, the wail of sirens. It's overlapping shouts, flashing lights, debris falling like deadly rain. But writing chaos well isn't about stacking loudness on loudness until readers can't breathe. It's about focusing on specific, visceral details that immerse the senses without overwhelming them. Instead of trying to describe everything happening at once, zero in on what your character would realistically notice.

Maybe it's the smell of burning plastic hitting harder than the noise. Maybe it's the sight of a woman screaming for a child who isn't answering. Maybe it's the way the ground shakes so violently that it feels alive and angry. In chaos, characters often focus on strange, sharp things because the brain tries to find some kind of order in disorder. By picking the right details, you create the illusion of total madness without losing the reader in confusion.

Good chaos scenes also have movement—but not random movement. Even in disaster, there's usually a current people are swept along by. A crowd running in one direction. A flood rising steadily higher. A fire driving survivors deeper into the city. Let your scenes of chaos have a direction, even if your characters are fighting against it. That gives your scenes momentum, makes them cinematic without being confusing.

Now, stillness is a different animal—and just as deadly. In disaster fiction, stillness isn't peace. It's often a warning. The eerie silence after a quake when the dust is still hanging in the air. The moment after a building collapses when the survivors are too stunned even to scream. The weird hush before a second wave of a tsunami hits. Stillness stretches tension tight as a wire because readers know, instinctively, that it won't last. Writing stillness means shifting the focus from external action to internal tension. It's not about nothing happening. It's about everything waiting to happen.

Stillness scenes are where fear blooms fully. Without immediate motion to distract them, characters are forced to feel. They hear their own ragged breathing. They realize how dry their throat is. They notice the shaking of their hands. Sensory details turn inward, magnifying the human vulnerability underneath the survival instinct. If chaos is about external overwhelm, stillness is about internal collapse—and it's often far scarier.

If you're using ChatGPT to brainstorm these moments, you can prompt for things like "sensory descriptions of a destroyed city during a moment of stillness" or "how chaos would feel during a building evacuation." You can also generate emotional beats: "how survivors react during a silent pause after a disaster wave passes." These small, vivid details are what will make your scenes breathe instead of blur.

When designing your scenes of chaos and stillness, it's important to use **rhythm**. Think of the story like a song: fast beats, slow beats, crescendos, rests. Let chaos scenes pulse with short, sharp sentences—fragments of action, snippets of shouted dialogue, images flashing like snapshots. Then let stillness scenes unfold slower, longer, heavier. Longer sentences. Focused thoughts. A different tempo. Readers will *feel* the change without you ever needing to explain it.

And don't be afraid to **layer** chaos and stillness even within the same scene. A character might be sprinting through burning streets (chaos) but suddenly freeze when they see someone they thought was dead (stillness). A fight might end in a sudden, shocking silence. A wall of water might be roaring toward the city, but the moment right before it hits might be deadly quiet. The best disaster fiction doesn't treat chaos and stillness like separate acts. It weaves them together, moment by moment, so readers are constantly being pulled in, pushed forward, stunned into holding their breath.

Another smart move is to use **character perspective** to shape how the chaos or stillness feels. A trained firefighter moving through a burning building will focus on very different things than a terrified teenager trapped inside. A doctor triaging patients in a flooded ER will experience the noise and motion differently than a grieving mother searching for her child. Every scene of chaos or stillness should feel personal because survival is personal. Don't try to describe everything. Describe what *this character* would notice, fear, hope for in this moment.

Symbolism can work wonders too. Maybe the chaotic collapse of a cathedral mirrors the internal collapse of a character's faith. Maybe the stillness after a firestorm is broken by a single bird call, signaling that life, battered and bruised, is still fighting back. Using chaos and stillness symbolically deepens the emotional resonance of your scenes without needing heavy-handed explanation.

And timing matters. Not every disaster scene needs a big boom or a long, reflective pause. Knowing when to unleash chaos and when to let stillness settle is part of controlling the emotional pacing of your story. Use chaos to shock, to disorient, to drive characters into action they're not ready for. Use stillness to break their hearts, to show what they've lost, to ask hard questions about why they're still fighting.

In the climax of your story, the interplay between chaos and stillness should be at its most intense. Maybe the final collapse happens so fast the characters can barely react. Maybe the final goodbye happens in total silence, except for the creak of broken wood and the rush of wind. Maybe the last stand happens in a storm of action—and the aftermath is a slow, broken walk through ruins. However you choose to do it, the rhythm of chaos and stillness should leave readers feeling wrung out, breathless, alive.

Because survival isn't just about racing from explosion to explosion.

It's about standing still in the ruins, listening to your own heartbeat, and deciding that somehow, against all odds, you're still not ready to stop.

Exploring Different Perspectives: Victims, Heroes, Villains

A disaster story becomes so much richer when you step outside a single point of view. Sure, it's easy to follow the survivors, the ones fighting to live another day. But disasters don't just create survivors—they create victims, heroes, and villains too. Sometimes, all in the same person. Exploring different perspectives doesn't just make your world feel bigger. It makes it feel real, complicated, painful, and alive. When you show a disaster through more than one lens, you turn the event from background noise into the very heart of human struggle.

First, let's talk about victims. In every disaster, there are people who don't make it out, or who are caught in the collapse in ways they can't control. Victims in your story aren't there just to raise the body count. They show the true cost of the disaster. They remind your readers that survival isn't guaranteed, and that loss isn't reserved for the bad guys. Victims have their own stories, even if they only flicker briefly across the page. A woman clutching a wedding photo in the rubble. A child calling for a parent who won't answer. A first responder trapped beneath the wreckage. Showing these lives, even in passing, gives emotional weight to every chaotic moment your main characters survive.

Victims also open the door to the kind of moral decisions that define disaster fiction. Do your survivors risk everything to try to save a stranger—or leave them behind? Does trying to help cost more lives? Writing these moments forces your characters—and your readers—to confront the ugly reality that sometimes, no matter how hard you try, you can't save everyone. And that trying might get you killed too.

Now, heroes. Disaster stories are naturally built for acts of heroism. Not the shiny, perfect heroism of comic books. The messy, terrifying kind where someone does the right thing even though it hurts, even though they're scared, even though they know it might not matter in the end. A hero might be a firefighter charging into a collapsing building. But they might also be a teenager sharing their last bottle of clean water with a stranger. Or an exhausted doctor stitching wounds in a flooded hospital long after the official evacuation.

Real heroism in disaster fiction often comes down to sacrifice. Someone choosing to protect others at a cost to themselves. But it can also be smaller: choosing hope when despair is easier, choosing kindness when cruelty would be safer. Writing heroism means showing characters making choices that are harder than surviving. It's easy to run. It's harder to stay and help. It's easy to give up. It's harder to keep believing when there's almost no reason left.

And then there are the villains.

Disasters don't just bring out the best in people. They also bring out the worst. Fear, greed, hunger, rage—they all fester in chaos. Sometimes villains in disaster fiction are big and obvious: warlords taking over shattered cities, politicians hoarding resources for the wealthy. But sometimes they're much quieter, much closer. A neighbor who locks their door against someone begging for shelter. A leader who lies to survivors to maintain control. A former friend who, faced with starvation, turns brutal.

Writing villains in disaster fiction works best when you make them understandable—even sympathetic. Maybe the leader who hoards food honestly believes it's the only way to prevent total collapse. Maybe the looter stealing medicine isn't just greedy—they're trying to save a child. The best villains aren't moustache-twirling caricatures. They're survivors who made a different choice. They remind your readers that in a world stripped of rules and comforts, the line between hero and villain can blur fast.

If you're using ChatGPT to brainstorm different perspectives, you can prompt for things like "point-of-view scenes from a disaster victim" or "reasons a survivor might turn villainous after a major collapse." You can also brainstorm complex moral choices: "how a character might justify sacrificing strangers to save their family." By exploring these different mindsets, you'll make your world feel fuller—and much harder to judge from a distance.

Another layer to explore is **shifting perspectives inside your main group**. Maybe the protagonist starts as a hero, saving others—but as supplies run low and losses mount, they start making colder choices. Maybe a secondary character who seems selfish and cowardly early on risks everything in the climax. Disaster changes people, sometimes for better, sometimes for worse. Tracking these shifts makes every character feel alive and unpredictable.

You can also layer perspectives across **different settings**. What does the disaster look like from a luxury skyscraper? From a crowded slum? From the mayor's office? From the hospital ward? Every location creates a different experience of the same event. In disaster fiction, the setting isn't just physical—it's emotional. Showing the collapse from multiple angles reminds readers that disaster never hits everyone equally, and survival sometimes comes down to luck as much as courage.

Another tool is to **blend victim, hero, and villain inside the same character**. Maybe a hero sacrifices one group to save another. Maybe a villain redeems themselves at the last moment. Maybe a victim lashes out and becomes a threat. In real disasters, people don't stay in one box. Neither should your characters. The more tangled their roles become, the more human and heartbreaking your story will feel.

Perspective also controls **what truths the readers know**. If you're writing from a single limited perspective, readers only know what that character sees, hears, fears. If you open multiple points of view, readers can know more—and dread the moment the characters discover what they don't yet see coming. Multiple perspectives let you layer suspense, irony, and heartbreak in ways a single point of view can't.

But use perspective shifts carefully. Too many, and the story gets scattered. Pick the ones that matter most—the ones that show a vital piece of the emotional or survival puzzle. And make sure each shift *feels* different. A child's terrified view of a disaster won't sound like a soldier's cold analysis or a doctor's weary triage. Voice matters. Sensory focus matters. Emotional core matters. Let every new perspective add a new flavor to the unfolding collapse.

Ultimately, exploring different perspectives in disaster fiction isn't about showing how different people survive differently. It's about showing that survival itself is a messy, brutal, beautiful thing. It's about showing that nobody is just one thing—not victim, not hero, not villain.

It's about showing how disaster strips people down to their barest selves, and how what's revealed is never simple, never clean, but always, always human.

The Outsider's View: Global Disaster from One Room

Sometimes in disaster fiction, the biggest, scariest events aren't witnessed out in the middle of the chaos. Sometimes the world falls apart, and your characters are stuck in a single room, watching, waiting, guessing. Maybe it's a hospital lockdown during a pandemic. Maybe it's a basement during nuclear fallout. Maybe it's a hotel room during a terrorist siege. Whatever the setup, the outsider's view—experiencing global disaster from one confined space—can create some of the most claustrophobic, intense, and emotional storytelling in the entire genre.

When characters are trapped in one room while the world outside burns, everything changes. They can't act on a grand scale. They can't rush into the streets to save people. They can't stop the larger disaster unfolding. They can only survive—and imagine. That sense of *not knowing* exactly what's happening magnifies fear in ways no explosion or flood ever could. It turns the world into something abstract and monstrous. The disaster stops being a backdrop and starts being a suffocating presence just beyond the walls.

Writing a disaster from one room means shifting your focus completely inward. You trade wide shots of collapsing cities for tight shots of cracked hands, fevered glances, whispered arguments. Every creak of the building, every flicker of the power, every distant rumble becomes a warning sign that the collapse is creeping closer. It's a slow kind of terror, one that eats away at the characters' nerves over hours, days, weeks.

The outsider's view works because it mirrors a truth about real disasters: most people aren't on the front lines. They hear about it secondhand. They wait for news that may never come. They wonder if the next noise outside the door is help—or something worse. Capturing that helplessness, that enforced passivity, turns your characters' survival from a physical battle into a psychological one. And that can be even more devastating.

If you're using ChatGPT to brainstorm these kinds of scenes, you can prompt for ideas like "sensory details inside a sealed room during a disaster" or "emotional stages of survivors trapped without information." You can also brainstorm practical survival questions: "how people might ration food and water while waiting for rescue" or "conflicts that might arise in a small trapped group." These prompts help build a vivid, painful world inside four walls.

When writing a disaster from one room, **the passage of time becomes one of your biggest weapons**. Outside, disasters often happen fast—floodwaters rise, earthquakes strike, fires spread. Inside, trapped survivors experience time stretching painfully long. Every hour feels like a lifetime. Days blur. Weeks grind down sanity. Tracking the slow, grinding weight of time helps you show how survival isn't just about staying alive physically—it's about staying intact mentally.

Use small, concrete signs of time's passage. The slow dimming of batteries. The gradual spoiling of food. The growth of stubble on faces. The tightening belts around waists. The scratch marks someone absentmindedly makes on the wall. These quiet changes show the relentless advance of time far more effectively than just mentioning dates.

Information control is another major element. Trapped characters don't know everything. Maybe they have a broken radio picking up faint transmissions. Maybe they hear rumors from passing survivors through a door. Maybe they see fires in the distance but don't know what caused them. This drip-feed of fragmented, incomplete information drives tension sky-high. Readers stay just as hungry as the characters for answers—and just as fearful about what the answers might be.

Emotionally, the outsider's view forces characters into confrontation with themselves and each other. When there's nowhere to go, nowhere to run, old secrets surface. Grudges fester. Despair infects conversations. Alliances form and fracture. Silence grows heavy. Writing these emotional spirals means focusing on body language, micro-expressions, breathing patterns—tiny signs that show how close someone is to snapping. In a locked room, everything matters. Every look. Every word. Every mistake.

Another advantage of the outsider's view is that **readers imagine the worst**, often more vividly than you could describe it. If characters are hearing distant gunfire but can't see the battle, readers fill in the blanks with their own fears. If characters smell smoke but don't know what's burning, readers will picture everything they love going up in flames. Leaving some horrors unseen gives them more power. It personalizes the disaster to each reader's worst fears without needing graphic detail.

You can also use **the changing environment inside the room** to mirror the collapse outside. Maybe the air grows hotter, fouler, heavier. Maybe cracks form in the walls. Maybe pests invade. Maybe the building itself starts to sag, warning that even this fragile haven won't last forever. These changes ratchet up the tension steadily, making it clear that staying still is only a temporary survival strategy—and that choices will have to be made, sooner or later.

One of the hardest and most powerful choices in a one-room disaster story is **when—or if—to leave**. Maybe the characters stay holed up as long as they can, but supplies run out. Maybe the noise outside stops—not because the world got better, but because it got worse. Maybe someone inside the room loses patience, or hope, and opens the door too soon. Leaving the shelter becomes a high-stakes, gut-wrenching decision that can easily turn deadly. Timing this choice—and building toward it carefully—is critical for making the final acts of your story feel earned.

In terms of structure, the outsider's view often follows a **claustrophobic arc**: initial denial or hope ("this will pass soon"), creeping dread ("why haven't we heard anything?"), growing fractures ("we can't stay here forever"), final desperation ("better to die trying than die waiting"). Tracking this emotional trajectory scene by scene keeps your story moving forward even when the characters are physically stuck.

Another emotional beat to explore is **the tension between memory and survival**. Trapped characters cling to memories of the outside world—the smell of coffee shops, the feel of crowded streets, the noise of ordinary life. Over time, those memories grow distant, dreamlike, painful. Maybe someone insists on recreating small rituals—washing up every morning, praying at dusk—to hold onto their humanity. Maybe someone else can't bear to remember, shutting down emotionally to survive. These responses show how survival is not just physical but psychological warfare.

Symbolism plays beautifully here too. A window boarded up against the light. A locked door. A cracked mirror. The way survivors see the world, and themselves, becomes twisted and haunted inside those four walls. Every physical object in the room gains emotional weight, representing hope, fear, betrayal, or loss. And when—or if—the characters finally step outside, the world they find should feel profoundly alien. Empty streets. Ash falling like snow. Ruined buildings. Or maybe survivors who have changed so much they barely seem human anymore. That first step out of confinement into the broken world beyond is the ultimate emotional release—and it should hit like a punch to the gut. Because a disaster isn't just something that tears the world apart outside the window. It's something that seeps inside the walls, inside the heart, until survival becomes not just about beating the world out there—but beating the slow collapse inside yourself too.

Creating a World Shaped by Ruin

In disaster fiction, the world isn't just a backdrop. It's a living, breathing character shaped by everything that's gone wrong. When you write a world shaped by ruin, you're not just describing wreckage. You're showing the slow collapse of civilization, the twisted beauty of what's left behind, and the brutal new rules that survivors have to live by. Getting the world right makes every step your characters take heavier, more dangerous, and far more emotional. Because when the world itself is broken, survival means learning how to live with, through, and sometimes *inside* that brokenness.

The first thing to realize is that a ruined world isn't just about rubble and wreckage. It's about **absence**. The missing sounds of traffic. The dead phones. The blank TV screens. The shops with their windows smashed out and their lights forever dark. Absence is a kind of ghost that haunts the survivors, a constant reminder that the old world is gone and it's not coming back. When you're building your ruined world, think about what's *missing* first—and then layer in what's been left behind.

Weather plays a huge part. Without human maintenance, cities decay faster than you might expect. Roads crack and buckle. Nature creeps back fast—grass pushing through sidewalks, vines clawing up abandoned buildings. Floods and fires and freezes hit harder without people repairing the damage. Writing a ruined world means thinking not just about what broke during the disaster, but what kept breaking afterward. Every day the survivors walk through ruins, the world falls apart a little more.

One powerful trick is to show how survivors interact with the ruins differently depending on how long it's been. Early on, they might pick through wreckage with hope—looking for food, supplies, loved ones. Later, they might avoid certain places altogether. Later still, ruins stop being strange—they become normal. A collapsed bridge isn't a tragedy anymore; it's just a landmark. An abandoned hospital isn't a rescue site—it's a hunting ground for supplies. That emotional shift in how characters see the broken world is a huge part of showing how ruin reshapes people as much as places.

If you're using ChatGPT to brainstorm ideas, you can prompt for "how a modern city might decay after an earthquake" or "what signs of life would remain five years after a global flood." You can also generate emotional beats like "how survivors might memorialize ruined landmarks" or "rituals survivors might invent to deal with a ruined world." Building these details in gives your story a lived-in, battered, breathing feeling that pure destruction can't achieve.

Ruins aren't just physical. They're societal too. Governments collapse. Emergency services vanish. Money might still exist in survivors' pockets, but it's meaningless compared to food, water, medicine. The laws that once held society together erode fast when survival becomes the only real currency. Writing a world shaped by ruin means showing how new systems emerge—maybe tribalism, barter economies, local warlords, wandering families forming their own codes of justice.

Culture changes too. Survivors might develop new superstitions, new taboos, new stories. Maybe children born after the collapse only know electricity as a fairy tale. Maybe certain ruins are considered cursed—or sacred. Maybe old holidays are abandoned, replaced by new memorial days marking the disaster's anniversary. Showing how ruin reshapes not just the ground but the soul of humanity gives your world incredible emotional depth.

Another smart move is to think about **zones of survival**. Not everywhere falls apart at the same speed. Some areas might still cling to a semblance of order—military enclaves, self-sufficient towns, remote villages. Other areas might be complete dead zones, ruled by chaos, lawlessness, or death. Survivors will know where these lines are, even if they shift over time. "Don't cross the river after dark." "Stay out of the city center." "No one survives the southern woods." These whispered rules add texture and tension to your ruined world.

And don't forget about **unexpected beauty**. A city half-sunken under floodwater, lit by the slanting gold of a dying sun. A forest reclaiming a suburban wasteland, trees breaking through roofs, deer grazing in deserted shopping malls. Disaster reshapes the world brutally—but sometimes it also strips away the ugly clutter and reveals something eerily beautiful underneath. Letting your characters notice this beauty, even fleetingly, reminds readers that ruin isn't just death—it's change. Painful, devastating change, but change nonetheless.

A ruined world also changes how characters move and think. A simple trip across town might become a dangerous expedition. Crossing a river might require a homemade raft or finding a long-forgotten bridge. Finding shelter might mean choosing between a cracked skyscraper that could collapse in the next aftershock or sleeping exposed under the stars. Every decision becomes more complicated, more dangerous, more exhausting. And every misstep can be fatal.

Memory plays a powerful role too. Survivors who remember the old world will carry grief like a second skin. The ruined world isn't just physically harder—it's emotionally heavier. Every ruined playground, every abandoned home, every broken streetlight is a wound. Characters who grew up after the disaster might see things differently—more pragmatically, less mournfully. That generational split gives you rich emotional material to explore.

Symbolism in a ruined world hits hard too. A rusted-out car becomes a symbol of broken dreams. A dead tree in the center of a town square becomes a marker for lost hope—or stubborn survival. A wall of missing persons posters fluttering in the wind becomes a monument to all the lives that vanished without warning. These visual echoes of what was lost will haunt readers long after the last page.

When you think about the emotional arc of your story, the ruined world should mirror the characters' inner journeys. Early on, the ruins might seem terrifying, endless, insurmountable. Later, as survivors adapt, the ruins might feel familiar, even navigable. In the end, the ruins might still be deadly—but they are *understood*. The characters don't tame the world. They learn to live inside its brokenness. And that's a powerful metaphor for survival itself.

You can also use the ruined world to make small victories feel huge. Finding an intact water pump. Growing a small crop of tomatoes in a shattered courtyard. Repairing a bicycle to make travel possible again. These tiny wins matter more against a backdrop of endless decay. They're sparks of life in the ashes—and readers will feel them keenly because the world has been built up so relentlessly around them.

Ultimately, creating a world shaped by ruin isn't just about smashing things. It's about building something new in the rubble. It's about showing how disaster doesn't just destroy—it transforms. It's about giving your characters a place that is both terrifying and strangely beautiful, hopeless and stubbornly alive.

It's about reminding readers that even when the old world falls, the human spirit somehow, miraculously, finds ways to endure.

Because survival isn't about rebuilding what was lost.

It's about learning to live with the ruins—and finding a way to call them home.

When Nature Takes Over: Post-Apocalyptic Landscapes

One of the most striking images in any disaster story is the way nature reclaims what humanity has lost. Crumbling skyscrapers tangled in ivy. Highways buckled by tree roots. Wild animals roaming through abandoned cities. When writing a post-apocalyptic landscape, you're not just describing ruins—you're showing a world where nature has started writing its own story again. And often, it's a story that's beautiful, brutal, and completely indifferent to whether humans survive it.

When you think about how nature takes over, it helps to remember that it doesn't happen neatly or all at once. Different disasters create different kinds of reclamation. A nuclear disaster creates dead zones where nothing grows for years, and then strange mutated plants and hardy species start creeping back in. A pandemic or sudden societal collapse leaves cities mostly intact, but human absence gives plants, weather, and animals the chance to slowly, steadily erode what people built. A climate disaster—floods, droughts, superstorms—reshapes entire regions, making deserts out of fields and swamps out of suburbs.

Nature moves fast once we stop holding it back. Without people cutting the grass and patching the roads, weeds push up through cracks in the pavement within months. In just a few years, vines can pull down fences and climb telephone poles. Roofs collapse under the weight of unchecked storms. Rivers flood their banks. Wildlife moves back into cities, bold and unafraid. Writing these changes in layers makes your world feel alive, even as it's falling apart.

If you're using ChatGPT to brainstorm natural reclamation, you can prompt for ideas like "how a city would decay over 5 years after a pandemic" or "what forests would look like in a post-apocalyptic world." You can also focus on specific settings: "a suburban neighborhood swallowed by floodwaters and overgrown with moss" or "a desert creeping over a once-bustling industrial area." These detailed images give your story grounding and depth.

One important thing to think about is **how different landscapes reclaim differently**. In tropical environments, nature would race back with thick vines, towering grasses, wildflowers choking the streets. In colder climates, decay would be slower, with snow and ice battering structures until they rot and collapse. Coastal areas might be drowned entirely, creating ghost cities half-sunken under the sea. Mountains might protect small pockets of civilization longer—or isolate them completely. Tailoring the post-apocalyptic takeover to your specific setting makes it feel more real.

Nature reclaiming human spaces also changes **the rules of survival**. In a newly overgrown world, dangers shift. Roads become impassable. Buildings collapse without warning. Animals roam freely—and they aren't always friendly. Food sources shift too. Survivors might forage for wild berries and hunt animals that have moved into the cities. Clean water becomes a daily battle. Even old threats like insects, mold, and disease grow deadlier without the buffers civilization once provided.

One powerful emotional angle to explore is **how survivors view the returning wilderness**. Some characters might see it as beautiful—a strange, wild rebirth. Others might see it as hostile, a green invader that took over everything they knew. Others might feel both at once. That complicated relationship between humans and nature gives your story emotional richness. It's not just about fighting the elements—it's about realizing that maybe the world isn't fighting back at all. Maybe it's just moving on.

Symbolism thrives in post-apocalyptic landscapes. A crumbling church overrun with ivy. A playground swallowed by wildflowers. A freeway bridge snapped in half by earthquake and overgrown with trees. These images aren't just striking—they tell a story without words. They show loss, rebirth, indifference, and the tiny stubbornness of life all at once.

The emotional power of these images comes from the contrast between memory and reality. Survivors who remember what a place *used* to be—loud, busy, alive—feel the weight of what's lost much more heavily when they walk through its ruins. A child born after the disaster, though, might look at the same wild city and see nothing strange. To them, vines growing through window frames and wolves in the subway tunnels are just normal life. That generational divide—between memory and adaptation—is one of the richest veins you can mine in post-collapse storytelling.

Another layer to explore is **what new dangers nature brings**. Flooded basements filled with toxic mold. Wildfires sweeping through dry overgrowth. Predators returning to old hunting grounds. Even once-safe plants becoming deadly when people no longer remember how to tell them apart. Survival skills change. It's not enough to have guns and canned food—you need knowledge of the natural world. Herbal medicine. Weather reading. Animal tracking. The survivors who adapt to this new wild world thrive. The ones who cling too tightly to the old rules don't.

Movement through a nature-reclaimed world should feel different, too. Paths are no longer straight lines. Survivors have to move around rivers where roads used to be. They have to climb over collapsed buildings, machete their way through thick undergrowth. Even inside cities, movement feels like trekking through an alien jungle built on top of a dead civilization. Writing these changes in texture and difficulty grounds readers physically inside your world.

Another great trick is to use **echoes of the old world** poking through the new. A rusting streetlight jutting out of a field of wild wheat. A shopping mall roof caved in, with saplings growing through the shattered skylight. A broken-down car now home to a fox's den. These echoes remind characters—and readers—that the world wasn't always this way. That something huge and tragic happened to let nature take it all back.

Still, not all ruins are abandoned. Some survivors build new lives among the ruins. Maybe they plant crops on rooftops, use abandoned factories as fortresses, build floating villages in flooded towns. Nature isn't just a threat—it's a toolkit for the new world. And those who embrace it instead of fighting it have the best chance at creating something that feels like a future, not just a long, slow death.

If you time it right in your story, you can show **the seasons of the new world** too. Spring reclaiming ruins with wild, chaotic life. Summer turning abandoned cities into steaming jungles. Autumn stripping the forests bare, exposing ruins once hidden. Winter freezing everything, a long silent pause in the chaos. Letting readers feel those natural rhythms inside the ruined world reminds them that life moves on, with or without humanity.

In the end, when nature takes over, it isn't revenge. It isn't cruelty. It's indifference. The vines grow whether people are watching or not. The rivers swell whether or not we have bridges to cross them. The wolves hunt whether or not we call them pests or predators.

The earth turns, the seasons shift, and life endures—even when the works of mankind crumble into dust.

Because post-apocalyptic landscapes aren't about the death of the world.

They're about the death of one version of it—and the birth of something wild, broken, and strangely beautiful in its place.

Science and Technology in Disaster Narratives

Science and technology always sit in the background of modern life, humming quietly, making everything easier, faster, safer—or so we think. But when disaster strikes, that quiet hum either becomes a lifeline or a ticking time bomb. In disaster narratives, science and technology aren't just window dressing. They're forces that can save, betray, or reshape the world. They can be the reason the world collapses in the first place—or the last, fragile hope that something better can be rebuilt from the ruins.

The first way to think about science and technology in disaster fiction is as **the cause**. Stories about pandemics, nuclear meltdowns, climate disasters, rogue AI, or genetic experiments gone wrong all use human knowledge and ambition as the match that lights the fuse. It's not always evil science either—sometimes it's science that was trying to help. A cure for a disease mutates into something unstoppable. A new energy source destabilizes the environment. An attempt to control the weather triggers a chain reaction of catastrophe. The tension here isn't about blaming knowledge itself—it's about how our use (or misuse) of knowledge can have unintended consequences.

If you're brainstorming with ChatGPT, you can prompt for things like "scientific experiments that could accidentally cause global disaster" or "technology failures that could lead to societal collapse." You'll quickly realize that some of the scariest disasters aren't caused by malice—they're caused by optimism. Good intentions gone terribly wrong often hit harder emotionally because they show how fragile even our best ideas are.

Another powerful angle is to show **science and technology as failing heroes**. Survivors huddle around cracked radios, praying for broadcasts that never come. Engineers try to fix a broken dam with makeshift tools. Doctors run out of antibiotics and are forced to fall back on centuries-old treatments. The slow death of reliable technology—power grids, hospitals, communication systems—becomes a silent, gnawing enemy in the background. Writing these failures makes the collapse feel real, like the rug has been yanked out from under modern life.

And yet, technology can also become **a symbol of stubborn hope**. A single working water purifier. A jury-rigged solar panel keeping a radio alive. A home-built drone scouting ahead for danger. In a world that has lost so much, these scraps of functioning technology shine like beacons. They remind readers—and characters—that not everything is broken beyond repair. That survival sometimes depends not just on strength or ruthlessness, but on ingenuity, creativity, and stubborn cleverness.

One thing to remember is that technology changes **meaning** after a disaster. A smartphone isn't a tool for communication anymore—it's a flashlight, a memory vault, a paperweight. A car isn't freedom—it's a trap if the roads are gone and fuel is scarce. A laboratory isn't a place of discovery—it's a tomb or a fortress. Showing how familiar objects take on strange, desperate new meanings makes your world feel textured and real.

Science in disaster fiction doesn't just mean technology, though. It also means **understanding the forces your characters are up against**. Flood survivors might need to understand how water behaves. Pandemic survivors might need basic knowledge of infection control. Nuclear disaster survivors might learn to fear the invisible threat of radiation, building Geiger counters from scratch or using old textbooks to figure out what places are safe. Knowledge becomes as valuable as food—and sometimes even rarer.

And science changes who survives. Characters with technical skills—mechanics, doctors, engineers, chemists—become precious. A car mechanic might suddenly be the most important person in a survivor group. A nurse with basic triage training might become the de facto leader. Someone who knows how to read old maps, fix a diesel generator, purify water, or set a broken bone has power far beyond what they would have had in the old world.

Skill replaces wealth. Knowledge replaces title.

Another tension point is **how much technology survivors can—or should—trust**. Maybe a broken warning system led them into danger once. Maybe the last transmission they heard was a lie. Maybe the old technologies are contaminated or dangerous now. Survivors might cling to ancient devices hoping for rescue—or they might reject all technology as cursed remnants of a fallen world. These emotional scars can shape characters deeply, defining who they trust, how they plan, and what kind of world they dream of rebuilding.

Technology can also act as **a lure**. Maybe a working radio promises hope—and leads characters into a trap. Maybe the promise of a functioning desalination plant drives survivors across a wasteland. Maybe a rogue AI still controls a section of ruined city, offering sanctuary in exchange for obedience. Technology's seductive promise of safety, control, or salvation can be as much a danger as an opportunity.

When designing how science and technology fit into your disaster story, think about **how long it's been since the fall**. In the first days and weeks, survivors scramble to keep familiar tools working. In the first years, scavenging becomes more desperate, with fewer repairs possible. In the first decades, technology becomes mysterious—old cell-phones and computers sitting like relics in abandoned homes, unreadable and useless. The timeline of decay shapes everything about how technology is perceived and used.

Science can also **offer a future**, if your story tilts toward hope. Maybe a survivor scientist discovers a new way to generate clean water. Maybe a group of engineers rebuilds a fragment of the power grid. Maybe survivors reforge a broken world with fragments of old knowledge and new improvisation. Science doesn't have to just be the villain or the ghost of the old world—it can be the seed of what's next, battered but alive.

One of the richest emotional beats in disaster fiction is **the fight to hold onto knowledge**. Maybe characters preserve books. Maybe they teach children by candlelight, trying to pass on the old world's wisdom before it's lost. Maybe a dying engineer leaves behind notebooks scrawled with diagrams and desperate advice. These moments are about more than survival. They're about legacy. About refusing to let the collapse erase everything humans once knew, once built, once dreamed.

In stories where hope survives the wreckage, science and technology aren't just about machines.

They're about the stubborn human belief that even when everything breaks, we can still make something better from the pieces.

That the mind's spark isn't so easily extinguished.

Because disaster stories aren't just about how the world ends.

They're about whether, in the ashes, we dare to imagine a new beginning—and whether we're brave enough, and smart enough, to build it.

Writing the Collapse of Infrastructure

When a disaster hits, it's not just the buildings that crumble. Infrastructure—the invisible skeleton of modern life—goes down too, and when it does, everything gets harder, scarier, and far more desperate. Infrastructure is what keeps water clean, lights on, food moving, and medical supplies reaching hospitals. When you write a disaster story, showing the collapse of infrastructure isn't just about adding realism. It's about showing how quickly life as we know it shatters, leaving survivors scrambling in a world that no longer plays by any familiar rules.

The collapse usually starts with **power**. Electricity goes out—and with it, a thousand other systems start falling like dominoes. Without power, communication fails. Cell towers die. Emergency broadcasts cut off. Water treatment plants stop working, and sewage backs up. Streetlights blink out, plunging cities into eerie, dangerous darkness. Refrigerators stop humming, and food starts to spoil. Even those lucky enough to have batteries and generators soon run into a wall: without resupply, everything eventually runs dry.

Power going out isn't just an inconvenience in disaster fiction. It's a transformation. It shifts the setting from a recognizable, manageable place to something primal and wild. Writing the lights going out should feel like flipping a switch on your entire world—not just physically, but emotionally. Suddenly, the old world really is gone.

Next comes **communication**. People are used to being connected 24/7. When the phones die, the Internet collapses, and radios go silent, the isolation becomes a second disaster all its own. No news from loved ones. No updates about the scale of the catastrophe. No way to coordinate rescue or warn about new dangers. Writing this silence creates an atmosphere of uncertainty, fear, and creeping paranoia. It also forces characters to fall back on face-to-face communication, handwritten messages, word of mouth—all painfully slow and unreliable compared to what they had before.

Then, **water and sanitation** systems fail. Most people don't realize how much clean water depends on electricity until it's gone. Water treatment plants can't run. Pumps fail. Tap water first becomes unreliable, then contaminated, then deadly. Toilets stop working, and waste starts piling up in streets and homes. Disease spreads fast. Survivors have to find new sources of water—wells, streams, rain—and figure out how to purify it. Boiling. Filtration. Improvised chemical treatments. A disaster world quickly divides between those who understand basic water safety and those who die of preventable infections.

After that, **transportation** falls apart. Gas stations depend on electric pumps to move fuel. Roads become blocked with abandoned vehicles. Airports shut down. Trains grind to a halt. Shipping stops. The intricate, invisible web that moves goods across countries snaps in an instant. Suddenly, cities that rely on daily shipments of food, medicine, and fuel start to starve. Supermarkets are emptied within hours—and there's no resupply coming. Writing the collapse of transportation turns survival into a local problem. There's no cavalry coming. There's no escape to some safe place just over the horizon. Survivors are stuck where they are, with what they have.

If you're brainstorming with ChatGPT, you can prompt for ideas like "how infrastructure failures cascade during a major disaster" or "what secondary disasters happen when services like waste removal or traffic control collapse." You can also generate survival challenges: "ways survivors might collect clean water without a functioning supply system" or "how blocked roads affect evacuation attempts." These little complications build a world where every step forward is earned the hard way.

Healthcare is another domino that falls fast. Hospitals lose power, too. Emergency generators buy time—but not much. Without fresh supplies, without communication, without order, hospitals turn into nightmare zones. Overwhelmed. Understaffed. Out of medicine. No clean water. No functioning operating rooms. Even if survivors reach a hospital, they might find little more than chaos, desperation, and grief. Writing this collapse sharpens the emotional stakes brutally. In a disaster world, a simple injury—a cut, a fever, a broken bone—can become a death sentence.

Food supply chains are another crucial piece. Modern grocery stores rely on "just in time" delivery models—meaning they carry very little extra stock. Without daily deliveries, shelves are stripped bare in days, sometimes hours. Perishable foods rot without refrigeration. Even canned goods eventually run out. Survivors have to shift fast to scavenging, hunting, growing—and fighting for—food. Hunger changes people. It frays tempers, destroys trust, and drives brutal choices. Writing the slow, grinding onset of hunger adds another layer of desperation to your disaster story that feels deeply real.

Then comes the collapse of **law and order**. Police, firefighters, emergency workers are overwhelmed, cut off, or just stop coming. Maybe they're trying to save their own families. Maybe they're dead. Maybe the system they served doesn't exist anymore. Without enforcement, old laws stop meaning much. New laws—laws of survival, laws of the strong—take their place. Some communities might form militias. Others might descend into chaos. Writing this collapse gives you endless story possibilities: alliances, betrayals, the rise of new powers from the ruins of the old.

One thing to remember is that **infrastructure collapse is rarely clean or complete all at once**. Some pockets might cling to power, water, or communication longer than others. A wealthy district might have private generators. A rural area might be slower to fall because it was less dependent on fragile systems to begin with. Survivors will know where these pockets are—and so will looters, desperate migrants, and warlords. Holding onto even a scrap of infrastructure becomes a beacon for hope—or a target for violence.

Writing infrastructure collapse isn't about listing services that fail. It's about showing how every small thing characters used to take for granted—turning on a tap, flipping a light switch, calling for help—becomes a memory. It's about showing the slow, grinding realization that survival isn't just about surviving the initial disaster. It's about surviving the endless chain of consequences afterward.

Infrastructure collapse also offers rich ground for showing **character development**. Maybe a city-dweller learns to filter river water by trial and painful error. Maybe a former IT specialist becomes a scavenger or a farmer. Maybe a child raised in the collapse doesn't even understand what a supermarket was. Watching characters adapt—or fail to adapt—to the loss of infrastructure shows their resilience, resourcefulness, and humanity.

If you time it right, you can use infrastructure collapse as a **series of waves**, each worse than the last. First the lights go out. Then the water stops running. Then the food runs out. Then the infections start. Each wave strips away another layer of normalcy, another piece of the characters' old selves. Each wave forces them to dig deeper—or give up entirely.

And don't forget the emotional weight. Infrastructure isn't just physical. It's memory, comfort, identity. A world where a parent can't get clean water for their child. A world where a doctor has to watch patients die because the machines are dead. A world where someone stands in the middle of a city street that used to hum with life, now silent and broken. Writing these moments of loss grounds your story in something far more gripping than explosions: grief, resilience, and the stubborn will to endure. Because disaster fiction isn't just about what breaks first. It's about what breaks last—and what refuses to break at all.

The Journey through Ruins: Road Stories in Disaster Fiction

Disaster fiction and road stories go together like dust and wind. When the world collapses, staying still often isn't an option. Supplies run out. Threats close in. Safe zones crumble. Survivors are forced onto the road, into the wastelands of ruined cities, broken highways, flooded fields. Writing the journey through ruins turns your story into more than just a survival narrative—it becomes a pilgrimage through everything the characters, and the world, have lost.

The key thing about road stories in disaster fiction is that **movement equals survival**, but it also equals danger. Every mile traveled brings characters closer to something they need—food, family, safety—but also exposes them to new threats they can't predict. Writing that tension, that sense that every step forward is a gamble, keeps readers wired tight, breathless, glued to the journey.

A good journey-through-ruins story doesn't just string together a series of obstacles. It tracks an emotional arc. Early in the journey, characters might be full of hope—or at least grim determination. They have a goal. A destination. A plan. But as the miles grind on, as the ruins stretch endless and empty, cracks appear. The group fractures. The goal blurs. The journey itself becomes the test—of endurance, of loyalty, of faith.

When you're writing the physical side of the journey, **the landscape matters**. A destroyed world shouldn't feel like a flat, grey wasteland (unless you want it to for a very specific reason). It should have texture. Landmarks. Layers of decay and survival. Maybe a character marks each night's camp with a stone cairn. Maybe a ruined mall becomes a moment of scavenged victory—or a trap. Maybe crossing a broken bridge becomes a desperate gamble. Make every mile *feel* like something: a risk, a memory, a small heartbreak, a small hope.

If you're brainstorming with ChatGPT, you can prompt for ideas like "landmarks survivors might encounter in a ruined city" or "hazards along a journey through a post-apocalyptic landscape." You can also generate emotional beats: "how characters' morale changes after weeks on the road" or "small victories and defeats during a survival journey." These layers turn the journey into more than just walking from point A to point B—they make it a living, brutal, beautiful odyssey.

One of the most powerful things you can do with road stories is **show how the world changes as characters move through it**. Different regions collapse differently. Maybe coastal towns are drowned ruins, with saltwater eating away at everything. Maybe cities are skeletal remains patrolled by desperate survivors. Maybe rural areas are deceptively beautiful—green, quiet, but hiding dangers like isolated warlords or invisible environmental threats. Each new environment challenges the characters in fresh ways, forcing them to adapt again and again.

Movement through ruins also strips away **layers of civilization**. Early on, characters might cling to old rituals—checking in at empty gas stations, trying to use dead cellphones, trading paper money no one honors anymore. But as the journey grinds on, they shed those habits. They stop looking for law enforcement. They stop expecting help. They stop talking about "when things get back to normal."

They start living completely inside the collapse—and that transformation is one of the most emotionally powerful parts of any disaster road story.

Another thing to remember: **the road takes things away**. It's not just about moving forward. It's about losing pieces along the way. Supplies dwindle. Friends fall behind. Dreams crumble. Physical injuries accumulate. Hope thins out.

A well-timed death or betrayal on the road doesn't just hurt the characters—it makes the journey itself feel hostile, alive, merciless. Survival becomes not about who's strongest, but about who can bear the weight of all they've lost.

Still, the road also offers **moments of unexpected beauty**. A sunrise over a deserted city. A deer walking calmly through a ruined park. A survivor teaching a child to fish at a stream running through a collapsed highway. These quiet moments are vital. They remind both characters and readers why survival is worth the cost. They create contrast that makes the next danger hit even harder.

One classic road-story tension to use is **choice of direction**. There's rarely a clear path forward. A safer, longer route—or a risky shortcut. A chance to detour to search for a loved one—or stick to the survival plan. These choices split groups, create conflicts, and reveal true character. Writing these crossroads moments builds natural, organic drama into the journey.

Another device you can use is **mythologizing places**. Survivors might talk about safe havens—"There's a settlement past the mountains," "There's clean water beyond the burned forests"—whether or not these places actually exist. Hope itself becomes a map that can lead characters to salvation—or death. Writing how rumors shape the journey creates emotional stakes that aren't just about geography. They're about belief. About needing something better to exist, even when evidence says otherwise.

Pacing matters hugely in a road story. You want to vary the rhythm—periods of tense travel, bursts of violence or disaster, stretches of exhausted quiet. Walking for days under blistering sun. Waiting out a storm in a half-collapsed barn. A sudden ambush. A flood. A safe night under the stars. This rhythm keeps readers from getting numbed by constant danger or lulled into boredom by constant stillness.

And don't forget that **the road itself changes the survivors**. Maybe a character who was cautious becomes reckless. Maybe a selfish loner learns to trust—just a little. Maybe a leader loses heart and has to be carried by the group. The journey isn't just about the world collapsing outside. It's about people collapsing, rebuilding, shattering, healing, carrying each other when they can, leaving each other when they must.

If you time it right, **the end of the journey** shouldn't feel like a neat destination. Whether the survivors reach a safe zone, find a missing loved one, or simply endure another day, the real climax is emotional. How have they changed? What have they lost? What tiny, battered piece of themselves have they kept alive?

And was it worth it?

Because in the end, the journey through ruins isn't just about crossing broken landscapes.

It's about crossing the broken spaces inside the soul—and finding, somehow, that even there, a path forward still exists.

Shelter Stories: Claustrophobia, Conflict, and Survival

Finding shelter during a disaster sounds like a victory—but in disaster fiction, it often turns into a whole new kind of battleground. When you cram survivors together in a small, closed space for days, weeks, or even longer, survival shifts from battling the outside world to battling each other—and themselves. Claustrophobia sets in. Paranoia grows. Old tensions surface. New ones are born. Writing shelter stories is about understanding that confinement doesn't just protect your characters. It pressures them, breaks them, and sometimes reveals what they're truly made of.

The first thing to get right when writing a shelter story is **the physical environment**. Tight spaces create constant, inescapable pressure. Maybe it's a basement crammed with canned goods and mildew. Maybe it's a subway tunnel reeking of oil and stale air. Maybe it's a survival bunker where the lights flicker and the recycled air tastes metallic. Wherever you set it, the shelter itself should almost feel alive—a character that looms over everything, shaping emotions, choices, and conflicts.

Details matter in confined settings. The creak of the floorboards overhead. The smell of unwashed bodies. The way whispers seem loud in a silent room. Writing sensory details pulls readers deep into the claustrophobia. Every sound feels bigger. Every argument feels more dangerous. Every breath feels like it's burning up limited oxygen. If the outside world was terrifying, the inside world becomes suffocating.

If you're using ChatGPT to brainstorm, you can prompt for ideas like "shelter designs during an apocalypse" or "conflicts that arise when survivors are trapped together." You can also build sensory maps: "how a storm shelter smells after two weeks underground" or "the sounds survivors hear inside a flooded subway system." These details make your shelter setting pulse with life—and threat.

One major source of tension in shelter stories is **the management of limited resources**. Food, water, medicine, batteries—all of it is finite, and every day the supplies shrink. Every meal is a calculation. Every drink of water is a choice between fairness and survival. Writing these dwindling resources sharpens every interaction between characters. Maybe someone hoards. Maybe someone lies. Maybe someone gives up their share out of guilt—or demands more out of fear.

Scarcity breeds conflict. It doesn't take long for old alliances to fracture when the stakes become survival versus loyalty. And not everyone reacts the same way. Some cling to fairness and group cohesion. Others turn ruthless, calculating who's worth saving and who's dead weight. Shelter stories are the perfect place to explore **the slow moral decay of desperate people**. Maybe not all at once. Maybe not with big betrayals. But with small, almost invisible steps: hiding an extra can of food, lying about a water cache, whispering doubts about leadership when the others are asleep.

Leadership and hierarchy naturally emerge in shelters too—but often not cleanly. Someone has to organize rationing, decide when to risk venturing out, settle disputes. But authority under survival conditions is fragile. Leaders are respected until a decision goes bad—or until someone stronger, louder, or more desperate challenges them. Writing these power shifts adds drama to even the smallest scenes: a heated argument over whether to open the door to a stranger, a quiet mutiny brewing over dwindling supplies.

Claustrophobia itself becomes a psychological force inside the shelter. At first, survivors might be grateful just to have a roof over their heads. But over time, the walls seem to shrink. Privacy vanishes. Tempers flare over tiny things—snoring, smells, the way someone taps their foot incessantly. Characters begin to crave open space, fresh air, silence, and freedom they can't have. This mounting pressure should crack your characters open slowly but surely, revealing vulnerabilities, grudges, secrets, and rage.

Shelter stories also give you a chance to explore **grief and guilt in close quarters**. There's nowhere to hide from sorrow when you're packed into a small space. Maybe a character mourns a lost family member. Maybe another carries guilt for the people they couldn't save. Maybe a survivor blames themselves for leading the group into a shelter that's now turning into a coffin. Grief has different shapes—quiet depression, explosive anger, irrational guilt—and when you trap people together with it, the emotional fallout is unavoidable.

Another rich vein to mine is **the arrival of outsiders**. Maybe someone begs to be let in. Maybe a wounded stranger stumbles to the door. Maybe a group larger than the shelter can handle forces their way in. New blood upsets the delicate balance inside the shelter. Trust fractures. Factions form. Writing these encounters asks hard questions: Who deserves to survive? Who decides? What are we willing to risk to hold onto our humanity?

Pacing inside a shelter story is delicate. You don't want endless stretches of nothing happening. At the same time, you don't want constant action, because part of the horror is in the waiting—the grinding uncertainty of when (or if) things will get better. Good shelter stories alternate between stretches of building tension—quiet dread, slow resource decay, subtle emotional fractures—and sharp spikes of action: a fight, a discovery, a betrayal, a decision to venture out.

Shelter stories can also build deep relationships—or destroy them. Being trapped forces intimacy. People share memories, regrets, hopes they wouldn't otherwise reveal. Friendships can deepen under pressure—but they can also snap like brittle wire. Writing these evolving relationships in small, honest beats—shared jokes, whispered confessions, ugly fights—makes the emotional landscape of your shelter as dynamic as any battlefield.

One powerful motif to weave into your shelter story is **hope versus despair**. Some characters will cling to hope stubbornly. They'll believe rescue is coming, that the world outside will heal, that surviving means more than just staying alive. Others will lose hope completely. They'll fall into fatalism, violence, even suicide. The battle between these worldviews—the believers and the broken—creates natural emotional conflict that's even more gripping because it feels so personal, so raw.

You can also use **symbolism** inside the shelter. A dying battery representing the group's last flicker of hope. A boarded-up window showing how completely cut off from the world they've become. A crack forming in the shelter's ceiling or walls, growing larger over time, mirroring the psychological cracks growing between the survivors. Symbols like these give your shelter story an emotional weight that readers will feel even if they can't always articulate why.

And finally, remember: **shelters are supposed to be safe**. When they fail—or when staying inside becomes more dangerous than braving the outside—you deliver one of the most gut-punching emotional moments in disaster fiction. Maybe the shelter floods. Maybe raiders breach the doors. Maybe disease spreads faster in confinement. Whatever the trigger, the realization that nowhere is truly safe changes your characters forever.

Because survival isn't just about finding walls to hide behind.

It's about facing what happens when the walls themselves start closing in.

Weather as a Character: Hurricanes, Wildfires, and Blizzards

When you're writing a disaster story, one of the most powerful, terrifying forces you can unleash isn't an army or a monster—it's the weather itself. Hurricanes, wildfires, blizzards, floods, droughts—these aren't just background hazards. They can become active forces in the story, almost like living, breathing characters. When you treat weather like a character, you don't just describe it. You let it act. You let it change the story. You make it personal, unpredictable, relentless. And that's when it becomes unforgettable.

The first thing to understand is that **weather has its own mood and agenda**. It doesn't care about your characters' plans, hopes, or fears. It moves according to its own terrible rhythms. A hurricane doesn't care if the last boat is about to leave the island. A blizzard doesn't care if the wounded survivor is just a hundred yards from safety. Weather creates an unfeeling, indifferent antagonist that's all the more horrifying because it cannot be reasoned with, bribed, or defeated—only endured.

Writing a hurricane, for example, isn't just about strong winds and rain. It's about pressure building long before the storm hits. The humidity thick enough to choke on. The eerie calm before the first squall. The sirens, the boarded windows, the mass exodus from coastal towns. Then the gradual collapse: power flickers, roads flood, the howling of the wind drowns out every shouted word. A hurricane scene isn't just an action set piece—it's a slow ratcheting of fear, a rising tide of claustrophobia and desperation.

Wildfires, on the other hand, move fast and unpredictably. They're alive in a way few other natural disasters are. They race with the wind, jump highways, circle back around when you least expect it. Survivors trapped by wildfire don't just face heat—they face smoke thick enough to choke on, embers raining from the sky, the sound of trees exploding from within as their sap boils. Writing wildfire scenes means capturing not just the speed and ferocity of the flames but the *panic* they create—the way paths close behind survivors faster than they can run.

Blizzards are different again. They kill slowly, silently. Visibility drops to nothing. The world becomes a uniform sheet of white where landmarks vanish and every step risks getting lost forever. Frostbite creeps up unnoticed. Hypothermia dulls minds until people sit down in the snow to die without realizing it. Writing a blizzard means writing **silence** as much as fury—the howling winds outside, the muffled breathing inside a snowbound shelter, the terrible knowledge that warmth, light, and safety are slipping further away with every passing hour.

If you're brainstorming with ChatGPT, you can prompt for things like "how a wildfire changes landscape and movement" or "psychological effects of being trapped during a blizzard." You can also generate pacing ideas: "slow burn survival tension in a hurricane lockdown" or "rapid escape scenes in wildfire conditions." Tailoring the weather to the emotional needs of your story gives it the bite and presence of a true antagonist.

Symbolism is another powerful tool when using weather as a character. A hurricane isn't just wind and water—it's nature's rage unleashed. A wildfire isn't just a blaze—it's chaos and destruction, sweeping away the old world whether people are ready or not. A blizzard isn't just snow—it's isolation, the slow erasure of the human footprint. Using weather symbolically allows you to mirror your characters' inner journeys. If they're losing hope, bury them under snow. If they're trying desperately to escape their past, chase them with fire. If they're clinging to love against impossible odds, show them fighting through a hurricane's roar.

One trick to writing weather effectively is **using sensory overload**. In a hurricane, don't just say "it was raining hard." Describe the rain battering skin like needles, the wind ripping shingles off roofs, the scream of metal twisting in the gusts. In a wildfire, show the sting of smoke in the eyes, the blistering heat on exposed skin, the roar of the flames like a freight train bearing down. In a blizzard, focus on the numbness creeping up fingers, the endless white devouring the horizon, the terrifying moment when up and down feel the same.

And yet, sometimes the scariest part of weather is **what you can't see**. The levee that might break in the next surge. The flames hidden by thick smoke until it's too late. The blizzard that cuts off the only road to safety while the survivors argue inside. Writing these unseen dangers builds suspense naturally. The weather becomes a constant, creeping threat, a monster just beyond the edge of visibility.

Another important dynamic is **how survivors interact with the weather emotionally**. Some will treat it with superstitious fear—believing the disaster is punishment, or fate, or the world cleansing itself. Others will try to fight it with bravado and stubbornness. Others will respect it as an unstoppable force and adapt accordingly. These different reactions create tension inside survivor groups. Who wants to evacuate too soon? Who wants to hunker down and wait it out? Who loses hope first? Who gambles everything on a break in the storm that never comes?

Weather can also create **moral dilemmas**. Do you risk crossing a flooded bridge to save someone trapped on the other side? Do you abandon an injured group member to move faster away from a wildfire? Do you leave shelter to search for supplies, knowing a blizzard could trap you outside forever? When weather controls movement, communication, and survival itself, every decision becomes more dangerous, more complicated, more painful.

Another great technique is **letting the weather shape your story's structure**. Maybe the hurricane is the ticking clock—survivors have 24 hours to get inland before the storm surge hits. Maybe the wildfire creates a shifting battlefield, survivors constantly adjusting plans as roads are cut off, shelters burn, winds change. Maybe the blizzard traps a group together, forcing them to face old grudges, new betrayals, or quiet deaths. Structuring your story around a weather event gives it natural momentum and escalation.

And timing matters. Let the weather build in stages. Early warnings. Small signs. Growing fear. False security when the sky clears for a moment—then the real disaster hits harder than anyone expected. Good disaster pacing with weather is about stretching the rubber band just tight enough before letting it snap.

When you think about it, writing weather as a character is about more than just physical threat.

It's about stripping characters down.

Taking away comfort.

Taking away control.

Forcing them to face themselves, each other, and the terrible realization that no matter how clever or brave or strong they are, sometimes survival means bowing before forces so much bigger than you.

Because in a disaster story, the sky itself can turn against you.

And the only thing more terrifying than fighting the storm...

is realizing the storm doesn't even know you're there.

Disease and Pandemic Disasters: Invisible Killers

Some disasters roar onto the page—earthquakes shaking the ground, hurricanes tearing the skies open. But in disease and pandemic narratives, the disaster creeps in. Quiet. Relentless. Unseen. It slips through crowded markets, dusty train stations, broken quarantine lines. It's not a monster you can shoot or a storm you can outrun. It's an invisible killer already breathing down your neck—and by the time you realize it, it's already too late. Writing pandemic disasters means tapping into a different kind of fear: not explosive panic, but the slow, gnawing horror of something you can't see hollowing the world out from the inside.

The first thing to remember when writing about disease is **the delay**. Unlike other disasters, the full scope of a pandemic takes time to reveal itself. At first, it's just whispers. A few unusual cases at a local hospital. A rumor of sickness in another country. Officials saying it's under control. Ordinary people ignoring the early warnings because they want to believe life will go on. Writing this early phase is about building tension quietly—showing the cracks forming before anything actually collapses.

When the sickness spreads, it doesn't move like an explosion. It moves like a tide. Relentless. Inevitable. Cities don't fall in a day. They empty out slowly. Store shelves clear. Streets grow quieter. Masks appear. Schools close. Airports shut down. Fear grows, but so does denial. Writing this creeping collapse is about pacing—letting the readers see the world unravel step by step, just slowly enough that people inside the story can pretend it isn't happening... until they can't.

If you're brainstorming with ChatGPT, you can prompt for ideas like "early warning signs of a pandemic" or "how societal collapse unfolds during a disease outbreak." You can also focus on survivor psychology: "how different characters respond emotionally to a spreading invisible threat." These layers give your pandemic story depth beyond simple infection scenes.

Fear of others becomes a massive theme in pandemic fiction. Every cough, every handshake, every crowded space becomes a potential death sentence. Writing that fear means showing how community—the very thing that keeps humans alive—turns poisonous. Friends pull away from friends. Families quarantine inside their homes. Strangers on the street become threats simply by existing. The world shrinks, not because of walls or borders, but because trust itself collapses.

Pandemics also create **information chaos**. Early on, survivors don't know what's true. Different governments offer conflicting advice. Scientists disagree. Conspiracy theories bloom like mold. Some say the disease isn't real. Some say it's a weapon. Some say the end is coming, and others say it's all fine, go about your business. Writing the swirl of misinformation mirrors the way fear and uncertainty feed off each other, speeding up the social collapse even faster than the virus does.

And **infrastructure doesn't just fail—it rots**. Hospitals overflow. Supplies run out. Power grids weaken as workers get sick or abandon their posts. Garbage piles up in the streets. The systems that made modern life feel safe die a slow, stinking death. Survivors aren't just fighting the disease—they're fighting the collapse of the very world that used to keep them alive.

Another emotional angle to explore is **grief without closure**. In a pandemic, people die alone. Quarantine means loved ones can't be at the bedside. Funerals are forbidden or rushed. Writing this kind of loss shows a different, deeper kind of emotional wound. Survivors aren't just mourning—they're haunted by the way they couldn't say goodbye, by the way the world demanded they turn away when someone needed them most.

One of the most chilling parts of pandemic storytelling is **the randomness of survival**. The disease might strike the healthy and spare the weak. It might mutate, changing the rules halfway through. It might offer false hope—a treatment that fails, a vaccine that comes too late. Writing this randomness forces readers to live inside the same uncertainty your characters feel. Survival isn't a reward for being good, or smart, or strong. It's a brutal lottery. And that truth changes people.

In some pandemic stories, the disease itself evolves into **a second disaster**. Maybe it causes neurological damage that changes behavior. Maybe it weakens survivors to the point that other threats—starvation, violence, natural disasters—finish what the virus started. Maybe the real threat becomes human desperation: looters, warlords, splinter governments rising from the ashes. The disease starts the collapse, but it's human fear, selfishness, and rage that finish it.

If you want to build extra richness into your story, consider **different survivor groups**. Some might become isolationists, living in sealed bunkers. Others might form traveling caravans, believing motion is safer than walls. Some might turn to faith, others to science, others to madness. How each group responds to the invisible killer reveals their true nature—and offers endless chances for alliances, betrayals, and heartbreak.

Pacing a pandemic story is different than pacing an earthquake or explosion narrative. You need room for **creeping dread**. Long scenes of uncertainty. Characters waiting for symptoms. Watching others cough. Wondering if that scratchy throat means the end. The horror isn't in big action scenes—it's in small, intimate, terrifying moments of doubt, isolation, and slow decay.

But that doesn't mean you can't have sudden spikes of terror too. Maybe the shelter gets compromised. Maybe a fever sweeps the group. Maybe a desperate mob overruns a safe zone. These spikes give the story rhythm—calm dread punctuated by frantic horror.

And don't underestimate the emotional weight of **hope turning to ash**. Maybe a vaccine seems close—only to fail spectacularly. Maybe a loved one seems to recover—only to relapse. Maybe a safe haven city holds out—only to fall overnight. In a pandemic story, false hope isn't cruel writing. It's honest. It mirrors the way real people cling to anything, any chance, even in the darkest times.

Symbolism runs thick in disease narratives too. Masks hiding faces—and truths. Empty playgrounds. Flickering hospital lights. Abandoned homes with dinner still on the table. Each symbol shows a world that didn't explode—it *faded*, rotted, dissolved while everyone was looking the other way.

In the end, writing a pandemic disaster story isn't about the disease itself.

It's about what fear does to people.

It's about how fragile society really is when trust evaporates and survival becomes personal.

It's about what we're willing to do—to ourselves, to each other—to live just one more day.

Because the scariest thing about an invisible killer isn't just that it's out there.

It's that it turns everyone, even those we love most, into something to fear.

Alien Invasion and Otherworldly Catastrophes

Some disasters feel all too human—plagues, floods, bombs, the slow unraveling of civilization. But sometimes, in the wild playground of disaster fiction, the thing that shatters the world isn't something we caused. It's something *else*. Something from beyond the stars, another dimension, or even beyond human understanding. Alien invasions and otherworldly catastrophes open up a different kind of storytelling: one where the enemy isn't just unknown—it's unknowable. And survival doesn't just mean beating the odds. It means trying to understand a threat bigger, stranger, and more merciless than anything Earth has ever faced.

When you write an alien invasion or otherworldly disaster, the first thing to decide is **what kind of threat you're dealing with**. Are the invaders violent and obvious, mowing down cities with energy weapons? Are they quiet and insidious, infiltrating minds, rewriting DNA, replacing loved ones with something almost—but not quite—human? Or are they simply indifferent, reshaping the planet for their own purposes without even noticing we're here, like ants scurrying around a demolished anthill?

The kind of invasion you choose shapes everything about your story's tone. Blazing sky battles and collapsed monuments create fast-paced, high-action survival tales. Silent takeovers, slow mutations, or creeping cosmic corruption lean into psychological horror and existential dread. You don't have to lock yourself into one mode, either. A great alien invasion story often shifts: from awe, to fear, to terror, to desperate survival.

If you're brainstorming with ChatGPT, you can prompt for ideas like "types of alien invasion scenarios" or "ways an otherworldly event could slowly transform a city." You can also explore emotional beats: "how characters might react to losing their concept of reality after a cosmic event" or "how survivors adapt to an unknowable enemy." Playing with these layers makes your invasion story feel alive, terrifying, and unpredictable.

First contact is one of the richest parts of writing these stories. How do people react when the skies fill with ships? When people start disappearing? When the laws of physics begin to twist? Initial responses might be a mix of awe, denial, hysteria, and hope. Governments might call for calm—or collapse overnight. Faiths might fracture or rally. Scientists might try to communicate—or realize too late that communication is impossible. Writing this early phase is about showing confusion more than certainty. Nobody *really* knows what's happening yet—and in the fog of that confusion, terrible mistakes get made.

One of the most powerful emotional currents in alien disaster stories is **the shrinking of the human ego**. In ordinary disasters, there's still a sense that if people pull together, they can survive. But facing something utterly alien strips that away. It makes humanity feel tiny, irrelevant, powerless. Writing that existential fear—the realization that we're not the masters of the universe, maybe not even important enough to save—hits deep and hard.

Another vital decision: **what do the aliens want, if anything?** Some classic approaches include:

- **Resources**: stripping Earth for materials, water, or biomass.
- **Slaves or hosts**: using humans for labor, reproduction, or experiments.
- **Territory**: clearing Earth for colonization, the way humans might clear a forest without much thought for the wildlife.
- **Annihilation**: pure eradication, for reasons we can't begin to guess.
- **Curiosity**: studying us, reshaping us, changing us—not from hatred, but from cold fascination.

Or maybe the worst possibility: **they don't even notice us**. We're just collateral damage in their larger, incomprehensible plans.

If you lean into the "unknowable" angle, you move closer to **cosmic horror**, where the true terror comes not from what the aliens do, but from realizing we were never important to begin with. This shifts your story into a darker, more philosophical tone, where survival becomes less about winning and more about maintaining some sliver of meaning in a meaningless universe.

Resistance stories are another classic arc in alien invasion fiction. Survivors become guerrilla fighters, scavengers, rebels hiding in the ruins. This kind of story gives you the satisfying arc of survival against impossible odds—but it works best when you show that every tiny victory costs something precious. Writing scrappy human resistance isn't about painting humanity as invincible. It's about showing that even in the face of certain defeat, we refuse to vanish quietly.

Otherworldly catastrophes don't have to be classic "alien landings," either. Maybe it's a tear in the fabric of reality itself. Maybe it's a pulse of energy that mutates life randomly. Maybe it's creatures from another dimension spilling through cracks in the sky. The stranger the event, the more you get to play with atmosphere: broken gravity, strange new ecosystems, eerie distortions of time and space. Survivors might have to navigate a world that doesn't just look different—it *works* differently now.

Symbolism runs deep in these stories too. Alien invasions can mirror colonialism, ecological destruction, fear of the unknown, or the collapse of familiar systems. Survivors trekking through ruined cities now crawling with alien flora and fauna can feel like refugees in a world that has moved on without them. An invasion can make your characters question everything—what it means to be human, what it means to have hope, whether survival is even the right goal anymore.

Another layer you can explore is **collaboration and betrayal**. In every alien invasion story, some humans will side with the invaders—out of fear, selfishness, desperation, or genuine belief that cooperation is the only way to survive. Writing these human villains adds an extra twist of emotional pain: betrayal doesn't just come from the skies. It comes from the people you thought you could trust.

And don't forget the **personal cost**. Just because the disaster is vast doesn't mean you have to lose emotional intimacy. Focus tightly on a handful of survivors. Show their losses. Their desperate dreams. Their moments of hope and despair. Let readers feel the enormity of the invasion through the small, searing heartbreaks of ordinary people trying to hold onto each other when the world ends.

Timing matters in alien catastrophe stories too. You can start your story **during the invasion**, with cities falling and skies burning. You can start **after**, when the new rulers have settled in and survival becomes a long, grinding struggle. Or you can start **at the first signs**, when nobody's sure if the strange lights and vanishing towns mean the end—or a new beginning.

However you time it, remember that alien and otherworldly disasters aren't just about wiping the slate clean. They're about the terror—and the awe—of facing forces bigger than anything we ever imagined. Forces that don't think like us, don't care like us, don't even see the world the way we do.

Because survival isn't just about fighting monsters.

It's about clinging to what makes us human in a universe that might not even know we exist.

Climate Change and the Slow Apocalypse

Most disaster stories are built around sudden, violent moments—the earthquake, the tsunami, the bomb, the invasion. But one of the most chilling forms of disaster is the one that creeps in so slowly that people barely realize it's happening until it's too late. Climate change is the slow apocalypse, and writing about it forces you to dig into a different kind of fear—not fear of a single collapse, but fear of a long, grinding unraveling that touches every part of life.

When you write a climate change apocalypse, you're not writing about a singular event. You're writing about **accumulated decay**. About systems stretched thinner and thinner until they finally snap. It's droughts that turn fertile farmland into desert. It's coastal cities swallowed a little more each year by rising seas. It's superstorms leveling towns that never saw a hurricane before. It's wildfires that burn longer and hotter every summer, until forests become memories. It's heatwaves killing crops, blackouts crippling cities, disease vectors spreading farther and faster than ever before.

The emotional weight in a climate change story comes from **the slowness of collapse**. People adapt. Deny. Hope. Pretend. They move inland when the coasts flood. They build seawalls and levees. They invent new ways to grow food in hostile environments. They tell themselves they can innovate their way out of it. But piece by piece, the world shrinks. The options narrow. The luxuries vanish.

What was once extraordinary—the 110-degree day, the once-in-a-century flood—becomes normal. And that normalization is the true terror: the idea that people can get used to anything, even the death of their own world.

If you're brainstorming with ChatGPT, you can prompt for ideas like "daily life in a post-climate collapse city" or "emotional beats for a family slowly losing their farm to drought." You can also explore story settings: "a refugee caravan fleeing rising seas," "a marketplace in a desertified former city," "a flooded metropolis where people live on rooftops." Building your slow apocalypse world through small, everyday details makes it feel chillingly real.

Climate disasters don't happen evenly, either. Some places get hotter, some get colder. Some flood, some burn. Writing regional diversity in climate collapse mirrors real life, where wealthier nations might wall themselves off behind green technology while poorer ones are abandoned to the storm. That unequal suffering creates powerful storytelling opportunities—conflicts over resources, climate refugees, broken alliances, and desperate migrations.

A major emotional engine in a climate change narrative is **the generational divide**. Older characters might remember the "before"—seasons that made sense, reliable harvests, blue skies without smoke. Younger characters grow up thinking endless droughts and toxic air are just how the world works. That split in memory and expectation creates deep emotional tension: regret, guilt, resentment, and the desperate hope that maybe the next generation can find a better way forward.

Another dynamic to explore is **false hope and exploitation**. In a world of creeping climate disaster, there will always be voices promising salvation. Politicians swearing that technology will save everyone. Corporations selling snake-oil solutions that only buy a little more time for the wealthy. Writing about how people cling to these promises—even when they know deep down they're lies—adds brutal realism to your slow apocalypse.

Survival in a slow apocalypse looks different too. It's not just about scavenging for supplies after a sudden event. It's about adapting to a world that demands more every year and gives less in return. Survivors might farm in skyscrapers, trade water like gold, migrate with the seasons like ancient nomads. Small luxuries—a fresh apple, a clean rainstorm—become treasures. Writing these adaptations shows how resilient—and how fragile—human ingenuity really is.

Communities fracture and reshape in the face of long-term collapse. Cities shrink. Governments fall. New alliances form around access to clean water, arable land, or old tech that still works. Maybe a group of survivors builds a floating city in the flooded ruins. Maybe a desert commune survives by perfecting solar desalination. Maybe bitter, climate-hardened tribes wage wars over the last remaining green spaces.

The future doesn't have to be completely dead. It just has to be *different*—and it has to be hard-earned.

One of the hardest, and most powerful, things to capture is **the emotional erosion** that mirrors environmental erosion. Hope fades slowly. Trust wears thin. Despair becomes an everyday emotion. Writing how characters struggle to maintain meaning, relationships, and dreams in a world where the horizon keeps shrinking is what gives your story emotional weight beyond the facts of environmental disaster.

And yet, even in the slow apocalypse, **seeds of hope can survive**. Maybe it's a child born into a dying world, and the fierce, almost irrational love of a parent determined to carve out a better life for them. Maybe it's a tiny community that refuses to give up, finding ways to live lightly, sustainably, cooperatively. Maybe it's a discovery—new crops, old wisdom, forgotten tech—that offers a fragile lifeline. Hope doesn't have to be big to matter. In fact, in a story about creeping loss, *small* hope often feels much more powerful.

Symbolism works beautifully in climate collapse stories. A cracked riverbed where a thriving river once ran. A ghost city submerged beneath gray waves. A battered greenhouse still nurturing a single stubborn tomato plant. These images do more than decorate your story—they *speak*, wordlessly, about memory, loss, endurance, and the stubborn human will to find life even in ruin.

Another emotional theme you can lean into is **guilt**. Some characters might feel responsible for the world their generation destroyed. Others might rage at the unfairness of inheriting a broken planet. Some might bury their guilt under denial, greed, or fatalism. Writing these emotional scars deepens the psychological realism of your world and makes survival feel even more personal.

When pacing your slow apocalypse story, remember it's not about a single explosion of action. It's about **layers of tension**. Drought leading to famine. Famine leading to migration. Migration leading to conflict. Conflict leading to collapse. Readers should feel the grind, the slow wearing away of options, the narrowing of the future, until survival itself feels like a radical act of rebellion against despair.

Ultimately, writing climate change and slow apocalypse stories is about capturing a different kind of horror.

Not the sudden terror of the bomb or the flood.

But the long, slow grief of watching something beloved die inch by inch, year by year.

And the stubborn refusal to go quietly into the scorched night.

Because survival in the slow apocalypse isn't about outrunning the end.

It's about finding reasons to live—and reasons to hope—even as the sky turns hotter and the rivers run dry.

Choosing the Tone: Bleak, Hopeful, or Bittersweet

Tone is one of the most powerful invisible forces shaping any disaster story. It colors everything—how the ruins feel, how the survivors act, how readers experience every loss, every small victory, every final decision. Before you even finish building your crumbling world or sketching your desperate characters, it's worth asking yourself: what emotional *flavor* will carry your story? Bleak? Hopeful? Bittersweet? Because the tone you choose will quietly control everything, from pacing to dialogue to the way your final scenes leave readers feeling long after they close the book.

Let's start with **bleak**. A bleak disaster story doesn't just put characters through hell. It lets them lose. It says that survival isn't always possible. That sometimes the disaster wins, no matter how hard you fight. Writing in a bleak tone means stripping away comforts early and often. Characters make desperate choices—and often regret them. Safe zones fail. Hope turns toxic. The environment grows harsher, not softer. Relationships break under the weight of fear and scarcity.

But writing bleak isn't about piling on misery until it becomes absurd. It's about showing that in some worlds, endurance isn't rewarded. Some characters won't be saved. Some struggles won't have a triumphant ending. Done right, bleak disaster fiction can hit harder than any explosion. It forces readers to sit with uncomfortable truths: that not every story has a happy ending, that not every hero gets a reward, that sometimes surviving changes you so much that the person you were might as well have died anyway.

If you're brainstorming with ChatGPT for bleak disaster story ideas, you can prompt for things like "emotional arcs ending in sacrifice or failure" or "scenes where survival demands heartbreaking choices." Bleak stories don't kill hope completely—they let it flicker just long enough for readers to mourn it when it's snuffed out.

Now, **hopeful** disaster fiction is a different beast. It's not about pretending everything is fine—it's about showing that even when everything breaks, something better can be built in the ruins. Hopeful disaster stories still have pain, loss, fear—but they also have stubborn resilience. Survivors band together. Communities rebuild. Humanity adapts. Writing hopeful disaster fiction means focusing on the sparks that refuse to be extinguished: kindness in the middle of chaos, sacrifice for a better future, belief that tomorrow might not be as bad as today.

Hopeful doesn't mean *easy*. It means choosing to show that the disaster doesn't get the final word. That people are messy, stubborn, brilliant creatures who can find ways to survive—and sometimes even thrive—against impossible odds. Readers of hopeful disaster fiction want to believe that collapse isn't the end of the story. It's the beginning of something new, rough, and beautiful.

If you're plotting a hopeful tone, you can prompt for things like "unexpected moments of kindness during disaster" or "small victories that build into larger survival successes." Hopeful doesn't mean cheesy. It means honest victories earned through grit, sacrifice, and human connection.

And then there's **bittersweet**—my personal favorite, and arguably the most emotionally complex tone you can choose. Bittersweet disaster stories live in the space between despair and hope. They recognize that survival often comes at a cost. That some things will never be rebuilt. That not everyone makes it. That even victories taste a little like ashes. But they also recognize that endurance itself has value. That new life grows from the cracks. That even broken things can be beautiful.

Bittersweet tones allow you to have real, heavy losses—deaths, betrayals, irreversible changes—and still offer something meaningful at the end. Maybe the protagonist makes it to the safe zone, but without the people they started with. Maybe the city burns, but a child plants seeds in the ashes. Maybe a character dies, but their sacrifice saves the next generation. Writing bittersweet stories means leaning into the complexity of real emotions, refusing simple answers, and trusting readers to sit with sorrow *and* hope at the same time.

If you want to shape a bittersweet tone, brainstorm with ChatGPT for things like "endings where survival comes with loss" or "characters finding purpose after personal devastation." Bittersweet stories hurt—but they also heal. They offer no clean victories, no neat conclusions. Just the messy, hard, beautiful truth that life goes on.

One way to lock in your story's tone early is to think about **your ending first**. Not the plot ending—the emotional ending. When the last scene fades out, how do you want readers to feel? Gutted? Uplifted? Haunted? Inspired? The answer to that question will help you steer every major choice—who lives, who dies, who changes, who stays the same, and what pieces of the old world are left standing.

You also want to weave your tone into **the small moments**. In a bleak story, even a sunrise might feel cold, empty, meaningless. In a hopeful story, a sunrise might feel like a fresh beginning. In a bittersweet story, a sunrise might be beautiful and heartbreaking at once—a reminder of everything lost, and everything still stubbornly alive.

Tone isn't something you slap on at the end. It's in the weather. The dialogue. The way characters move, the way they hope or despair or fight.

Another trick is to match **the physical world to the emotional one**. In a bleak story, the environment might grow steadily worse—wastelands, poisoned air, dead oceans. In a hopeful story, survivors might reclaim land, find clean water, see green shoots piercing through broken concrete. In a bittersweet story, nature might reclaim ruined cities in a way that's both beautiful and sad—a world moving on with or without human dreams.

Tone can also shift within a story—but carefully. A story might start grim and end hopeful, showing a climb from darkness into light. Or it might start with fragile hope and slowly slide into grim acceptance. Or it might oscillate, letting characters (and readers) taste both despair and defiance over and over. When tone shifts, it should feel natural—driven by the characters' journey, not just imposed by the author.

One thing to avoid is **tone whiplash**—where a story's emotional temperature changes so fast it feels jarring or false. Keep your tone transitions gradual. Let a hopeful moment be undercut by a creeping shadow. Let a bleak moment be interrupted by a stubborn act of kindness. Let a bittersweet moment linger, giving readers time to feel both sides of the emotional coin.

And remember: whatever tone you choose, it should feel **earned**. If the story has been relentlessly grim, don't tack on a saccharine happy ending at the last minute. If the story has been about hope and resilience, don't cynically yank it away in the final paragraph just for shock value. Trust the emotional truth you've built across the story.

Stay honest to the journey.

Because the best disaster stories aren't just about surviving collapse.

They're about surviving what collapse does to the human heart.

And whether that heart beats with bitterness, with hope, or with a fragile, aching mix of both—that's up to you.

Resource Wars: Fighting Over What's Left

When the disaster hits, the first instinct is to survive. But when the disaster drags on, when the supplies start to run low and no cavalry comes riding over the hill, survival stops being a private struggle. It becomes a war. A war fought over water, over food, over medicine, over fuel, over anything that still has value. Writing resource wars in disaster fiction taps into one of humanity's oldest, rawest instincts—not the will to destroy, but the will to take what is needed, no matter the cost.

The first thing you have to realize is that **resource wars don't start big**. They start small. Two families fighting over a working well. A scuffle over a bag of rice. A few gunshots in a supermarket parking lot when there are only five cans left on the shelf. These early conflicts are often chaotic, personal, and vicious. Writing these small eruptions of violence gives your world a sense of rising, inevitable tension—like watching the first cracks spider-web across a dam.

As resources grow scarcer, **violence gets organized**. Gangs form. Militias rise. Local warlords stake claims over wells, farmland, warehouses. Writing this escalation is about showing how quickly human groups revert to tribalism when survival is on the line. "Us" and "them" lines get drawn in blood. Maybe your characters cling to old national borders—or maybe those collapse completely and new alliances based purely on survival emerge.

If you're brainstorming with ChatGPT, you can prompt for things like "how resource wars start in post-disaster societies" or "conflicts that arise over limited supplies." You can also get emotional story beats like "betrayals within survivor groups over scarce resources" or "alliances of necessity between former enemies." Building these tensions makes your story feel alive, dangerous, and emotionally gripping.

Water is often the first flashpoint. Without water, people die in days. Wells become strategic targets. Rivers become battle lines. Controlling a working water filtration system becomes more valuable than owning a thousand guns. Writing about water wars lets you strip survival down to its most brutal, essential core.

It's not about ideology.

It's about thirst.

Food is next. Starvation changes people. It shrinks morality. Characters might start by sharing equally—then shift to rationing based on strength, usefulness, loyalty. In extreme cases, cannibalism lurks at the edges of survival horror, and the decision to cross that line—or refuse to—can define entire arcs. Writing hunger means writing slow deterioration: weakness, hallucinations, hopelessness, and the primal, gnawing drive that strips away civilization one painful day at a time.

Fuel and energy spark different kinds of conflicts. Control over vehicles, generators, heaters, and cooking equipment means control over movement, protection, and comfort. Survivors might rig old solar panels, scavenge diesel, or build crude windmills. Territories with remaining fuel sources become fortresses—or death traps. Writing energy conflicts lets you explore the tactical, strategic side of resource wars—sieges, raids, alliances.

Medicine becomes a bargaining chip, too. In a collapsed world, a simple antibiotic is worth more than gold. Insulin. Painkillers. Even basic first aid supplies. Medicine wars often carry an extra emotional punch because they pit survival against compassion. Who gets the last vial of penicillin—the child with pneumonia or the adult leader holding the group together? Writing these choices breaks characters wide open, showing readers who they really are when the easy answers run out.

One of the best parts of writing resource wars is **moral ambiguity**. In a stable world, raiding a food truck is theft. In a collapsing one, it might be the only way to save your family. Readers should feel torn. They should root for characters even as they cross lines they would have condemned before the disaster.

Maybe a character loots medicine—and leaves others to die.

Maybe a character kills to protect their share—and loses themselves in the process.

Maybe a character refuses to fight—and is punished for their mercy.

Group dynamics shift under the pressure of resource scarcity. In peaceful times, the strongest or smartest might lead. In desperate times, the most ruthless might take over. Leaders who cling to old-world values may be betrayed by those willing to do whatever it takes. Writing the slow erosion of loyalty and trust under the grinding weight of starvation, thirst, and fear gives your story raw emotional power.

Another layer to explore is **resource propaganda**. Survivors might lie about what they have to avoid being targeted. Leaders might promise resources they don't actually control to rally followers. Factions might demonize others to justify raids. Information itself becomes a weapon.

Writing these manipulations turns your resource war into not just a physical battle—but a psychological one.

If you want to go even deeper, you can explore how **resource control reshapes society**. Maybe a group that controls the last clean water source demands total loyalty in exchange. Maybe they reinvent feudalism, with warlords offering protection in return for absolute obedience. Maybe trade flourishes again—not with money, but with goods: clean water for antibiotics, fresh crops for ammunition.

Economies collapse and are reborn under desperate new rules.

And don't underestimate **the emotional toll**. Survivors fighting over scraps don't just lose their homes and loved ones. They lose pieces of themselves. Writing how guilt, trauma, and regret pile up inside characters makes survival cost something real. A character who wins a battle for supplies might lose their faith in humanity. A character who refuses to fight might watch their family starve.

Survival becomes a slow erosion of self.

Pacing is critical in resource war stories. Early skirmishes should feel personal, messy, chaotic. As time goes on, conflicts should become more strategic, more brutal, more coordinated. Every act of violence should push the world a little further from what it used to be—and push the characters a little closer to what they swore they would never become.

Symbolism can work powerfully here too. A broken well becomes a symbol of lost community. A burned field becomes a grave for the old world. A single unripe apple becomes a symbol of fragile hope—or bitter betrayal.

These images stay with readers long after the last shot is fired.

Because writing resource wars in disaster fiction isn't just about fighting for survival.

It's about showing what survival *costs*—and whether, after all the blood and grief and betrayal, it was ever really survival at all.

Writing Disaster Stories for Young Adult Audiences

Disaster stories hit differently when you're writing for a young adult audience. Teenagers live at the edge of everything already—emotion, change, fear, rebellion, hope. When you throw them into the middle of a disaster, it isn't just a fight for survival. It's a fight for identity, for agency, for a future they might not even be sure exists anymore. Writing disaster fiction for young adults means tapping into that raw emotional current, respecting it, and channeling it into stories that are just as powerful—and sometimes even more honest—than anything written for adults.

The first thing to understand is that **YA disaster fiction isn't about watering things down**. It's not about making everything safe or pretty or easy to digest. Teens can handle darkness. They live with fear, uncertainty, and grief already. What they don't usually tolerate well is hopelessness without meaning. A YA disaster story should hurt. It should scare. It should challenge. But it should also leave a crack open—a place where resilience, growth, and the stubborn will to keep going can take root.

If you're brainstorming with ChatGPT, you can prompt for things like "disaster story ideas centered on teenage protagonists" or "emotional arcs for young survivors in catastrophic settings." You can also explore thematic ideas: "coming of age during societal collapse" or "finding hope and identity after disaster."

When you're writing for teens, **the protagonist's age matters**. They should be old enough to take action, but young enough to still be growing, questioning, stumbling toward understanding. Typically somewhere between 15 and 18 years old feels right. Old enough to have a real impact on the story, young enough that they're still figuring out who they are when the world falls apart.

In a YA disaster story, **relationships are everything**. Friendships. First loves. Found families. Rivalries that flare under pressure. Betrayals that cut deeper because trust means everything when the world outside is crumbling. Writing disaster fiction for teens means focusing not just on survival logistics—how to find clean water, how to avoid roving gangs—but also on emotional survival. How do you keep trusting people when betrayal could mean death? How do you keep loving someone when loss is inevitable?

Identity becomes a survival issue, too. In the middle of a disaster, teens aren't just fighting external enemies. They're fighting internal battles about who they want to become. Do they harden and survive at any cost? Do they cling to their old values, even when it gets them hurt? Do they carve out a new identity in the ashes of the old world? Disaster accelerates that journey brutally, and writing it honestly gives your YA story a heartbeat that readers will feel on every page.

Another powerful tool is **giving teens real agency**. In many disaster stories, adults either vanish, fail, or become the antagonists. Teen protagonists have to make decisions—sometimes bad ones—with real consequences. They can't just tag along behind adult heroes. They *are* the heroes. And they're messy, imperfect, scared, reckless heroes, which makes them all the more real and relatable.

Pacing is a little different in YA disaster fiction too. Teens are impulsive. They don't always plan. They react with gut and heart and fierce loyalty. Your story should move fast. Emotions should spike high and crash hard. Moments of tenderness, rage, terror, and hope should come quick and raw. Long, slow stretches of technical detail—how to build a water purifier from scratch, for example—are less important than the emotional stakes of whether the purifier works in time to save a friend.

Another essential point: **let your characters fail**. Especially early on. Survival isn't neat. Teens might make rash decisions that cost lives. They might trust the wrong person. They might cling to old-world ideals when the new world demands something harder. Failure is a huge part of growth, and YA readers expect characters to earn their survival and their wisdom.

But at the same time, **don't strip away all their power**. YA disaster fiction shines brightest when it shows young people stepping up—not because they were born ready, but because they had no choice. Show them scared. Show them hurt. Show them breaking down. But also show them getting back up, even when it feels impossible.

Themes in YA disaster stories often mirror traditional YA themes but sharpened under extreme pressure.

- **Coming of age** becomes coming of survival.
- **Finding your voice** becomes saving your life—and the lives of others.
- **First love** blooms under the shadow of loss and fear.
- **Identity** becomes a weapon against despair and erasure.

Symbolism works beautifully here too. Maybe a battered necklace becomes a symbol of everything the protagonist refuses to give up. Maybe a ruined school becomes a battleground for a new beginning. Maybe a single growing plant in a wasteland becomes proof that life fights back, even in the worst conditions. YA readers don't need everything spelled out—but they feel deep symbols sharply, instinctively.

Hope is the engine of YA disaster fiction. Even in the bleakest, most brutal worlds, there should be sparks of it. A friendship that survives when the city falls. A new community built out of ruins. A sunrise after a night of terror. YA readers are wired for hope—not because they're naïve, but because hope is part of growing, learning, becoming. Your story doesn't have to promise that everything will be okay. It just has to show that something better is still possible.

One thing to avoid is **talking down** to the audience. Teen readers can spot condescension a mile away. Don't simplify language unnecessarily. Don't censor real fear, real anger, real grief. Trust them to walk into hard emotional places and find their own way out. Trust them to recognize complexity—that sometimes people you love let you down, that sometimes survival demands impossible choices, that sometimes the right thing doesn't feel good at all.

Dialogue in YA disaster fiction should feel immediate, emotional, and a little rough around the edges. Teens don't give long speeches about philosophy. They snap. They joke. They blurt things out at exactly the wrong time. Let the dialogue breathe and crack and bleed a little—it will feel more alive.

And don't forget that **small victories matter enormously**. Finding a lost sibling. Saving one person. Making it through one more night. In a YA disaster story, the road ahead doesn't have to be easy—or even clear. It just has to be worth walking. Readers don't need the world to be fixed by the end. They just need to believe it's still worth fighting for.

Because writing YA disaster fiction isn't about protecting young readers from fear or grief or pain.

It's about handing them the truth—and the reminder that even at the end of the world, there's still a way forward.

That even when everything falls apart, they can rise from the wreckage—not perfect, not whole, but stronger and more fiercely alive than ever.

Turning a Disaster Story into a Gripping Short Story

Disaster fiction usually conjures images of sprawling epics—hundreds of pages of survival, collapse, and rebuilding. But disaster stories can be even more powerful when packed into the tight frame of a short story. In fact, the intensity of a disaster—the urgency, the life-or-death stakes, the raw human emotion—makes it a perfect match for the short story form. Writing a disaster short story isn't about shrinking the disaster. It's about focusing it down to a sharp, unforgettable point.

The first thing to realize when turning a disaster story into a short story is that **you can't tell everything.** You don't have space to show the entire collapse of a city, the whole course of a pandemic, the full history of the alien invasion. Instead, you need to pick **one slice** of the disaster. One moment. One decision. One emotional heartbeat. That narrow focus is what gives a disaster short story its punch.

If you're brainstorming with ChatGPT, you can prompt for things like "single moments of high tension in disaster settings" or "emotional turning points during survival." You can also work backward: pick the emotional gut-punch you want the story to leave, and build everything around that.

Characters in a short disaster story need to come alive fast. You don't have chapters to peel back their layers slowly. Instead, show who they are through immediate action and reaction. Maybe the way a character refuses to leave an injured stranger behind tells us everything about them. Maybe the way another character hoards supplies and lies without flinching shows their core in a single scene.

Characterization needs to be efficient—but not shallow.

Dialogue can pull double duty here. A single line of speech can reveal loyalty, fear, guilt, or desperation. A whispered "I'm sorry" at the wrong moment can fracture an alliance. A shouted command can reveal a hidden cowardice or courage. Keep dialogue tight, emotional, and layered with unspoken meaning.

Setting also needs to be established with a few vivid strokes. You don't have the luxury of five pages describing the ruined cityscape. Instead, pick two or three sharp details—a tilted bus buried in ash, a silent sky choked with smoke, a cracked clock tower still ticking against all odds—and let the reader's mind fill in the rest.

A good disaster short story feels bigger than its word count because it sparks the reader's imagination to build the larger ruin beyond what's shown.

Another key is **limiting the timeline**. A disaster short story usually covers a few hours, a day, maybe even just a few minutes. You're zooming in on one flashpoint—the crucial choice, the heartbreaking realization, the last desperate act. Keeping the timeline tight keeps the tension high and the emotional stakes immediate.

Conflict should be immediate and intense. No slow burns. Open in motion, open in danger. Start when the character already knows they're in trouble—or better yet, when they think they're safe and discover they're wrong.

The best disaster short stories grab the reader by the throat from the first line and don't let go until the final breath.

And speaking of final breaths—**endings** matter even more in short form. A short disaster story should leave a bruise. It might end in triumph, survival bought at terrible cost. It might end in heartbreak, with rescue just out of reach.

It might end with a single stubborn act of hope. But whatever ending you choose, it should feel inevitable—not random, not convenient.

Every choice in the story should funnel naturally toward that ending.

One way to build a strong ending is to **mirror the beginning**. If the first scene opens with a character lighting a fire to signal for help, maybe the final scene shows them putting it out—accepting that no one is coming. If it opens with a survivor refusing to trust anyone, maybe it ends with them taking a desperate risk to save a stranger.

Circular structure gives a short story emotional weight and makes it feel complete, even in a small space.

Themes in a disaster short story should be simple but sharp. Trust. Sacrifice. Isolation. Hope. Fear. Choose one or two emotional threads and weave everything through them—setting, dialogue, action, even the smallest details. In a short story, thematic unity makes every sentence pull in the same emotional direction, creating a story that feels cohesive and powerful.

If you want to add an extra emotional punch, **symbolism** works beautifully in short disaster fiction. A single object can carry enormous weight—a photograph clutched through a flood, a pocketknife passed from dying hand to living one, a broken necklace representing lost innocence. Symbolism gives readers something to hold onto emotionally long after the last word.

Pacing is naturally faster in short stories, but that doesn't mean constant chaos. You can—and should—have small moments of stillness, reflection, or decision. A breath between the collapse of a building and the next sprint for safety. A heartbeat where a character hesitates, knowing it might cost them everything. These pauses sharpen the action that follows, like pulling back a slingshot before letting it fly.

One thing you can experiment with is **narrative structure**.

- Start at the end and work backward.
- Start in the middle of the disaster and reveal what happened through flashbacks.
- Use letters, journal entries, or emergency broadcasts to tell the story sideways.
  Disaster fiction lends itself to fragmented, desperate storytelling, and readers are often willing to jump in without needing everything explained upfront.

Another powerful technique is **limiting point of view**. Stick closely to one character's experience. What they see. What they fear. What they misunderstand. A disaster seen through the tight lens of one mind feels scarier, more immediate, and often more emotionally devastating. And don't forget: **not all disaster stories are about survival.** Some are about sacrifice. Some are about choosing dignity in the face of certain death. Some are about finding a scrap of beauty in a ruined world, even if there's no one left to see it. Letting go of survival as the only possible "win" opens up richer, riskier, more haunting possibilities. Because the best disaster short stories aren't small just because they're short.

They're small the way a blade is small—sharp, purposeful, devastating.

Expanding a Disaster Story into a Full Novel

Sometimes a disaster story idea bursts out in a few thousand words—a flash of survival, a brief glimpse of ruin, a snapshot of a crumbling world. But some ideas won't stay small. They grow in your mind, stretch against the edges of the short story format, and demand room to breathe, fall apart, and rebuild. Expanding a disaster story into a full novel isn't just about adding pages. It's about deepening the world, the characters, the themes, and the emotional journey until readers feel like they're living inside the collapse.

The first step in expanding is to realize **what part of your short story was only the tip of the iceberg**. A powerful disaster short story usually hints at a much bigger world: cities burning beyond the horizon, survivors fighting battles you don't see, whole systems falling like dominoes off the page. Expanding into a novel means taking those hints and pulling them into the light. It's about asking yourself, "What else is happening beyond this single event?" and then building the roads that connect it all.

If you're brainstorming with ChatGPT, you can prompt for things like "ways to expand a survival story into a full disaster novel" or "secondary plots for disaster fiction." You can also dig into world-building questions: "what new dangers emerge months after a major catastrophe?" or "how does a small community survive long-term after societal collapse?"

Characters are your first anchor for expansion. In a short story, you might focus tightly on one protagonist's crisis. In a novel, you have the space to flesh out a cast: allies, rivals, family members, strangers with their own agendas. Some of them will stay loyal. Some will betray. Some will simply break under the pressure.

Expanding your character web naturally expands your story's emotional reach.

Give each major character **an arc**—something they want, something they fear, something they might lose. Survival is important, but it's not enough. They need emotional goals too. Forgiveness. Redemption. Power. Connection. Having multiple emotional throughlines braided together makes your novel feel rich, layered, and alive.

Setting comes next. A short disaster story might take place in one house, one bunker, one city block. A novel can roam wider. What's happening in the countryside? In other cities? Across borders? You don't have to tell the whole world's story—but you can suggest it. Refugees passing through, rumors of distant safe zones, glimpses of larger societal collapse happening just out of sight.

A great disaster novel feels like it's sitting on top of a vast, shifting, dangerous world.

When expanding, **time also stretches**. A short story might cover an hour, a night, a week. A novel can show months—or years—after the initial event. You can show how survivors adapt, how societies splinter or reform, how trauma and loss settle into the bones of the world.

You can show not just the disaster—but the *aftermath*.

And this is where you get to layer in **new kinds of conflict**.

- In the beginning, the enemy is survival itself: fire, water, disease, fear.
- As time goes on, the enemies become other survivors, shifting alliances, corrupted leaders.
- Later still, the enemy might be despair, loss of purpose, the question of whether survival even matters

anymore.

Pacing becomes crucial in a novel. Disaster fiction is naturally front-loaded with action, but a novel needs rhythm. Moments of frantic escape need to be balanced with moments of fragile quiet. Scenes of horror need to be balanced with scenes of beauty—maybe a child discovering a single living flower among the ruins, or two survivors sharing a joke in the middle of the dark.

Stretching disaster across a novel means creating an emotional landscape, not just a physical one.

You'll also want to **build in new stakes and turning points**. In a short story, survival through one crisis might be enough. In a novel, you need layered goals:

- First, get out of the burning city.
- Then, find a safe place.
- Then, deal with the people already there.
- Then, face the environmental collapse you didn't know was coming.
  Each arc builds toward a new emotional or physical climax, carrying the reader deeper into the story rather than dragging it out.

One powerful trick when expanding is to **use flashbacks or memory**. Characters carrying trauma from the initial disaster react differently to new threats. Maybe a survivor freezes at the sound of helicopters because they remember being strafed during the collapse. Maybe a character keeps a radio turned on to static, because once, long ago, it meant they weren't alone.

Memory weaves the past and present together, making the disaster feel deeper and more personal.

Another technique that helps is introducing **the slow disaster** underneath the big one. Maybe after the earthquake or virus or invasion, a second, slower collapse sets in—crop failure, political fragmentation, rising waters. This layered approach means survival isn't about winning a single battle—it's about enduring wave after wave of hardship, each one asking more of the characters than the last.

Themes naturally deepen in a novel too. In a short story, you might focus tightly on trust or betrayal. In a novel, you can weave multiple themes: survival vs. morality, hope vs. despair, loyalty vs. self-preservation.

Every relationship, every decision, every setting detail can tie back to these themes, reinforcing them again and again until readers feel them bone-deep.

Expanding into a novel also gives you space to explore **world-building details** that were only hinted at before:

- How did governments fall?
- What new power structures rose in the ruins?
- What myths and legends are survivors telling themselves to cope?
  You don't have to answer every question—but suggesting that there are answers out there makes the world feel huge and alive.

Symbolism becomes even more important stretched across a novel. A broken bridge might first appear as a literal obstacle. Later, it becomes a symbol of the characters' severed relationships. Finally, rebuilding—or choosing not to rebuild—that bridge might be a major emotional moment.

Symbols carried carefully through the story give the novel emotional resonance beyond simple survival.

And don't forget that a novel allows for **multiple climaxes**.

You might have:

- A physical climax (the fight for resources, the escape from disaster).
- An emotional climax (a character's breaking point, betrayal, or redemption).
- A thematic climax (choosing hope when giving up would be easier).

Each one needs to feel earned, growing naturally from everything that came before.

The bigger the collapse, the bigger the cost—and the bigger the emotional payoff when (if) something good survives.

Because expanding a disaster story into a novel isn't just about writing more.

It's about digging deeper.

Making readers not just watch the collapse, but *live* it.

Making them feel every heartbreak, every desperate choice, every fragile moment of stubborn, furious hope.

Because a disaster novel, at its best, isn't just a story about the end of the world.

It's a story about the stubborn refusal to let it be the end of *everything*.

Shaping Your Disaster Story into a Screenplay

Disaster stories are made for the screen. Explosions, floods, fires, crumbling cities, desperate last stands—it's pure cinematic gold. But turning a disaster story into a screenplay isn't just about describing big scenes. It's about shaping the story visually, emotionally, and structurally so it plays out with the pace, clarity, and impact a movie demands. A screenplay isn't just a novel without the extra words—it's a blueprint. And if you're serious about adapting your disaster story for the screen, you have to think like a builder, not just a storyteller.

The first thing to understand is that **screenplays are lean and fast**. Every scene, every line of dialogue, every moment has to move the story forward. There's no room for wandering internal monologues or lush descriptions of sunsets over ruined cities. You have to show everything through action, behavior, dialogue, and visual moments.

In a disaster screenplay, if you can't see it, hear it, or feel it happening in the moment, it doesn't belong on the page.

If you're brainstorming with ChatGPT, you can prompt for things like "visual ways to show emotional states in a disaster movie" or "disaster scene ideas that can be filmed without heavy exposition." You can also ask for action-based storytelling techniques: "showing a character's fear without them saying it aloud," for instance.

Structure becomes king when you're screenwriting. The classic three-act structure is your best friend here:

- **Act One**: Set up the world and the characters—and then hit it with the disaster.
- **Act Two**: Show the consequences, the struggle to survive, and the emotional breakdowns and betrayals that come with it.
- **Act Three**: Deliver the climax—an escape, a final sacrifice, a new beginning.

Screenplays live and die by momentum. Every ten pages or so (roughly every ten minutes of screen time), something big should shift—an escalation, a reversal, a discovery, a death. If too many pages go by without something changing, the energy drains out of the story, and audiences start looking at their phones.

Characters in a disaster screenplay need strong visual goals and motivations. What does your protagonist want when the disaster hits? Save their family? Reach higher ground? Find a cure? These goals have to be crystal clear on screen. Viewers don't have access to the characters' thoughts, so they need to see desire and fear in action—grabbing a radio, running toward danger, refusing to leave a fallen comrade.

Dialogue has to **snap and reveal**. In a disaster movie, people are under extreme pressure. They don't give speeches. They don't usually sit down and talk about their feelings for twenty minutes. Good disaster dialogue is short, emotional, full of subtext. A single line—"I told you we shouldn't have stayed!"—can reveal years of resentment boiling to the surface in the middle of an earthquake or firestorm.

When shaping your story, you also have to think in **scenes** rather than chapters. Each scene should do at least two things at once:

- Advance the plot (get closer to survival, or push closer to failure).
- Reveal character (show fear, courage, selfishness, loyalty).

If a scene doesn't do both, cut it or rewrite it. Screenplay storytelling is a tightrope walk—one foot in plot, one foot in emotion, every step forward.

The disaster itself must evolve. It can't just be "bad thing happens" for 90 minutes. It has to shift.

- First, the earthquake hits—immediate chaos.
- Then, the fires start—secondary danger.
- Then, the survivors realize aftershocks are coming—or the levee is failing—or the air is poisoned.

Each escalation forces new decisions, new sacrifices. Writing the disaster like a living thing—escalating, mutating, cornering the characters—keeps the story moving forward naturally.

Visuals matter enormously. In prose, you can write, "The city lay in ruins under an apocalyptic sky." In a screenplay, you have to write what the camera sees. "A toppled skyscraper lies across Main Street. Smoke snakes into a blood-red sky. Car alarms wail in the eerie silence." Specific, sensory images grab the audience. Vague, generic disaster scenes lose them.

One powerful technique is to **anchor emotional moments to visual ones**.

- A character promises to protect a child—then gets separated in the stampede.
- A character hesitates at a crumbling bridge—flashbacks to their past trauma flicker in the flashing lightning.
- A survivor reaches the top of a flood barrier—only to see an endless sea swallowing their home.

When emotion and action happen at the same time, the scene punches through the screen and grabs the heart.

Pacing your screenplay means building peaks and valleys.

- High tension (escaping the tsunami).
- Brief recovery (sheltering overnight in a ruined building).
- New threat (disease spreads among survivors).
  If everything is chaos, chaos loses its bite. If everything is stillness, tension evaporates. Good disaster screenplays pulse with shifting intensity.

Another trick: **use silence and stillness to make chaos hit harder**.

Let the camera linger on an empty swing moving in the wind—then cut hard to a wall of water crashing over the playground.

Let survivors sit in exhausted, shivering silence—then smash the silence with the roar of an approaching firestorm.

Contrast gives disasters emotional weight.

If you're adapting a short disaster story into a screenplay, you'll often need to **expand the world around the core moment**.

- Introduce secondary characters that embody different responses to the disaster (cowardice, hope, brutality, sacrifice).

- Show glimpses of how different areas are collapsing differently (wealthy vs. poor, urban vs. rural).
- Seed information about the larger cause of the disaster without bogging down in exposition.

One thing screenplays do beautifully is **hint at bigger worlds through tiny details**. A radio transmission crackling in the background. A glimpse of looters in a distant street. A child's crayon drawing of burning cities.

You don't have to explain everything. You just have to show enough to let the audience's imagination run wild.

Finally, the **ending** matters more than ever. In disaster screenplays, endings must feel both inevitable and earned. Maybe the characters survive—but at great cost. Maybe they fail—but leave behind a glimmer of hope for others. Maybe survival wasn't the real victory at all—maybe it was refusing to give up their humanity in a world gone savage.

The audience doesn't need a happy ending.

They need a *satisfying* one.

One that feels true to the journey you've taken them on.

Because a disaster screenplay, at its best, isn't just explosions and screaming and running from fire.

It's about people—flawed, brave, desperate people—trying to hold onto themselves while the world falls apart around them.

And when the credits roll, the audience should feel like they've survived something, too.

The Art of Dialogue in High-Pressure Situations

Disaster stories run on adrenaline. Every second counts. Every breath matters. And in those heart-stopping moments, dialogue isn't just characters talking—it's survival language. Writing dialogue in high-pressure situations isn't about clever speeches or big emotional monologues. It's about rawness. Urgency. The desperate, unfiltered way people actually speak when the walls are crumbling and the clock is ticking.

The first thing to understand is that **pressure compresses language**. People don't explain. They don't wax poetic. They don't give their full backstory before deciding to climb out the window to escape the fire. In high-stakes moments, dialogue gets stripped down to the essentials: orders, warnings, questions, gut reactions.

Short. Snapped. Raw.

If you're brainstorming with ChatGPT, you can prompt for things like "how people speak under stress" or "emotional reactions in life-or-death situations." You can also explore tension beats like "dialogue that hides fear with anger" or "characters saying one thing while meaning another in a crisis."

In a disaster scene, **people rarely say exactly what they feel**. Fear comes out as shouting. Love comes out as desperate orders. Guilt comes out as blaming someone else. Writing dialogue with emotional layering—where the surface words and the deeper feelings don't quite match—is one of the most powerful ways to create tension without needing long descriptions.

For example:

- "Don't be stupid, you'll get yourself killed!"
  Translation: "I'm terrified of losing you and I don't know how to say it."
- "Go! I'll catch up!"
  Translation: "I know I won't, and I don't want you to watch me die."

Good disaster dialogue says more than what's spoken. It leaves emotional aftershocks between the lines.

Another essential trick is **letting silence do some of the talking**. High-pressure moments aren't always filled with words. Sometimes people freeze. Sometimes they choke on the words they want to say. Sometimes a look, a hesitation, or a turned back speaks louder than dialogue ever could. Writing those silences—their weight, their meaning—gives your story emotional texture.

Interruptions are natural under pressure.

People cut each other off.

They start sentences they don't finish.

They shout over each other, mishear things, repeat themselves without realizing it.

Writing these messy rhythms makes scenes feel more alive. A polished, perfectly structured conversation will feel fake when the roof is literally coming down on the characters' heads.

Here's what high-pressure dialogue often sounds like:

- "Get back! Move, move—no, the other way—"
- "Where's the bag? Where's the—damn it, where's the bag?"
- "Don't you dare give up on me. Not now. Not here."
  Fast. Overlapping. Bursting out like a dam breaking under too much strain.

Another huge tool is **conflicting goals inside the same moment**.

Maybe one character wants to fight back. Another just wants to run. Another freezes up entirely. Their dialogue colliding—pleading, ordering, yelling—creates instant, organic tension.

You don't have to invent extra conflict.

Stress makes people want different things—and that's all you need.

Word choice under stress often reverts to instinctive habits.

- A soldier barks out orders.
- A parent uses a child's nickname automatically.
- A doctor slips into clinical shorthand even while bleeding out.

These little quirks ground the character and reveal their deepest instincts—who they are when everything else is stripped away.

You can also use **callbacks** for emotional punch. Maybe in a quiet earlier scene, a character joked, "If the world ends, I'm sticking with you."

Later, when everything really *is* falling apart, the same character gasps out, "Still sticking, right?"

That moment, that echo, lands harder because it's layered with memory, fear, and love—all without needing a single flowery speech.

Pressure reveals truth.

In normal life, people hide things—fear, guilt, love, resentment.

But in a disaster, when there's no time to think, the truth blurts out.

- A secret confession.
- A bitter accusation.
- A desperate apology.
  These truth-bombs crack relationships open like dropped glass, and they change the story forever.

Another great tool is **timing emotional confessions badly**.

Disaster doesn't wait for perfect emotional setups.

- Someone might scream "I love you!" while dragging a bleeding friend to safety.
- Someone might confess betrayal seconds before the floodwater hits.
  These messy, mistimed, high-stakes declarations feel much more real than a neat, pre-planned heart-to-

heart.

Swearing, stammering, and babbling have their place too. Under extreme stress, dialogue gets sloppy.

- "Oh god oh god oh god."
- "We're not gonna make it, we're not gonna—"
- "Shut up! Shut up and *move!*"

You don't want every line to be noise—but sprinkling real, messy emotional explosions through your dialogue makes the polished, strategic moments shine even brighter by contrast.

Misdirection in dialogue is another goldmine.

Characters might lie to protect others—or themselves.

They might say "I'm fine" while clutching a broken arm.

They might say "We'll make it" when they know the odds are almost zero.

Writing lies under pressure adds painful irony that hits readers right in the gut when the truth inevitably surfaces.

And don't forget: **humor doesn't vanish under pressure**.

In fact, gallows humor thrives in disasters.

- The soldier cracking a joke about cafeteria food while under fire.
- The medic teasing a patient while stitching up a gunshot wound.
- The exhausted survivor quipping, "Well, guess this cancels my dentist appointment."
  Humor under stress isn't disrespectful—it's survival. It's a defiant middle finger at death.

Scene pacing matters too. In disaster dialogue, you want scenes to move in waves:

- A burst of action (running, fighting, falling).
- A gasp of dialogue (yelling, confessing, snapping).
- Another burst of action.
- A tighter, tenser exchange of words.
- Maybe a final emotional gut-punch line before everything explodes again.

This rhythm—action, dialogue, action, revelation—keeps tension high without exhausting readers.

Lastly, **end scenes on a sharp line** when possible.

- A brutal command.
- A desperate confession.
- A question left unanswered.
  Don't always resolve the tension. Let the dialogue *hang* in the air like smoke as the scene cuts or shifts. It leaves readers leaning in, emotionally raw, wanting more.

Because dialogue in high-pressure disaster scenes isn't just about moving the plot.

It's about ripping characters open.

It's about showing who they are when everything polite and practiced falls away.

It's about making readers feel the heartbeat, the fear, the desperate hope, right there in the room, in the fire, in the flood, in the crumbling city.

And if you get it right, even a single shouted word—*Run!*—can carry the weight of the whole world falling apart.

Writing Characters on the Edge of Panic

There's nothing quite as electric in a disaster story as a character teetering right on the brink of panic. That razor-thin line between holding it together and falling apart is where some of the most human, heartbreaking, and suspenseful moments live. Writing characters on the edge of panic isn't just about making them scream and cry—it's about capturing the internal battle, the way fear erodes reason moment by moment, breath by breath, until all that's left is survival instinct, or collapse.

The first thing to realize is that **panic is a process**, not an instant switch. People don't usually go from calm to total meltdown in a blink. There's a ramp-up. Writing that slow build—the tightening chest, the racing thoughts, the physical fidgeting, the small mistakes—is what makes it feel real.

It's not just about writing a character *being* panicked.

It's about writing a character *trying not to be.*

If you're brainstorming with ChatGPT, you can prompt for things like "physical symptoms of panic" or "small mistakes characters make under extreme stress." You can also ask for psychological details: "how characters try (and fail) to hide panic from others."

When you're writing a character slipping toward panic, **show the early signs** before the big blowup.

- Short, shallow breathing.
- Snapping at others without meaning to.
- Dropping things.
- Repeating questions or instructions as if trying to anchor themselves.
- Fixating on something meaningless because it's easier than facing the real danger.

These little cracks in the armor tell readers what's coming—and build delicious, slow-burning tension.

Internal thoughts start racing too. Logical planning gets drowned out by what-ifs, regrets, desperate prayers. You might write the character's internal dialogue in fragments—half-sentences, broken loops.

- *Where's the exit, where's the exit, there's got to be an exit—*
- *Don't fall, don't fall, don't fall—*
- *I can't, I can't, I can't—*
  Panic speeds everything up in the mind, even if the body freezes.
  Writing this mental chaos gives readers a direct line into the character's terror without needing paragraphs of exposition.

Physical reactions are huge, and they're messy.

- Sweating even if it's freezing.
- Trembling hands that fumble critical tasks.
- Tunnel vision—only seeing the immediate threat and missing other dangers.
- Dizziness, nausea, sudden weakness in the knees.

Letting physical symptoms slip into the action scene itself makes panic feel invasive and unavoidable.

One of the most effective techniques is to **write characters trying to suppress the panic**—and failing.

- Someone tries to steady their hands by gripping something—but their knuckles go white.
- Someone tries to shout orders—but their voice cracks.
- Someone tries to tell a joke—but it falls flat, edged with hysteria.
  The effort to maintain control, the moments where it almost works and then breaks—that's where the emotional gold is.

Dialogue under panic pressure gets weird too.

- Characters repeat themselves.
- They shout without realizing.
- They lie to themselves and others ("I'm fine, I'm fine!")
- They bark orders that don't make sense.
  Dialogue can also start to fragment mid-sentence:
- "We have to—we can't just—there's no time—"
- "Get it, get the thing, the thing by the door, hurry, *hurry!*"

Writing this jumbled, pressured speech captures the feeling of thoughts derailing faster than they can be spoken.

Other people's reactions to a panicking character create brilliant extra tension.

- One character might try to snap them out of it—sometimes gently, sometimes violently ("Slap me if I freeze up!")
- Another might feed the panic, making everything worse ("We're all dead anyway!")
- Another might abandon the panicking character completely, leading to guilt and resentment later.
  Writing these interactions makes panic contagious and volatile, turning one person's fear into a group meltdown—or a hard choice about who gets saved and who doesn't.

Another great layer is **the moment the character realizes they're losing control**—but can't stop it.

- They hear themselves screaming and hate it.
- They know they're making mistakes and can't slow down.
- They see fear in others' eyes and realize it's reflecting their own.

That terrible self-awareness deepens the emotional impact. It's not just terror. It's shame. Regret. Isolation.

One thing you want to avoid is **melodrama**.

Real panic isn't constant screaming and flailing. It's jagged. It spikes and dips.

- A character might hyperventilate one minute—then go eerily calm the next in the numbing freeze of shock.
- A character might laugh uncontrollably at the worst moment because their mind can't process what's

happening.
- A character might stubbornly insist everything's fine while tears run down their face.

Writing panic in a messy, unpredictable way makes it feel real—and makes the audience invest emotionally, because they recognize it.

Timing the moment of full collapse is key too.

Don't let panic derail a scene for pages and pages.

- Let the panic burst happen—then force action.
- A character might shove the panic aside just long enough to do something heroic or reckless.
- They might collapse right when they're most needed—and someone else has to step up.
- Or they might not collapse at all, just carry that brittle edge of fear through everything, dragging it behind them like a broken wing.

Symbolism can sneak into panic writing, too.

- A character's hands shaking while trying to light a match—a symbol for fading hope.
- A radio crackling static as a background to a character's mental static.
- A locked door becoming a metaphor for their trapped mind.

Layering panic into physical objects or environment details lets readers feel the pressure without you having to spell it out.

And don't forget that **panic has aftermath**.

Survivors don't just wipe their faces and move on.

They carry the shame of losing control.

They wrestle with the fact that others saw them at their weakest.

They fear it happening again—and sometimes that fear makes the next panic come faster.

Writing the echoes of a panic attack—the tension under a survivor's skin, the jumpiness, the flashes of remembered helplessness—makes your characters feel layered, wounded, and vividly real.

Because writing characters on the edge of panic isn't about making them look weak.

It's about showing that bravery isn't the absence of fear.

It's fear clawing at your throat, your mind screaming at you to run—and moving forward anyway.

It's about being human at your rawest—and still reaching for survival.

Evoking Emotion without Sentimentality

One of the greatest challenges when writing disaster stories—or honestly, *any* intense fiction—is hitting the reader right in the heart without slipping into sticky, over-sweet sentimentality. You want your readers to *feel* something deep and real. You want their stomachs to knot, their throats to tighten, their hands to grip the pages a little harder. But you don't want them rolling their eyes, muttering, "Okay, we get it," when a moment tries too hard.

Writing raw, powerful emotion without tipping into melodrama is an art—and mastering it is what separates an *okay* disaster story from one that leaves scars.

The first key is understanding that **real emotion is messy, contradictory, and often unsaid**.

In real life, people don't give long, polished speeches when their world falls apart. They don't always cry at funerals. They don't always say "I love you" at exactly the right time.

Real emotions come out sideways—through small actions, awkward silences, misplaced anger, bad jokes, stubbornness.

Writing these crooked, imperfect expressions of feeling will always land harder than writing a character sobbing perfectly on cue with swelling music in the background.

If you're brainstorming with ChatGPT, you can prompt for ideas like "small actions that reveal deep emotions" or "natural emotional reactions under stress." You can also focus on misfires—"things characters do when they're grieving but can't talk about it" or "how people show fear without admitting they're afraid."

Less is more when you want emotion without sentimentality.

- A character carefully folding a dead friend's jacket says more than a thousand weeping monologues.
- A character whispering "Don't go" as someone slips away says more than pages of desperate pleas.
- A survivor noticing the empty chair at a fireside gathering—and quietly adding wood to the fire for no one—cracks the heart without a single word about grief.

Trust the reader.

You don't have to explain everything.

You don't have to shove emotions in their face.

You can *suggest* emotion through what characters notice, what they choose to ignore, what tiny rituals they hold onto even after everything else is gone.

Readers are emotional creatures. If you give them the space, they'll meet you halfway—and when they do, the feelings will be theirs, not just yours.

Avoid emotional clichés.

Disasters are emotional by nature. Death. Loss. Fear. Love. Hope.

But if you describe grief the same way everyone else does—fists pounding the ground, anguished wails, slow-motion screams—you're only reminding readers of every disaster movie they've ever half-watched.

Instead, look for **fresh angles**:

- Maybe the strongest character breaks down, not when someone dies, but when they find an untouched birthday cake in a ruined store.
- Maybe the character who never cries finally does—but only because they sprain their ankle trying to save a dog, and everything just crashes down at once.
- Maybe the survivor who everyone thought was cold has a breakdown not over death, but over a broken music box that played their mother's lullaby.

Emotion doesn't have to come at the "big" moments.

Sometimes it sneaks up during the quiet ones—and those moments are often the ones readers remember the longest.

Show emotional conflict.

Pure sadness is fine, but emotional complexity is unforgettable.

- The survivor feels both grief and relief when their injured friend dies, because now the group can move faster.
- The leader feels guilt for surviving—and rage at being blamed for living.
- The parent feels crushing love for their child—and bitter resentment that they're trapped by that love in a dying world.

Layered emotions feel *real* because real people almost never feel just one thing at a time. Writing that complexity makes your story deeper, rawer, and far from sentimental.

Restraint is powerful.

Holding back emotion until it cracks through can create devastating impact.

- A character stays stoic through the whole journey—until someone offers them a sip of clean water, and they can't hold back the sobs anymore.
- A leader makes all the hard calls—until they're alone, stitching up a wound, and their hands won't stop shaking.
- A survivor never mentions their lost sister—until they see a crayon drawing in an abandoned building and simply sit down, too numb to move.

Choosing when to break the emotional dam—and when to hold it back—shapes how readers experience the story.

Use the setting as emotional echo.

Sometimes the world does the crying so your characters don't have to.

- Rain hammering on a tin roof while a survivor buries a friend.
- A storm knocking over a makeshift grave marker.

- A burnt-out city street where the only thing still standing is a children's playground.
  These images carry emotional weight without needing a single word of melodrama.

Characters covering emotions are often more powerful than characters wallowing in them.

- The kid who jokes about everything because if he stops laughing, he'll start screaming.
- The medic who saves lives mechanically, refusing to remember the names of the dying.
- The soldier who polishes their weapon obsessively to avoid thinking about the family they left behind.
  When readers see these coping mechanisms, they *know* what's really going on underneath—and the recognition hits harder than any tear-streaked confession.

Small, physical details matter.

- A trembling hand smoothing a photo.
- A backpack packed with useless things because a survivor couldn't bear to leave them behind.
- A sudden inability to meet someone's eyes.
  These physical cues say more about heartbreak, terror, or love than pages of emotional exposition ever could.

Let readers hurt a little.

It's tempting to soothe every emotional wound immediately—comfort after grief, hope after despair.

But sometimes the most powerful thing you can do is leave the hurt raw for a while.

Let characters sit in silence.

Let scenes end unresolved.

Let the weight of loss settle in the room like dust.

Readers will carry that pain longer—and they'll love your story more for trusting them to survive it.

Because evoking real emotion without sentimentality isn't about being cold.

It's about respecting the emotional intelligence of your readers.

It's about showing that even in the middle of collapse, the human heart beats in ways that are messy, complicated, angry, fragile—and beautiful.

Because the truest tears don't come when a story demands them.

They come when a story quietly leaves the door open,

and readers walk through on their own.

Finding Moments of Humor in Catastrophe

Disaster stories are heavy by design. Death, destruction, grief, and survival form the bones of the genre. But here's a secret: if you only ever give readers pain and terror, they'll eventually go numb. What keeps disaster stories feeling real, feeling *alive*, is not just the devastation—it's the unexpected, scrappy sparks of humor that survive even in the darkest times. Humor in catastrophe isn't about disrespect. It's about survival. It's about humanity thumbing its nose at despair and saying, "You're not taking everything from me."

The first thing to understand is that **humor in disaster stories is a pressure valve**.

When the stakes are relentless, even a tiny moment of absurdity can let readers exhale—before you ratchet the tension right back up again.

It's not about making the disaster funny. It's about showing that even when everything else is collapsing, people still find ways to laugh, because laughter is a weapon against despair.

If you're brainstorming with ChatGPT, you can prompt for things like "small humorous moments in survival scenarios" or "ways characters use humor to cope with trauma." You can also ask for character-specific ideas: "how a sarcastic character might lighten a tense disaster scene" or "gallows humor between soldiers after losing comrades."

One of the most natural ways to write humor in catastrophe is through **banter**.

Stress cranks up emotions, and when people are scared or exhausted, humor bubbles up without warning.

- A character makes a snarky comment while dragging a wounded friend to safety.
- A survivor jokes about their bad luck finding an empty can of beans after fighting through a looter mob.
- Two characters argue over which apocalypse movie got it "more wrong" while dodging actual falling debris.

This kind of humor doesn't kill the tension—it *sharpens* it. It reminds readers that these are real people trying to survive, not grim robots trudging toward doom.

Gallows humor thrives in disaster stories too. It's dark. It's sharp. And it's real.

- A paramedic cracks a joke about how their shift was supposed to end an hour ago—while stitching up a wound in a collapsing hospital.
- A pilot jokes about getting frequent flyer miles while crash-landing an evacuation plane.
- A survivor mutters, "Well, at least we don't have to pay rent anymore," while watching their apartment sink into a flooded street.

Gallows humor acknowledges the horror without letting it swallow the characters whole.

It's not about laughing *at* the tragedy—it's about laughing *in spite of it.*

Character-driven humor is another rich source.

Different personalities react differently to disaster.

- The sarcastic pessimist who comments on everything with dry wit.

- The cheerful optimist who makes terrible puns even when surrounded by rubble.
- The deadpan realist who points out the absurdity of trying to rescue a pet goldfish in the middle of a wildfire.

Letting humor emerge naturally from character voices makes it feel earned, not forced.

Another important trick is **timing**.

You don't want humor right in the middle of a death scene or during a heart-wrenching sacrifice moment. It feels disrespectful and can kill the emotional weight you're building.

But humor *right before* or *right after* a major emotional hit? That can be devastatingly effective.

- A survivor cracks a joke to cover their fear—then realizes the danger is even worse than they thought.
- A character makes a sarcastic comment about "dying in this stupid place"—then gets trapped, and the comment hangs in the air like a bad omen.

These emotional pivots—hope to horror, laughter to tears—make disaster stories feel raw, unpredictable, and real.

Absurdity is another great form of humor during catastrophe.

The world doesn't collapse neatly. It collapses stupidly.

- Survivors find a vending machine still working—and fight over the last pack of gum.
- A group takes shelter in a novelty museum full of life-size rubber dinosaurs.
- Someone clings desperately to a perfectly useless item, like a waffle iron, because it's the last normal thing they could grab.

Moments of absurdity remind readers that life, even at the end of the world, doesn't stop being weird.

Physical comedy can work too—carefully.

- A character trips while making a heroic speech.
- Someone struggles to look cool climbing out of a collapsed building and falls flat on their face.
- A survivor fights heroically with a locked door—only to realize it pushes open.

Small, clumsy, human moments ground disaster stories. They make characters lovable. They keep tension from becoming exhausting.

Another layer to explore is **humor as emotional armor**.

Characters might joke because it's the only way to keep functioning.

- The leader makes a joke at their own expense because they're terrified of losing the group's trust.
- The medic teases patients to distract them from their injuries—and themselves from their helplessness.
- The loner cracks jokes because real emotional connection feels too dangerous.

Humor used this way isn't just funny—it's heartbreaking. It shows how close characters are to breaking under the strain.

Running jokes can also be powerful emotional anchors.

- A survivor group teasing the youngest member about their terrible cooking—even when food is scarce.
- A running bet about who will find a working radio first.
- A promise to celebrate with something ridiculous (like a pizza party) once they survive.

When these jokes resurface later—especially after loss—they hit hard.

The joke reminds readers of who was lost, what was hoped for, what still matters.

And sometimes, letting characters find laughter again after all seems lost is the ultimate act of defiance.

It says:

"We're still here.

We're still human.

You didn't take that from us."

Symbolism through humor can be sneaky and powerful too.

- A character carving dumb faces into a ruined building's walls becomes a quiet symbol of refusing to disappear.
- A group laughing over a cracked snow globe in an abandoned store becomes a symbol of fragile hope.

These moments layer meaning without needing heavy speeches about resilience or humanity.

The key is remembering that **humor doesn't erase tragedy**—it coexists with it.

Disaster survivors aren't laughing because things are okay.

They're laughing because things are *not* okay—and somehow, they still have to live through it anyway.

Because in the end, finding humor in catastrophe isn't about mocking the fall.

It's about standing up in the ruins, coughing on dust, covered in bruises, and laughing anyway.

Because sometimes, the last weapon survivors have against the darkness...

is a crooked smile.

Flashbacks and Memories in a Disaster Story

Disasters happen fast. Fires, floods, wars, pandemics—everything changes in a moment. But no one walks into catastrophe without dragging the past behind them. Memories don't vanish just because the world collapses. They get louder, sharper, more complicated. Writing flashbacks and memories into a disaster story isn't just about backstory. It's about showing how survival isn't only about escaping the present danger—it's about carrying all the weight of who you were *before* everything fell apart.

The first thing to understand is that **flashbacks must feel urgent, not leisurely**.

Disaster fiction runs hot. The pace is fast. Readers are wired tight with tension. You can't slam on the brakes for a long, dreamy trip down memory lane.

When a flashback hits, it should feel sharp. Bleeding through.

Triggered by something—an image, a smell, a word—that rips the character out of the present for just a moment.

If you're brainstorming with ChatGPT, you can prompt for ideas like "sensory triggers that cause flashbacks" or "memories that could haunt a disaster survivor." You can also explore emotional layering: "how a flashback can change a character's decision under pressure."

Flashbacks in disaster fiction should feel like intrusions.

They aren't neat. They aren't tidy.

- A mother sees a broken bicycle in a ruined street—and flashes to her son's laughter the last time he rode his bike.
- A soldier smells diesel smoke—and is back in a war zone where a bad decision cost lives.
- A survivor hears a child's song through cracked speakers—and remembers the birthday party they never made it home for.

These flashbacks hit like emotional landmines. They knock the character sideways, just for a second. Long enough to show the reader that survival isn't just about bodies. It's about memories clawing at the mind.

Timing is everything.

A flashback during a quiet moment (waiting out a storm, tending to wounds) lets characters process old wounds.

A flashback *during* chaos—while running, fighting, escaping—creates layers of emotional tension. The character has to survive the present while being pulled under by the past.

The best flashbacks reveal emotional stakes, not just information.

It's not about dumping backstory.

It's about showing why this moment matters.

- Why the character refuses to leave a trapped stranger behind.
- Why the leader won't order another risky rescue.

- Why the tough survivor freezes at the sound of alarms.

Flashbacks show where the cracks are. They show what's been broken inside the character long before the world outside fell apart.

Flashbacks also change decisions.

The mother who lost a child might hesitate longer to save a stranger's kid.

The medic who failed once might push harder this time, risking everything.

The cynic who abandoned friends before might choose loyalty now, even when it seems stupid.

Writing flashbacks that actively *change* what happens in the present makes them part of the story's momentum—not just emotional decoration.

Physical triggers make flashbacks feel real.

- The sharp sting of smoke in the lungs.
- The cold weight of a soaked jacket against the skin.
- The metallic taste of blood.
  These sensory details can snap a character backward faster than any "Once upon a time" transition ever could.

You can also use **visual cues** to bridge between present and memory.

- A character reaches for a door—and suddenly they're five years old again, hiding behind the same door during a home invasion.
- A flash of lightning reveals a face—and it becomes another face, from another time, another life.
  Smooth, fast transitions between now and then make flashbacks feel like natural emotional reactions, not interruptions.

Another trick is **layering flashbacks over action**.

Instead of stopping the story cold, you weave flashes of memory into what's happening now.

- A survivor climbing a crumbling building flashes to climbing trees as a child—before a fall left permanent scars.
- A fighter running through a burning village hears their brother calling them back—not here, not now, but still loud enough to pull at their steps.

This technique lets you maintain tension in the present while deepening the emotional stakes.

Symbolism in flashbacks can magnify the emotional punch.

Maybe the protagonist flashes back to planting a garden with their father—and now they scavenge rotten fields where nothing grows.

Maybe they remember a perfect snow day with their friends—and now snowdrifts bury corpses outside the shelter.

Linking sensory memories to the broken reality of the disaster world makes grief and longing bleed naturally into the story.

Flashbacks also shape relationships.

Characters who share survival bonds usually carry scars they don't talk about right away. Flashbacks can show:

- Why one character trusts no one.
- Why another clings desperately to anyone who shows kindness.
- Why a third is so reckless, acting like every day is their last.

When the truth finally spills out—through confession, accident, or sheer collapse—the flashbacks have already prepared readers to feel it fully.

Guilt and regret are common flashback fuels.

In disaster fiction, almost everyone has left someone behind.

- Someone they couldn't save.
- Someone they abandoned in a moment of fear.
- Someone they swore they'd come back for—and didn't.

Flashbacks can sharpen guilt into an open wound—and make redemption arcs feel earned and brutal.

Memory distortion adds another layer.

Traumatized characters don't always remember perfectly.

Maybe they forget their mother's face but remember the pattern on her dress.

Maybe they misremember a betrayal, turning it over and over until they aren't sure who was right.

Maybe they cling to an idealized version of someone who was never really a hero.

Writing flawed, fragmented memories makes characters feel wounded, complicated, painfully human.

Pacing flashbacks across the story is key.

- Early flashes hint at trauma without revealing everything.
- Mid-story flashbacks deepen emotional stakes before a major choice or loss.
- Late flashbacks reveal critical truths that change the meaning of everything before.

A well-timed flashback can be the emotional twist that makes a disaster story unforgettable.

Don't overuse them, though.

If every moment triggers a flashback, the present story drowns under the weight of the past.

Use flashbacks like spice: carefully, meaningfully, sparingly.

Let readers hunger for the full story behind the scars—and when you finally show it, let it *hurt*.

Because disaster fiction isn't just about what breaks today.

It's about what was already broken—and how the end of the world makes those old fractures bleed all over again.

Because sometimes surviving the disaster is the easy part.

Surviving your memories?

That's the real battle.

Keeping Your Story Grounded When the World Is Not

When you write a disaster story, everything around your characters falls apart—cities burn, governments collapse, oceans rise, plagues spread. The world spins out of control. It's tempting, especially when the stakes are massive, to let the storytelling spin out of control too. Bigger explosions. Louder screams. More chaos. And more. And more. But the real secret to writing a gripping, unforgettable disaster story isn't making the destruction louder.

It's keeping your characters grounded when everything else is not.

Grounded doesn't mean boring. It means *anchored*. It means no matter how much the world breaks, readers can still find something solid to hold onto—someone real, someone vulnerable, someone human at the center of all the noise. When you do that, the collapse around them feels bigger, not smaller. Because now it matters.

Now readers care.

If you're brainstorming with ChatGPT, you can prompt for things like "ways to show human resilience in extreme settings" or "small human actions that ground a chaotic survival story." You can also explore emotional techniques like "how to keep tension character-focused during large-scale disasters."

The first way to stay grounded is **make your characters' stakes personal**.

Saving the world sounds great on paper, but it's abstract.

Saving your sister.

Saving your home.

Saving a handful of strangers who trusted you.

Those are stakes readers can feel in their gut.

A character trying to survive a wildfire isn't thinking about global warming statistics—they're thinking about getting to their kid's school before it burns down. A character in a city under siege isn't trying to broker world peace—they're just trying to find clean water and a safe place to sleep.

Make the apocalypse intimate.

Let readers experience it through blistered hands, exhausted lungs, whispered promises, desperate prayers.

When readers *feel* the collapse at skin level, you don't need to describe every fallen building. The fear, loss, and hope on one character's face will carry the entire world with it.

Small goals ground big chaos.

If your character's only goal is "save humanity," it's too big, too vague. Readers can't root for that in a deep, emotional way.

But if the goal is "get medicine for Dad before nightfall" or "reach the next town before the levee breaks," readers latch on hard.

Small, specific goals give structure to the chaos—and let you ratchet tension up one obstacle at a time.

Another way to stay grounded is **showing small, human rituals surviving the disaster**.

- Someone braiding their child's hair before a dangerous trek.
- Someone cleaning their boots meticulously even though everything else is filthy.
- Someone lighting a single candle every night for missing loved ones.

These small acts say:

"I am still here.

I am still human.

I still matter."

Grounding your story in these quiet rituals reminds readers that the characters aren't just surviving—they're *living* in the ruins, even when it hurts.

Focus on sensory details, not spectacle.

You can write "the city burned"—but that's far away.

Or you can write:

- The stink of melted plastic thick in the back of the throat.
- The heat so fierce it peels skin before flames even touch.
- The ash falling like dirty snow, sticking to sweat-slicked skin.

Small, immediate sensory details pull readers into the scene *right now*.

You don't need to describe every building collapse.

You need to describe what it feels like to breathe while the world is ending.

Another anchor is **relationships**.

In a disaster, trust is everything. Love is everything. Anger, betrayal, forgiveness—*those* are the fires burning even hotter than the landscape outside.

- The best friend who refuses to leave.
- The brother who lies to keep you safe.
- The stranger who risks everything for someone they barely know.

Writing strong, real relationships keeps readers locked on the emotional core of the story, no matter how much chaos rages around them.

Characters should stay reactive—and proactive.

Don't let characters stand around watching the world fall apart.

- Show them making choices.
- Show them taking action, even when it's the wrong action.
- Show them trying and failing and trying again.

Movement grounds emotion. It shows the struggle against despair and defeat.

Even a tiny act of agency—a survivor choosing to share their last bottle of water—matters more than a thousand pages of static description.

Remember fear shrinks focus.

In real disasters, people don't think about the *whole* flood, the *entire* fire. They focus on the next step. The next breath.

- Climb this stairwell.
- Cross this flooded street.
- Find that first aid kit.

Keeping your character's perspective tight in high-intensity moments makes the chaos feel *bigger*, not smaller, because it presses in around them on all sides.

Symbols can subtly anchor the story too.

- A cracked photograph kept safe in a survivor's pocket.
- A broken watch still ticking against all odds.
- A child's toy carried across a battlefield.

Symbols survive when words fail. They connect readers to loss, love, hope, and resilience without heavy exposition.

Tone management matters, too.

When everything is screaming and burning, a quiet moment matters more.

- A simple shared meal in the ruins.
- A memory of home murmured to a sleeping child.
- A sunset watched from a rooftop full of ash.

Disasters don't erase beauty completely.

Letting moments of quiet awe or fragile peace shine through makes the horror sharper by contrast—and keeps the story grounded in something real and human.

Characters' emotional journeys ground the external journey.

The world may end spectacularly—but what readers care about is whether your character:

- Lets go of guilt.
- Chooses forgiveness.
- Finds the courage to hope again.

- Realizes they're stronger than they ever believed.

The external survival arc mirrors the internal survival arc.

The goal isn't just "survive the disaster."

It's "survive yourself."

Because in the end, keeping a disaster story grounded isn't about describing every fallen building and burned forest and broken sky.

It's about remembering that the real weight of collapse falls on human hearts.

Readers don't cry because a city crumbles.

They cry because a father holds his daughter's hand and promises, against all odds, that they'll see tomorrow.

Because when the whole world is broken, the only thing that matters—the only thing that keeps readers reading and feeling and caring—is the stubborn, fragile, furious will of people refusing to be broken too.

Playing with Time: Jumping Back and Forwards in Time

Disaster stories usually scream forward with momentum—one catastrophe chasing another, one desperate decision leading to the next. But when you start playing with time—jumping backwards, forwards, spiraling between then and now—you unlock an entirely different emotional engine. Time manipulation lets you build suspense, deepen character arcs, create irony, and layer meaning in ways that straight-line storytelling sometimes can't reach.

Done right, it makes a disaster story feel bigger, deeper, and way more personal.

The first thing to understand is that **playing with time must serve the story, not confuse it**.

Jumping around for the sake of being artsy or clever can frustrate readers. But when the timing choices reflect the emotional heart of the story—when the structure *feels* like the chaos, memory, or uncertainty the characters are living through—then it's magic.

If you're brainstorming with ChatGPT, you can prompt for ideas like "ways to use flashforwards and flashbacks in disaster fiction" or "narrative structures that reflect chaos and survival." You can also ask for character-driven structures: "how a character's memories affect pacing in a survival story."

One simple, powerful way to play with time is **starting with the aftermath**.

You open the story after the worst has already happened:

- A lone survivor picking through ruins.
- A child growing up in the shadow of a long-gone disaster.
- A rescue team finding the remnants of a failed expedition.

Then you jump back to how it all fell apart.

Readers already *know* the ending—or think they do.

Now they read with a heavy weight of dread, piecing together how hope slipped through everyone's fingers.

Flashforwards create tension by showing consequences before causes.

You show the survivor limping through a wasteland—then flash back to the moment they first heard the sirens.

You show the broken community clinging to a dying town—then flash back to the day they thought the disaster was temporary.

This lets readers experience hope, denial, and early mistakes through the grim knowledge of where it all leads.

Flashbacks, on the other hand, deepen emotional stakes by showing what was lost.

Mid-chaos, a character remembers:

- A family dinner in the kitchen now reduced to ashes.
- A sibling's teasing laugh before the sickness took them.
- The last normal morning before the sky cracked open.

These memories don't slow the story—they sharpen it.

They remind readers what's at stake—and what survival actually *costs*.

Parallel timelines can work brilliantly, too.

You weave two stories at once:

- Then: The world falling apart.
- Now: The hard, bitter struggle to rebuild, to endure.

Each timeline informs the other.

What characters do in the past echoes into their present selves.

The survivor hardened by betrayal.

The leader shaped by a single choice that can't be undone.

The refugee who never forgave the friend who abandoned them.

Parallel timelines build emotional layering naturally—every victory feels heavier, every loss more permanent.

Another powerful technique is the **"unreliable memory" flashback**.

Characters might remember past events incorrectly.

- Survivors argue over what really happened at the evacuation.
- A leader's guilt twists memory into self-blame that might not be fair.
- A character flashes back to a betrayal—but the truth, revealed later, is more complicated.

Using memory gaps and distortions lets you create mystery and emotional complexity at the same time.

Jump cuts between time periods can mirror trauma.

In real life, trauma often fractures memory. People live half in the present, half in the past.

You can mirror that on the page:

- A character running through a collapsing building flashes to a playground as a kid—then back, stumbling through smoke.
- A survivor tending a wound flashes to a battlefield years ago—then jolts back, breath hitching.

These sudden, jarring transitions pull readers into the disorientation and emotional chaos the character feels.

When playing with time, **anchors are crucial**.

Each time jump needs something small but clear to orient readers:

- A change in environment (the ruins vs. the intact city).
- A physical marker (a character's missing hand, scars, or aged appearance).

- A narrative marker (chapter titles like "Two Months After" or "The Day Before").
- A sensory cue (rain in the present, sunshine in the memory).

You don't have to hit readers over the head with "FLASHBACK!" labels, but subtle anchors help them stay grounded even when time spirals.

The emotional arc should stay clear even if the timeline twists.

Readers should feel where the character is emotionally, even if they're jumping from before to after, from hope to loss and back again.

The emotional journey is the rope that guides them through the maze.

Purposeful reveals are one of the best rewards of time play.

Maybe early in the story, a character refuses to enter a flooded tunnel.

The reason isn't explained—until midway, a flashback reveals they lost someone there.

Or maybe a character's coldness makes them seem heartless—until a late reveal shows they had to leave family behind to survive.

These revelations hit harder because readers have carried the mystery like a splinter under the skin the whole time.

One amazing structure you can use is the **full-circle loop**.

The story ends where it began—but with devastating new meaning.

- The first line is "She waited by the river, just like he said."
- The last line, after all the chaos and loss and survival, is exactly the same—but now readers know *why* she waited, *who* she waited for, *what* was lost, *what* was found.

The same scene, the same words, but an emotional gut-punch instead of mystery.

This looping structure feels satisfying, inevitable, brutal, and beautiful all at once.

Foreshadowing thrives when you play with time.

Hints dropped in early scenes take on horrifying clarity later:

- A cracked photo on the wall at the start—whose absence you finally understand in flashbacks.
- A character flinching at a certain sound—whose origin you only discover after heartbreak.

Foreshadowing lets readers live with a growing sense of dread and wonder, even when the disaster's full scope hasn't been revealed yet.

Pacing must stay tight.

When you jump between times, every scene must matter.

Every flashback, flashforward, or sidestep must:

- Deepen emotional stakes.
- Reveal critical character truths.
- Escalate tension toward the final collapse or salvation.

Randomly drifting through memory swamps tension.

Sharp, purposeful cuts between times sharpen it.

And lastly, **make the final timeline collapse emotionally, not just logically**.

Maybe the story ends with all the timelines converging:

- The past you fled.
- The future you feared.
- The present you finally accept.

Maybe survival isn't just outrunning disaster.

Maybe survival is accepting the past, carrying it forward, and finding something stubborn and fragile and human in the ruins.

Because playing with time isn't about showing off.

It's about making readers *feel* the weight of memory, loss, hope, and survival folding over each other like storm clouds.

Because in a disaster story, time doesn't move in a straight line.

It twists. It fractures.

Just like the human heart.

Writing the Final Sacrifice: Heroic Deaths and Tragic Losses

If you're writing a disaster story, you're writing about loss. It's baked into the bones of the genre. Cities fall. Families fracture. The world as it once was is torn apart. But among all the losses, nothing cuts readers deeper than *the final sacrifice*—that moment when a character chooses death, chooses surrender, chooses to lose everything so that someone else might live, or hope might survive.

Writing heroic deaths and tragic losses isn't just about shock value. It's about meaning.

It's about making the reader feel like a character's last breath changed something real.

The first truth you have to embrace is that **not every death should be noble.**

In fact, most deaths in disasters are messy, stupid, preventable, or meaningless.

Someone trips at the wrong second.

Someone hesitates too long.

Someone gets caught in crossfire meant for someone else.

Those random deaths are painful—and they add to the realism and horror.

But the *final sacrifice*? That's different.

That's where death becomes a choice.

If you're brainstorming with ChatGPT, you can prompt for things like "ways a character might sacrifice themselves in a disaster scenario" or "emotional beats that make a heroic death feel earned." You can also explore different moods: "bittersweet sacrifices" or "sacrifices that spark new hope."

The most important rule? The sacrifice must feel earned.

Readers should see it coming, even if they're praying it won't happen.

- The medic who always puts others first.
- The older brother who swore to protect his siblings no matter what.
- The stubborn loner who finally, finally chooses someone else over himself.

The sacrifice shouldn't feel like a twist.

It should feel like destiny—the heartbreaking kind that makes perfect, terrible sense when it happens.

Set up the emotional dominoes early.

Give readers small moments that hint at who the character is—and what they're willing to do.

- A brief, bitter argument about who should carry the heavier burden.
- A tight, quiet promise to keep someone safe.
- A grim look at the wreckage of the past, the unspoken understanding: *someone has to pay the price.*

Plant those seeds early, so when the final moment comes, readers feel the weight of every step that led there.

The sacrifice must cost something personal.

It's not enough for the character to jump in front of a bullet because it's the "heroic" thing.

It needs to tear something open inside them.

- The character who finally lets go of the future they were clinging to.
- The leader who thought they were too important to lose—until they realize they're the only one who *can* be lost to save the others.
- The mother who fought like hell for survival but lays it down willingly to save her child.

Sacrifice isn't about dying.

It's about *choosing* to give up something you didn't think you could live without.

Details make the death unforgettable.

It's not about how many explosions or how much blood you describe.

It's about the tiny, human moments wrapped around the end:

- The glance over the shoulder before slamming the door and locking themselves on the other side.
- The whispered joke to ease someone else's fear, right before the final moment.
- The way a hand lingers a second longer on a friend's shoulder, as if saying goodbye without words.

It's the ordinary human things, right up against the extraordinary horror, that break hearts wide open.

A sacrifice should ripple outward.

It should *change* the surviving characters.

- A guilt that drives a survivor to become better.
- A legacy that gives others the courage to keep moving.
- A story told around campfires long after the fires of disaster have gone cold.

Even in disaster fiction, death should *matter*.

It should leave fingerprints on the living.

Don't rush the aftermath.

When a major character dies, *pause*.

Let the silence fall.

Let readers—and characters—sit in the shock, the grief, the empty space where that person used to be.

- Maybe no one says anything at all.

- Maybe someone whispers their name.
- Maybe someone refuses to acknowledge it happened.

The absence should echo.

Readers need that space to mourn—or rage, or deny—before the story moves forward again.

Avoid making every sacrifice "clean."

Not every heroic death looks pretty.

Sometimes the person isn't remembered as a hero.

Sometimes the survivors are too busy running to even bury them.

Sometimes the sacrifice works—but barely—and everyone is too broken to celebrate.

That ugliness, that messiness, makes survival feel earned.

It reminds readers that heroes don't get parades in a dying world.

They get forgotten boots, bloodstained shirts, and whispered memories.

Sometimes, the sacrifice doesn't even succeed fully—and that's okay.

Maybe the character buys *time* but not victory.

Maybe they save *someone*, but not *everyone*.

Maybe they *think* they're doing the right thing—and it turns out messier than they ever knew.

Writing sacrifices that are meaningful but complicated makes the story linger long after the last page.

Symbolism can deepen a final sacrifice.

Maybe the character leaves behind something small:

- A hand-drawn map to a safe place.
- A battered photograph tucked into a survivor's pocket.
- A scrap of a song hummed one last time.

These symbols carry the sacrifice forward even after the character is gone.

They give survivors—and readers—something tangible to hold onto.

And yes, sometimes, you twist the knife.

Sometimes the character promises to come back—and doesn't.

Sometimes the sacrifice is witnessed by no one.

Sometimes the character dies thinking they failed—only for their actions to save lives they never knew.

Pain is part of the gift you give readers.

Real pain. Earned pain. The kind that hurts beautifully.

Because a final sacrifice isn't about showing how brave your character is.

It's about showing how much was at stake—what was loved, what was lost, and what, somehow, was carried forward.

It's about reminding readers that even in the darkest ruin,

even when everything is broken and burned,

there are still people willing to throw themselves into the fire

so that someone else might have a chance to see the sunrise.

And those are the characters readers never forget.

Closing the Loop: Ending Your Disaster Story with Impact

Disaster stories start with collapse—but if you want your story to live on in readers' minds long after they turn the last page, the ending matters just as much as the beginning. Closing the loop doesn't mean tying everything up neatly with a bow. Disasters don't allow for neatness. What it means is making the emotional journey feel complete, even if the world is still broken, even if the wounds are still bleeding. A powerful ending isn't about everything being fixed. It's about everything feeling *earned.*

The first thing you need to think about is **the emotional arc, not just the plot arc.**

Survival is great, but survival alone isn't satisfying unless it means something.

- Has the character changed?
- Has the world inside them shifted, even if the world outside is still in ruins?
- Is there a sense of closure, or at least of a new beginning built out of the wreckage?

Readers need to feel like all the struggles, sacrifices, and horrors led *somewhere.* Even if that "somewhere" is just a stubborn heartbeat in the dark.

If you're brainstorming with ChatGPT, you can prompt for ideas like "ways to close a disaster story with emotional weight" or "types of endings that feel satisfying even in bleak stories." You can also explore different tones: "hopeful endings," "bittersweet endings," "tragic but meaningful endings."

One classic way to close the loop is a return to the beginning—changed.

You mirror the opening scene, but everything is different now.

- The story starts with a family breakfast. The story ends with one survivor sitting alone, eating a cold can of beans where a kitchen used to be.
- The story starts with a group crossing a bridge into a city. It ends with one person crossing the same bridge, leaving the ruins behind.
- The story opens with laughter echoing in a village square. It ends with silence—but a child chalks a drawing on the broken stones.

These mirrored moments slam the emotional change into sharp focus without needing paragraphs of explanation.

Readers *feel* the journey, not just see it.

Another way to close the loop is fulfilling a small, human promise.

Maybe it's not the grand "save the world" mission. Maybe it's the tiny, stubborn goals characters clung to through it all:

- Burying a loved one properly.
- Returning a lost item to someone who mattered.
- Reaching a shelter that always sounded too good to be true—and finding it, even if it's broken, even if it's empty, just finding it.

That small promise kept in the ashes of everything else hits harder than any bombastic victory speech.

Character choices should define the ending, not just external events.

It's easy to have a disaster "end" when the floodwaters recede or the last enemy is defeated.

But what makes an ending stick is when the characters choose who they're going to be afterward.

- The loner who decides to stay with a new family.
- The leader who walks away from power instead of clinging to it.
- The broken survivor who dares to hope again.

Letting the character's *decision* shape the ending gives readers closure because it shows growth, not just survival.

Tone matters—commit to it.

If your story is hopeful, lean into that stubborn light.

If it's bittersweet, let the ache linger.

If it's bleak, don't suddenly swerve into cheap optimism at the last second—it will feel false.

Authenticity matters more than happiness.

Endings don't have to be cheerful. They have to be *true* to the story you've told.

Symbolism can close emotional loops beautifully.

- A cracked photo carried through the entire journey finally being placed in a new home.
- A broken watch, stopped at the moment of disaster, being carefully set down and abandoned—moving on.
- A sprout growing in a burned field, small and stubborn.

Symbols don't need long explanations.

Handled right, they hit readers straight in the heart without a single extra word.

Silence is powerful.

You don't always need to explain what happens after the last scene.

Sometimes just ending on an image—a glance, a sunrise, a hand reaching out—carries more emotional weight than pages of explanation about rebuilding or resettling.

Disaster survivors often don't know what comes next.

Letting your story end with that same uncertainty can feel painfully honest—and incredibly moving.

The last line matters more than you think.

The last sentence of a disaster story should land like a blow—or like a whisper readers can't forget.

- "He didn't look back."
- "She laughed, even as the ash fell."
- "Together, they walked into the broken dawn."

Short, sharp, emotionally loaded final lines leave readers with a lingering ache—or a lingering hope.

Sometimes, you close the loop by leaving some things broken.

Not everyone survives.

Not everything is saved.

That's not failure.

That's truth.

The emotional payoff comes not from erasing pain, but from *carrying it forward* with dignity, with love, with something like hope stitched into all the cracks.

Reader investment is paid back by emotional honesty.

If readers have spent hours following your characters through fire and storm and grief, don't cheat them with a shallow ending.

Honor the pain.

Honor the journey.

Honor the fact that survival is messy, and endings are rarely clean.

Because the best disaster stories don't end with the world being rebuilt.

They end with the human spirit stubbornly refusing to vanish.

A few classic types of disaster endings you can explore:

- **The Quiet Survival**: A handful live, battered but breathing. The storm has passed. For now.
- **The Noble Sacrifice**: Someone dies so others can live. Their loss is the foundation for a new beginning.
- **The Cycle Continues**: The disaster is survived—but the seeds of the next are already visible.
- **The New Dawn**: A tentative rebuilding begins. A fragile, stubborn hope pierces the ruins.
- **The Sole Survivor**: Everyone is lost but one. Survival is the story—and the burden.

Closing the loop is about respect.

Respect for the characters.

Respect for the story you've built.

Respect for the emotional investment your readers made.

Because when you close a disaster story right, you leave readers not just with the memory of collapse, but with the echo of survival.

Not just with grief, but with the flicker of everything still worth fighting for.

Because even at the end of the world, even after everything falls apart,

there is always something worth saving—

even if it's just the stubborn beat of a single heart, still refusing to give up.

Testing Your Disaster Plot with ChatGPT Prompts

You've come up with a disaster story. The characters are taking shape. The setting is crumbling beautifully. The emotional arc feels real. But before you lock everything down—or worse, get stuck halfway through—you need to stress-test your plot. You need to find the leaks before the floodwaters hit. You need to find out if your story actually works under pressure, just like your characters.

And one of the best ways to do that fast and smart?

Testing your disaster plot with ChatGPT prompts.

Using ChatGPT as your plot sparring partner isn't just about getting more ideas. It's about challenging what you already have. It's about asking hard questions, exposing weak spots, finding deeper layers, and sharpening everything until it cuts.

The first way to test your disaster plot is **challenge the core disaster itself.**

Ask ChatGPT:

- "List ten unexpected consequences of a [disaster type]."
- "What's a twist on [disaster] that readers haven't seen before?"
- "What societal structures would collapse first during a [disaster]?"
- "How could the [disaster] affect daily life in small, personal ways?"

Why? Because most disaster plots live or die by how believable, layered, and fresh the disaster feels.

If the disaster is only a background boom and crash without ripple effects, it feels flat.

If the disaster touches everything—relationships, economies, psychology, faith—then it feels alive and terrifying.

Next, pressure test your protagonist.

Ask ChatGPT:

- "What flaws would a survivor of [disaster] realistically have?"
- "Give me three ways a character might react badly to sudden disaster."
- "What moral dilemma could break a normally good person during [disaster]?"

If your protagonist sails through everything bravely, logically, and morally perfect, readers will disconnect fast.

Real disaster survivors freeze. They snap. They lie. They crumble. They lash out. They regret.

Finding the fault lines in your protagonist makes their journey deeper—and their survival matter more.

Test your antagonist—or your opposition.

In some disaster stories, nature itself is the antagonist: fire, flood, virus, earthquake.

In others, the real enemy is other survivors: greed, fear, betrayal.

Ask ChatGPT:

- "What human conflicts could arise after [disaster]?"
- "How might desperation turn allies into enemies during [crisis]?"
- "What believable antagonist could emerge from a refugee camp after [event]?"

Even if nature starts the disaster, human nature usually deepens it.

Making sure you have layered, realistic antagonism—whether it's a crumbling government, a desperate warlord, or just the selfishness of scared people—raises the stakes.

Stress-test your emotional arc.

Ask ChatGPT:

- "Suggest emotional beats for a survivor during [disaster type]."
- "How might grief evolve over months after losing everything?"
- "What small emotional victories could keep hope alive after [catastrophe]?"

Disasters aren't just physical. They're emotional earthquakes.

If your plot is nothing but physical danger after physical danger, it eventually gets dull.

Mixing fear, hope, anger, guilt, love, betrayal, and forgiveness into the action keeps readers locked in at the heart level.

Challenge your timeline and pacing.

Ask ChatGPT:

- "What's a high-tension opening scene for a [disaster] story?"
- "Suggest major midpoint disasters that could escalate the plot."
- "How could a quiet moment deepen tension before the climax?"

Testing how your disaster escalates—and how moments of calm sharpen the tension—makes sure your pacing doesn't just sprint at full speed until readers burn out.

Probe your ending. Hard.

Ask ChatGPT:

- "List bittersweet endings for a [disaster type] survival story."
- "Suggest a final choice that forces the survivor to lose something important."
- "What's a quiet, powerful way to end a disaster story without a big battle?"

A disaster story doesn't need a "happily ever after."

But it does need *resolution*.

Even if the world stays broken, the character arc must close.

Testing different ending options helps you find the one that resonates—not just the one that "wraps things up."

You can also test your disaster world-building.

Ask ChatGPT:

- "What unexpected changes happen to society 5 years after [disaster]?"
- "What black-market economies might form after a [catastrophe]?"
- "How would daily life change for a child born after the disaster?"

Readers love disaster worlds that feel real at every level.

Not just flaming cities and ruined highways—but love songs rewritten for lost cities.

Street food made from desperate new crops.

Superstitions about storms and sirens.

Testing your world-building forces you to go deeper than rubble and ash.

You can even test how readers might react emotionally.

Ask ChatGPT:

- "What moment would make readers cry in a [disaster] story?"
- "What scene would make readers cheer despite the darkness?"
- "What gut-punch betrayal would devastate readers during [crisis]?"

Thinking from the audience's heart, not just the writer's head, shifts how you build each major moment.

You're not just telling a story.

You're creating an emotional rollercoaster people won't forget.

Finally, you can pressure test the overall *freshness* of your disaster plot.

Ask ChatGPT:

- "What overused tropes happen in [disaster genre] stories?"
- "How can I twist the [disaster] scenario to make it feel new?"
- "What character archetypes are tired in disaster fiction—and how can I flip them?"

It's brutal but necessary.

If your story feels too much like a hundred others, readers will tune out.

Testing for originality early can save you months of work—and turn a "pretty good" idea into an unforgettable one.

Because when you use ChatGPT to test your disaster plot, you're not asking it to write the story for you.

You're treating it like a mirror.

A sparring partner.

A firestorm you can throw your ideas into—and see what survives.

You're finding weaknesses before they become plot holes.

You're finding deeper emotions before readers get bored.

You're sharpening your story until it cuts clean, bleeds real, and burns into the mind like a memory of smoke and survival.

Because disasters don't give second chances.

And neither should your story.

Editing Your Disaster Story Quickly and Effectively

Finishing the first draft of a disaster story feels like surviving your own mini-apocalypse. You're standing there, a little dazed, a little battered, holding a messy pile of words that somehow tells the tale of people battling fire, flood, plague, collapse—and maybe even finding hope.

But you're not done. Not yet.

Now it's time to edit.

And if you want to keep your momentum—and keep the raw emotional power of your story intact—you need a fast, focused, and brutal editing approach that doesn't sand off all the edges that make disaster fiction so gripping.

The first thing to remember is **editing is not polishing.**

Not yet.

Editing disaster fiction is triage first.

You're not fixing typos and tweaking commas.

You're saving the story's life—shoring up weak foundations, re-breaking bones that healed wrong, making sure the emotional blood is still pumping strong through every scene.

If you're brainstorming your editing game plan with ChatGPT, you can prompt for things like "quick ways to tighten pacing in a survival story," "common mistakes in disaster fiction," or "editing checklists for high-intensity stories."

First pass: Big-picture survival check.

Ask yourself the hard questions:

- Does the story have a clear emotional arc, not just an event arc?
- Does the protagonist change—or at least get battered into something new?
- Does the disaster escalate naturally, with waves of tension and quiet moments mixed in?
- Is there a real ending—not just a stop, but a finish that feels earned?

If the answer to any of these is "kind of" or "not really," mark it.

You're going to need to fix it.

Fast.

Second pass: Scene-by-scene surgery.

Go through the story scene by scene, quickly.

Ask two questions per scene:

- What does this scene do for the plot?
- What does this scene do for the characters?

If a scene isn't doing both, it's either dead weight—or needs serious reworking.

Disaster fiction can't afford dead scenes.

Every step must push the survival struggle forward *and* pull readers deeper into the characters' hearts.

Third pass: Emotional continuity sweep.

Disaster stories are emotional rollercoasters.

But that doesn't mean characters should randomly flip moods like light switches.

Check:

- If someone is broken in one scene, they shouldn't be cracking jokes with ease the next unless there's a clear, believable reason.
- If someone hardens into a survivor, it shouldn't come out of nowhere—it should grow through moments of pain, failure, and loss.
- If there's a betrayal or death, make sure the emotional fallout doesn't magically vanish a few pages later.

Readers don't need constant sobbing and wailing—but they need emotional *truth*.

Fourth pass: Disaster logic check.

Real disasters obey brutal internal logic.

- If the city floods, are the characters consistently dealing with water damage, ruined electronics, blocked roads?
- If food runs out, is hunger starting to show—not just physically, but mentally and emotionally?
- If the government collapses, are there power vacuums, riots, new (and often terrible) leaders?

Cross-check your survival world against itself.

Make sure the disaster isn't just set dressing—it needs to bleed into everything.

Fifth pass: Tighten the pacing screws.

Disaster fiction demands momentum.

You should be able to feel the clock ticking even during quiet scenes.

Test pacing by asking:

- Is there a goal in every chapter—even if it's just "stay alive till morning"?
- Are there escalating obstacles and new threats regularly introduced?
- Does the tension rise overall, even if there are brief breathing spaces?

If you hit a section where the story drags—cut it, tighten it, or add a ticking clock.

Quick ways to tighten sluggish sections:

- Start scenes later, after the action has already begun.
- Cut internal monologues when action or dialogue could show the same emotion.
- Combine two scenes into one if they do similar emotional or plot work.

Sixth pass: Word sharpening.

Now—*now*—you start touching the prose itself.

Not polishing everything into boring perfection.

Just making sure every word cuts.

- Replace generic words with sharper, more specific ones. ("Bad" becomes "crumbling," "shattered," "rotting.")
- Kill any lines that explain what readers can already feel. ("He was terrified" can vanish if the paragraph already shows him trembling and gasping.)
- Keep action sentences quick and clear. Shorter sentences speed up tension scenes naturally.

Dialogue clean-up:

- Cut polite conversation. In disasters, people talk fast, rough, emotional.
- Let interruptions, stammering, unfinished sentences breathe in tense scenes.
- Make sure every line of dialogue either builds character, builds tension, or pushes the plot.

Seventh pass: Final emotional test.

Skim your manuscript fast—like a reader would.

Ask yourself:

- Where did I feel something?
- Where did I skim?
- Where did I want to cry, scream, cheer, or stop reading?

If you skimmed it, readers will too.

If you felt it? Good.

Make those scenes hit even harder if you can.

Optional but powerful: Use ChatGPT for feedback.

- "Where might the pacing lag in this disaster story?"
- "What emotional beats could be stronger based on this scene?"
- "Suggest ways to make this sacrifice moment even more heartbreaking."

Outside perspective—even from an AI—can catch things you're too close to see.

Finally: Know when to stop.

You can always tinker forever.

But disaster stories are raw by nature.

If your edit makes the story smoother but kills its wild, hurting heart—you've edited too much.

When the story is fast, fierce, aching, and honest—

When it punches and bruises and breathes and bleeds—

You're done.

Because disaster fiction isn't about perfection.

It's about *survival.*

And sometimes, survival is rough, dirty, and scarred—but beautiful all the same.

So edit fast.

Edit fiercely.

And then step back—and let your story stand, battered but unbroken, ready to break readers open too.

Designing a Gripping Opening Scene

The opening scene of a disaster story is everything. It's the door your readers walk through—and if that door is flimsy, confusing, or boring, they'll turn right around and leave. But if the opening scene crackles with energy, urgency, and human emotion, they'll lean in, heart pounding, ready to follow you straight into the fire.

A gripping disaster story doesn't ask politely for readers' attention.

It grabs them by the collar and says, *"Come with me. Don't blink. Don't breathe. We're already running."*

The first thing to realize is that **your opening doesn't need to show the full disaster yet—but it needs to pulse with the feeling of it**.

Maybe it's the moment just before everything collapses—the stillness before the quake, the tension before the sirens.

Maybe it's the moment the first cracks appear—confusion, then horror, then action.

Or maybe it's already mid-chaos—a character running through smoke, blood on their hands, desperate to find a way out

Wherever you start, it needs to *feel* alive. Immediate. Emotional.

If you're brainstorming with ChatGPT, you can prompt for ideas like "high-tension opening scenes for different types of disaster stories" or "emotional hooks for survival stories." You can even dig into sensory prompts: "what sights, sounds, and smells define the beginning of a disaster?"

Start with motion.

Disaster stories are about urgency. Fear. Instinct. Survival.

Your first scene should open *in movement*—physical, emotional, or both.

- Someone racing up a stairwell as water floods the lower floors.
- A character arguing over whether the radio warning is real.
- A kid waking up to the smell of smoke, the world shifting under their feet.

Stillness can be powerful later—but at the start, you want momentum.

You want readers stumbling into the story like your characters are stumbling through the rubble.

Anchor your reader immediately.

Even if everything's about to fall apart, readers need something solid to grab onto in the first few lines.

- Who is the character?
- Where are we?
- What's wrong—or about to be?

It doesn't take pages of description.

Just a few sharp, vivid strokes.

- "Lena tightened her grip on the steering wheel as the first tremor rattled through downtown."
- "The smell of salt and rot was stronger today. Strong enough that Jacob finally packed a bag."
- "No one screamed until the third siren."

These small openings place readers *inside* the moment without dragging them down with exposition.

Hit an emotional nerve immediately.

Disaster fiction isn't just about broken buildings and blood.

It's about broken hearts.

- Fear.
- Regret.
- Love.
- Anger.

If you can trigger an emotional response within the first page—better yet, within the first paragraph—you win.

Readers don't stick around for technical descriptions of floods or firestorms.

They stick around because they care about the *people* running, hiding, fighting.

Focus tight, not wide.

You don't need to explain the global pandemic, the meteor impact, or the political collapse on page one.

In fact, you shouldn't.

Readers trust you to fill them in as they need to know.

At the beginning, focus on one person, in one moment, with one immediate problem.

Big-picture disasters are scary.

But small, personal disasters make readers *feel.*

Start just before, just during, or just after the first real impact.

The best opening scenes often happen at a crossroads:

- Right before disaster (building tension, dread, denial).
- Right as disaster strikes (chaos, shock, adrenaline).
- Immediately after (numbness, confusion, frantic survival).

If you start too far before, readers get restless.

If you start too deep into chaos without context, they get confused.

The sweet spot is the tipping point—where life tilts from "normal" into "nothing will ever be the same."

Use sensory overload—but smartly.

Disasters attack all senses.

- The sound of twisting metal.
- The stink of burning plastic.
- The taste of ash at the back of the throat.
- The sharp, blinding flicker of emergency lights.

But don't dump five sensory details at once.

Thread them through the action.

Let the world bleed into the reader's mind naturally, making every step feel immediate and real.

Introduce stakes fast.

Not world stakes—*personal stakes.*

- A woman trapped with her injured father.
- A man desperate to reach his child's school before the flood.
- A teenager separated from their group as the fire spreads.

Readers don't stay for global headlines.

They stay for *people trying to save what matters most to them.*

Foreshadow deeper trouble.

Even if the opening chaos is huge, hint that worse is coming.

- The aftershocks will be bigger.
- The virus hasn't mutated yet.
- The levee hasn't failed—*yet.*

That lingering thread of dread makes readers need to know what happens next.

Use dialogue—but keep it tight and urgent.

Opening scene dialogue should sound like survival.

- "Where's Mom?"
- "Move! Don't look back!"
- "That wasn't an aftershock. That was something else."

Let characters talk like real people caught off-guard by fear, not like movie heroes giving speeches.

If you use a prologue, make it count.

Prologues can work if they're short, sharp, and hook hard.

Maybe you show a scientist realizing too late that the asteroid will hit.

Or a first responder realizing the virus has already spread beyond containment.

But if the prologue feels like a long info-dump, skip it.

Dive into the beating heart of the story instead.

A few ways to start strong:

- **Mid-action**: "The building collapsed before she could scream."
- **Mid-emotion**: "He had never been so terrified—and it wasn't even his life he was trying to save."
- **Mid-decision**: "It was too late to run. So Lena stayed and waited for the fire."

And don't be afraid to be a little ruthless.

Disaster fiction is about *shattering* the world, not gently nudging it.

Start with something broken.

Start with something stolen.

Start with something burning, sinking, crumbling, or falling.

Because the best disaster stories don't open with a polite knock.

They kick the door in.

They hurl readers straight into the storm, the smoke, the fire—and dare them to keep going.

Because survival starts the moment the ground shifts under your feet.

And a great opening scene makes sure readers feel that shift—in their bones, in their hearts, in every breath.

Naming Characters, Places, and Events That Stick

In disaster stories, survival isn't just about staying alive—it's about being remembered. The same goes for your characters, places, and even the events that shape your plot. If readers forget the hero's name halfway through, if the city feels like a blurry backdrop, if the disaster sounds like generic "bad stuff happened"—your story loses emotional punch.

Names matter.

Names *stick.*

And the right name can make a character or a ruined city or a final battle live in the reader's mind long after they close the book.

The first thing to remember is that **names carry weight long before readers even realize it**.

A name can hint at personality, history, danger, hope.

And in a disaster story, where everything else might be stripped away, names are sometimes the last thing characters cling to—the only thing that refuses to burn or drown or vanish.

If you're brainstorming, you can prompt ChatGPT with ideas like "names for survivors in a post-collapse city," "names for abandoned towns in an apocalyptic story," or "names for pivotal events after a major disaster."

Naming characters: Make them feel real and vivid.

You want names that are strong enough to survive the chaos—but still feel like they belonged to real people before the world fell apart.

Tips for survivor character names:

- **Keep it simple and strong.** Short, sharp names like "Maya," "Rex," "Luke," "Sam," "Dana" stick better in high-tension stories than complicated ones. Readers don't want to puzzle over six-syllable names when the floodwaters are rising.
- **Let the name hint at something deeper.**
  Maybe a survivor named "Hope" struggles with bitterness.
  Maybe a tough leader named "Grace" wrestles with mercy and cruelty.
  Subtle name irony can layer emotional complexity under the surface.
- **Cultural and regional realism matters.**
  If your story is set in coastal Louisiana, characters named Ayanna, DeShawn, or Patrice feel authentic.
  If it's rural Australia, names like Mick, Tash, or Rory might make more sense.
  Grounding names in believable places and backgrounds makes everything feel more real.

Naming groups and families:

In tight survival groups, nicknames emerge naturally.

- "Red" for the kid with the beat-up red hoodie.
- "Doc" for the former medical student who does triage.
- "Lucky" for the guy who keeps surviving impossible situations—even if it's sarcastic.

Small, affectionate (or bitter) nicknames humanize survivors without you needing long exposition dumps.

Naming places: Give your world texture.

An abandoned hospital named "Saint Gabriel's" feels different than one called "Mercy General."

A ruined suburb called "Silver Pines" hits differently than one called "Old Bridge."

Tips for place names:

- **Use ironic names.**
  Safe Haven turns into a killing ground.
  Sunny Hills becomes a cratered wasteland.
  This adds dark layers of meaning without needing to explain anything.
- **Use natural imagery.**
  Places named after rivers, trees, hills, stars—these names linger even after civilization dies.
- **Reference what survives.**
  Maybe survivors call a stretch of city ruins "The Glass Field" because shattered windows still glitter in the rubble.

Good place names give the setting character.

You're not just surviving in "the ruined city."

You're fighting your way through Echo Crossing, or Ashmarket, or Black Hollow.

Naming events: Give disaster moments identity.

In real life, disasters earn names fast.

- "9/11"
- "Katrina"
- "The Blitz"
- "The Blackout"

In your story, survivors would naturally name major events too.

- "The Long Silence" (after a communications blackout).
- "The Night the Sky Fell" (after meteors or bombs).
- "The Last Winter" (after a nuclear winter or deep freeze).

Event names help you time-jump and layer emotion without explaining every single thing.

Readers *feel* the weight when a character mutters, "It's not like before the Silence."

Naming organizations and enemies:

If your story has factions, groups, or new governments rising after disaster, names matter even more.

- Cold, mechanical names ("Sector 17 Authority," "Emergency Stability Corps") suggest authoritarian survival at the cost of freedom.
- Hopeful but battered names ("The Dawn League," "The Last Light") suggest fragile resistance.
- Brutal street names ("Bone Rats," "The Ash Kings") hint at new predators born from the ruins.

Good faction names sketch the whole mood of a group without a single info-dump paragraph.

Avoid cheesy or overdone names unless you're twisting them.

Names like "The New Order" or "Project Phoenix" have been done to death unless you give them a twist.

- Maybe "Project Phoenix" was supposed to save people—but became the reason everything burned.
- Maybe "The New Order" is ironically tiny and pathetic, not the mighty force it once claimed to be.

Fresh twists on old ideas make even familiar names feel chilling and new.

Use repetition to cement names emotionally.

Characters should say important names out loud—sometimes with fear, sometimes with bitterness, sometimes with desperate hope.

- "We're almost to Ashmarket. Just another mile."
- "Don't trust anyone from Sector 17. They shoot first."
- "Remember what happened the Night the Sky Fell. Don't trust the silence."

Hearing names spoken again and again cements them in the reader's mind—and deepens the emotional resonance every time they appear.

Let names evolve over time.

In real disasters, people rename things.

- "Freedom Plaza" becomes "Dead Man's Crossing."
- "The Gateway Bridge" becomes "The Last Stand."
- "Jonesville" becomes "The Hollow."

If survivors live long enough, they will rewrite the world in their own battered language.

Letting places and events shift names as the story progresses makes the world feel alive—and makes survival feel like something still being built, not just mourned.

Names tell hidden stories.

You don't have to explain every name's origin immediately.

Readers love mysteries.

- Why do they call it Red Hollow?
- What really happened on the Night of Cinders?
- Why does nobody go near the Cradle?

The slow, painful reveal of what those names *mean* gives you built-in emotional bombs later.

Because in disaster stories, survival is memory.

Survival is *naming* the things you lose—and the things you refuse to let go.

Good names stay.

Good names echo in the mind.

Good names turn ruined streets and broken people into something unforgettable.

Because even when the sky falls and the rivers dry up,

even when the cities crumble and the stars disappear,

the names remain.

And sometimes, they're the only thing that does.

Examples of Prompts for Disaster Story Design and Structure

One of the best things about using ChatGPT (or any brainstorming tool) for writing disaster stories is how it can *turbocharge* your creativity when you ask the right questions. A great prompt isn't just "give me an idea." It's a key that unlocks doors you didn't even realize were closed. It's the flare gun you fire into the dark ruins of your imagination to find hidden paths.

So if you want to design and structure a disaster story that actually sticks, burns, aches, and *matters*, you need to start asking *better prompts*.

A good disaster story prompt focuses on tension, survival, emotion, and stakes. It nudges you past the obvious "everything exploded" idea and digs into characters, worlds, and decisions that feel *real*.

Here's a guide to building and using strong prompts—and examples you can throw straight into ChatGPT (or your own brain) whenever you feel stuck or want to go deeper.

First: Structuring Your Disaster World

You want the disaster to feel layered, brutal, and believable. So start asking questions that make the world richer.

Prompts to try:

- "Describe a disaster scenario where the real danger isn't the event itself but the aftermath."
- "List five small daily life changes after a city loses all electricity permanently."
- "What unexpected professions become critical after a global collapse?"
- "Suggest disaster settings that aren't typical cities—something more unique like oil rigs, underground towns, cruise ships."

These kinds of prompts force you to think past the easy version of 'the world ended' and toward settings and worlds that feel unique and terrifyingly lived-in.

Next: Choosing the Right Kind of Disaster

There's no rule that says your disaster has to be a nuclear war or a zombie apocalypse.

The more specific and twisted your disaster is, the more memorable your story becomes.

Prompts to test:

- "Invent a slow-burn disaster that takes five years to fully destroy civilization."
- "Suggest environmental disasters that aren't earthquakes, tsunamis, or meteors."
- "Give me disasters where the initial survivors face unexpected second waves of collapse."

This pushes you toward less predictable, more personal, more gripping disasters.

Building Structure around the Collapse

A disaster story isn't just 'and then everything went bad.'

It's waves of tension, breathing moments, desperate recalculations.

Prompts to plan structure:

- "Outline a disaster story where Act 1 is denial, Act 2 is collapse, Act 3 is fragile survival."
- "Suggest a mid-point twist where the disaster survivors realize the true threat is something they caused trying to survive."
- "Give me a disaster story structure where the protagonist makes a terrible choice early—and it haunts the second half of the story."

When you shape your disaster story with these arcs in mind, you get stories that don't just escalate, they evolve—and stay in readers' hearts longer.

Creating Compelling Protagonists

No reader cares about the collapsing bridge if they don't care about the person trying to cross it.

Strong disaster protagonists are messy, scared, stubborn—and sometimes, not even very likable at first.

Character prompts:

- "Suggest personality flaws that would make surviving a disaster harder for the protagonist."
- "Create a disaster story where the protagonist's skill set is *completely wrong* for survival at first."
- "Give me examples of emotional scars a character might carry after living through the collapse of society."

These help you avoid creating bland survival machines and instead create people who readers desperately want to see claw their way through.

Designing Relationships in Chaos

Disasters forge or destroy relationships.

Often both.

Relationship-building prompts:

- "What relationships get stronger during disasters—and which ones break first?"
- "Suggest a survival group made of people who would normally hate each other."
- "Create tension in a survival group by giving each person a hidden agenda tied to pre-disaster secrets."

If you want real emotional explosions between characters, setting up complicated alliances and betrayals early makes everything hit ten times harder later.

Designing Set Pieces and Major Disaster Moments

You need iconic scenes that readers remember—the dam breaking, the bridge collapse, the fire racing over the hill.

Set-piece prompts:

- "Invent a survival challenge involving a destroyed landmark."
- "Create a survival scenario where the protagonist must cross an area they know is structurally unstable."
- "Describe a disaster set-piece that starts hopeful—and turns into a trap."

You can even get more specific:

- "Give me a tense scene in a flooded subway tunnel."
- "Suggest a survival sequence during a chemical spill in a suburban neighborhood."

Set pieces aren't just cool visuals.

They should rip at your characters' emotions and force choices under extreme pressure.

Building Themes and Symbolism

Great disaster stories aren't *just* about survival.

They're about identity, hope, loss, greed, sacrifice, betrayal.

Theme-building prompts:

- "Suggest themes for a disaster story about losing faith in humanity—and slowly regaining it."
- "What object could symbolize survival, guilt, or resilience in a post-collapse world?"
- "Create a disaster story where weather mirrors the emotional journey of the characters."

Themes make your disaster bigger than the broken buildings and shattered roads.

They make it about *something* that matters long after the last siren fades.

Testing and Twisting Your Story

Once you have a basic structure, keep testing it.

Break it.

Twist it.

Twisting prompts:

- "What's the worst decision my protagonist could make right now?"
- "Suggest a betrayal halfway through that would shatter the survivors' trust."
- "Invent a reveal where the original disaster was just the beginning of something worse."

Survival stories that seem predictable don't survive in readers' minds.

Always look for ways to make your story turn harder, hurt deeper, burn longer.

Finally: Ending with Power

The end of your disaster story must leave bruises—or hope—or both.

Ending prompts:

- "Describe a disaster ending where the protagonist sacrifices their freedom to save others."
- "Create a disaster story ending that feels both tragic and inevitable."
- "Suggest a quiet, hopeful ending for a disaster story without promising a perfect future."

Because the ending isn't just about who lives and who dies.

It's about what *survives* inside the readers' hearts after they close the book.

One More Trick: Randomized Disaster Story Generator

You can even create a lightning-fast generator by combining random prompts:

- **Disaster type:** Flood / Pandemic / Drought / Invasion
- **Setting:** Suburbia / Oil Rig / Mountains / Ghost Town
- **Character flaw:** Arrogance / Guilt / Cowardice / Selfishness
- **Twist:** Second disaster / Internal betrayal / No rescue coming

Throw a few random elements together, ask ChatGPT for combinations, and suddenly you're staring at story sparks you never would have found on your own.

Because the truth is, designing and structuring a disaster story isn't about following a formula.

It's about building something that feels like it could shatter at any second—and somehow, someone clings to the broken pieces and finds a way to go on.

Good prompts don't just give you ideas.

They give you momentum.

They give you danger.

They give you the fuel to burn down the world—and make readers feel every collapsing, breathtaking, *beautiful* second of it.

Examples of Prompts for Designing Compelling Characters

Disasters don't just break buildings—they break people. And that's exactly why characters in disaster stories must feel so real you could reach out and touch them. They need to hurt, fear, love, betray, and bleed in ways that make the end of the world not just an idea, but an experience.

If readers don't care about your characters, they won't care about the flood, the fire, the plague, the fall.

The world can collapse spectacularly, but it's the people readers follow through the wreckage who make or break the story.

So how do you design survivors, leaders, villains, heroes, and cowards that readers remember?

You start with *better questions.*

And you let those questions dig deeper than just "What's their job?" or "What's their hair color?"

If you're brainstorming with ChatGPT, you can prompt for things like "design a disaster survivor with a deep internal conflict" or "create a flawed leader forced to make impossible choices during an apocalypse."

Here's a collection of prompt types and examples you can use to craft characters who feel messy, human, and unforgettable.

First: Building Characters from Strengths and Weaknesses

Disaster survivors aren't superheroes.

They're people with sharp edges, regrets, and hidden strengths that only show under pressure.

Strengths/weaknesses prompts:

- "Suggest hidden strengths a timid character might discover during a major disaster."
- "Create a character whose greatest skill becomes useless after the collapse."
- "List character flaws that would make survival harder but more interesting."
- "What emotional wounds would a paramedic carry into a post-collapse world?"

The goal is to create characters who aren't perfectly equipped to survive—but *fight anyway*.

Second: Exploring Past Trauma and Backstory

Everyone brings baggage into a disaster.

Sometimes that baggage is what kills them—or saves them.

Backstory prompts:

- "Describe a guilt a character carries from before the disaster that shapes every choice they make."
- "What is the one memory a survivor clings to when hope runs out?"
- "What secret does a disaster character desperately hide from their group?"

- "How might a past betrayal make a survivor reckless—or overly cautious?"

Backstory isn't about dumping pages of flashbacks into the story.

It's about creating emotional landmines that explode at the worst possible times.

Third: Pushing Characters into Impossible Choices

Survival isn't neat.

Characters have to make ugly, gut-wrenching decisions.

Moral dilemma prompts:

- "Give me a survival choice where either decision could destroy the protagonist's soul."
- "Describe a situation where a character must choose between loyalty and survival."
- "Create a moment where a character must decide whether to lie or tell a truth that could shatter their group."
- "Suggest a scenario where saving one person means sacrificing ten others—and no rescue is guaranteed."

Impossible choices force real growth—and unforgettable regret.

Fourth: Designing Relationships Under Pressure

In disasters, alliances are fragile.

Love is dangerous.

Friendship might be the difference between life and death—or betrayal and doom.

Relationship prompts:

- "Describe a friendship that turns into bitter rivalry during a disaster."
- "Suggest a survival partnership built entirely on necessity, not trust."
- "How does a former teacher/student relationship shift when survival depends on both?"
- "Create tension in a romance strained by competing survival goals."

Relationships in disaster fiction should crack under the weight of fear, hunger, and guilt—then either shatter or forge into something stronger.

Fifth: Contrasting External and Internal Survival

Sometimes, the characters who survive best physically are the ones losing the worst internally.

Duality prompts:

- "Design a character who is a brilliant tactician—but emotionally collapsing."
- "Create a character who outwardly seems cowardly but displays unexpected courage when it matters most."
- "Describe a survivor who clings to rituals (prayer, cleaning, lists) to hold back emotional breakdown."

Showing survival as both external (body) and internal (mind, soul) makes characters feel fully alive—and fully vulnerable.

Sixth: Building Archetypes—and Then Breaking Them

Disaster fiction has tons of classic survivor archetypes:

- The hardened leader.
- The naive optimist.
- The reluctant hero.
- The embittered cynic.

These can work—but only if you twist them.

Archetype-twisting prompts:

- "Design a hardened leader who secretly wants someone else to take over."
- "Create a naive optimist who turns into a ruthless survivor."
- "What if the reluctant hero refuses the call—and someone else rises instead?"
- "Suggest a cynic who finds hope too late to save themselves."

Readers love seeing familiar types—but they *adore* seeing those types crack open and evolve.

Seventh: Naming Emotional Drivers

Characters need more than the desire to "stay alive."

They need deeply personal motivations.

Driver prompts:

- "What would make a character risk everything during a disaster?"
- "Describe a personal vow made before the world fell—and how it twists the character's choices."
- "What does the protagonist believe is unforgivable—and how are they forced to break that belief?"
- "Create a survival group where each member is driven by a different core need (revenge, redemption, family, freedom, faith)."

When characters fight for something more than breath, their struggles matter more.

Eighth: Stress-Testing Your Character

You know your character's surface.

Now it's time to push them until they break—and see what's underneath.

Stress-testing prompts:

- "How would this character react to being left behind?"
- "What would make this character betray someone they care about?"

- "If forced to abandon a loved one to save a group, would they?"
- "What mistake would haunt them forever—even if no one else knew?"

Stress-testing forces you to reveal character truth not with long descriptions, but through *action*.

Finally: Designing Flawed Leaders, Followers, and Outsiders

Not everyone in a disaster story should lead.

Not everyone should follow well.

And some people never fit anywhere.

Role prompts:

- "Create a would-be leader whose charisma hides terrible insecurity."
- "Describe a loyal follower who eventually questions orders—and what that costs."
- "Build an outsider character who survives alone—but secretly longs for connection."
- "Invent a survivor who manipulates groups without ever committing to any of them."

Disaster survival groups aren't neat, happy families.

They're messy, broken, hopeful, angry, scared tribes trying to outlast the end of the world.

Designing characters who reflect that messy truth makes every victory and betrayal land harder.

Because compelling disaster story characters aren't superheroes.

They're survivors—and not always good ones.

They limp, they fight, they bleed, they break.

They cling to hope when they shouldn't—and sometimes they let it go too soon.

And when you build them right, readers don't just root for them to survive.

They *need* them to survive.

They mourn them when they fall.

They carry them, long after the fires burn out and the last page turns.

Examples of Good Prompts for World Building in Disaster Stories

When readers pick up a disaster story, they're stepping into a broken world. And if that world doesn't feel vivid, raw, and brutally real, they'll never truly feel the terror, the hope, or the heartbreak you're trying to give them.

World-building in disaster fiction isn't about page after page of describing ruined buildings and fallen governments.

It's about **building a living, breathing, bleeding world** that grabs readers by the heart and drags them straight through the wreckage.

A good disaster world should feel three-dimensional. It should feel *lived-in*. It should feel *lost*.

And the best way to start building it?

By asking better questions.

If you're using ChatGPT or brainstorming on your own, the right prompts can force you to dig deeper, past the obvious crumbling cities, into the tiny details that make a survival world unforgettable.

Here's a breakdown of world-building categories—and great prompts you can use to explode your setting into something readers can't forget.

First: The Nature of the Disaster

What exactly broke the world—and how?

Disaster design prompts:

- "Describe a slow-burn disaster that took years to destroy society."
- "What unexpected chain reactions happen after [disaster type]?"
- "How does the environment itself become more dangerous after the collapse?"
- "Invent a disaster that changes seasons, wildlife, and weather patterns permanently."

Your disaster needs aftershocks—not just one event, but ripples that affect *everything*.

Second: Daily Life After Collapse

Survival isn't just fighting fires.

It's eating, drinking, sheltering, breathing.

Daily survival prompts:

- "How do people get clean water after [disaster]?"
- "Describe what a typical meal looks like for survivors."
- "Where do people live if houses aren't safe anymore?"
- "What small, forgotten skills become life-saving in a collapsed world?"

When you show survivors *living*—not just running or fighting—you make the world feel brutally alive.

Third: Community and Culture After Disaster

How do people organize after the world ends?

What rules matter?

What taboos emerge?

Community-building prompts:

- "Suggest three types of survivor groups formed after a major collapse."
- "What rituals do survivors create to mourn their dead after mass death events?"
- "How do small communities punish crimes like theft or betrayal when there's no police?"
- "What old holidays or traditions survive—and how are they twisted by the new world?"

Society doesn't stop—it mutates.

And mutated societies are pure gold for emotional storytelling.

Fourth: Geography and Changing Landscapes

Disasters reshape the land itself.

Landscape prompts:

- "Describe a city partially submerged after decades of rising floods."
- "What dangers hide in abandoned rural areas after society collapses?"
- "How does a desert expand when agriculture fails and the climate shifts?"
- "Create a mountain refuge that becomes both sanctuary and prison for survivors."

Landscape isn't just background—it becomes *character*.

It traps, saves, punishes, and defines the story.

Fifth: Technology and Its Breakdown

Technology doesn't just vanish overnight.

It fails, rots, mutates.

Technology prompts:

- "What low-tech inventions help people survive in a post-disaster world?"
- "How do old pieces of technology (radios, generators, solar panels) become priceless?"
- "Describe a black market built around salvaged pre-collapse tech."
- "How might survivors build new communication systems without the internet?"

Realistic tech decay makes the world feel less like a fantasy—and more like a terrifying near-future.

Sixth: Economy and Resources

Money changes—or dies.

Barter returns. Scarcity rules.

Economy prompts:

- "What items become more valuable than gold in a survival economy?"
- "Describe a 'currency' that develops among survivors (ammo, batteries, seeds, clean water)."
- "What brutal power struggles emerge over dwindling food supplies?"
- "How do trade caravans, raider gangs, or fortified markets operate?"

The economy of a collapsed world is raw, dangerous, and full of brilliant storytelling chances.

Seventh: Medicine and Health

Without hospitals, survival gets even grimmer.

Health prompts:

- "What home remedies or old medicines make a comeback after modern systems fail?"
- "Describe a field hospital made from salvaged materials."
- "What happens when a disease spreads among survivors with no antibiotics?"
- "What new dangers arise from untreated injuries, infections, or malnutrition?"

Every time a survivor trips and cuts their leg, readers should *feel* the risk of death—not just shrug it off like in superhero fiction.

Eighth: Belief Systems and Superstitions

When the world ends, so do old gods—and sometimes new ones are born.

Belief prompts:

- "What new religions or cults emerge from the ashes of civilization?"
- "How do survivors reinterpret old myths, prophecies, or religious texts after disaster?"
- "Suggest a superstition that develops around the signs of [disaster type]."
- "Describe rituals survivors use to ward off further catastrophe."

Beliefs help characters make sense of chaos—or spiral deeper into it.

Ninth: Wildlife and Nature Reclaiming the World

Nature doesn't stop.

It moves into abandoned places, mutates, takes over.

Wildlife prompts:

- "Describe how urban animals (rats, coyotes, stray dogs) change after human collapse."
- "What new predator rises in a broken ecosystem?"
- "How do survivors adapt to dangerous new environments—overgrown cities, toxic forests, flooded plains?"
- "What invasive species dominate after society collapses?"

Nature becomes both enemy and ally—and a constant, creeping reminder that humanity is no longer in control.

Tenth: Naming and Language Changes

When old structures fall, even language evolves.

Language prompts:

- "How does survivor slang evolve after a disaster?"
- "Invent nicknames for places, disasters, and survivor groups."
- "Describe how children born after the collapse speak differently than those who lived before."

Language evolution makes your world feel truly rebuilt—or barely hanging on.

And one bonus category: Secrets and Hidden Truths

Every good disaster world has mysteries buried under the rubble.

Secrets prompts:

- "What hidden cause of the disaster might survivors slowly uncover?"
- "Describe a forbidden place survivors fear to enter—but must."
- "What terrible truths does the new ruling group keep from the people?"

Hidden layers of history, lies, and lost knowledge make your survival story more than just action—it makes it a haunting exploration of memory and loss.

Why prompts matter so much in disaster world-building:

Because readers don't just want explosions.

They want places that feel *so real* they can smell the burning, taste the dust, hear the silence after the last radio signal fades.

They want to feel what it's like to pick their way through fallen cities.

To light a fire in a flooded world.

To wonder if that strange sound outside the camp fence is a lost dog—or something worse.

They want to survive—not just with your characters, but *inside* your world.

And the right prompts pull that world out of the rubble, piece by piece, until it's something no one can forget.

Examples of Prompts for Disaster Story Ideas

By the time you've built a crumbling world, created broken heroes, and sharpened your survival themes, you might think the hard part is over. But coming up with *truly gripping disaster story ideas* — the kind that grab readers by the gut and don't let go — still demands a special kind of magic.

Luckily, you don't have to wait for lightning to strike.

You can *summon* that magic by using better prompts.

Disaster fiction doesn't need more explosions for the sake of explosions.

It needs moments where the earth shakes and the human spirit either rises... or shatters.

And the right story ideas are built not just on catastrophe, but on **pressure, choice, survival, and emotional weight.**

Here's a toolbox full of high-powered prompts you can use to generate disaster story ideas that are raw, original, and unforgettable.

First: Twisting Classic Disasters

There's nothing wrong with using familiar disaster types — but the twist is what makes them yours.

Story idea prompts:

- "Write a flood story where the real enemy is an ancient secret exposed by the water."
- "Invent a wildfire story where the fire is only a symptom of something much worse underneath."
- "Describe an earthquake story where the survivors realize the city is sinking, not crumbling."

Instead of telling the same disaster story everyone expects, find the *unexpected shadows* hiding inside it.

Second: Slow Burn, Long Fall

Not every disaster strikes in one day.

Some stories are about the slow crumbling of everything once taken for granted.

Slow collapse prompts:

- "Imagine a drought that lasts a decade, slowly grinding society into dust."
- "Describe how a 'harmless' virus mutates into a multi-generational catastrophe."
- "Write about a global blackout where power never returns — and new civilizations rise from the darkness."

Slow disasters let you explore survival *and* transformation.

Third: Personal Disasters inside Global Collapse

Not everyone is trying to save the world.

Sometimes they're just trying to save *one person.*

Personal disaster prompts:

- "A teenager risks everything to find their missing sister during an urban evacuation."
- "A mother clings to a crumbling skyscraper with her child, waiting for a rescue that may never come."
- "A former con artist uses old skills to survive in a lawless refugee city."

The world falling apart is big.

One desperate heart fighting to survive in it? That's where readers *feel* the story.

Fourth: Survivors versus Survivors

Disasters don't just kill.

They reveal what people are willing to do to live.

Conflict prompts:

- "After the collapse, two groups fight over the last safe ground — a polluted, dying island."
- "Survivors living underground discover another group — and not everyone wants to share the supplies."
- "A peace treaty between camps is tested when a child goes missing."

Survivor versus survivor plots ramp up tension even when the original disaster has passed.

Fifth: Small Mistakes, Big Catastrophes

Sometimes disaster doesn't come from grand evil or freak accidents.

Sometimes it's one tiny misstep.

Accidental disaster prompts:

- "A hacker trying to expose a government cover-up accidentally crashes the entire banking system."
- "An experimental crop released early to stop famine mutates uncontrollably."
- "An abandoned scientific outpost turns out to have been holding back a global threat — until now."

This keeps the disaster *personal* — and readers wondering if they would've made the same mistake.

Sixth: Hopeful Disasters

Not every survival story has to be pure grimdark misery.

Hope can survive too — and that hope feels even brighter against a broken world.

Hope prompts:

- "A group of children raised in a post-collapse commune set out to find the 'Old World' everyone says is dead."
- "A builder starts creating small, walled gardens in flooded cities — and they become sanctuaries."
- "A radio DJ keeps broadcasting during a global pandemic — and their voice becomes the thread that holds

survivors together."

Stories that show humanity clawing back light after endless darkness leave a different kind of scar.

Seventh: Alien or Supernatural Disasters

Sometimes the world ends in ways science can't explain.

Strange disaster prompts:

- "One night, the stars vanish — and with them, the laws of gravity slowly unravel."
- "Something falls from the sky into a remote village — and whoever gets too close disappears."
- "A strange mist covers the oceans, and ships that enter it never return."

Weaving mystery into disaster multiplies the fear — because what you can't explain is often more terrifying than what you can.

Eighth: Microcosm Stories

Instead of covering the entire globe, tell a survival story in one tight, pressurized location.

Microcosm prompts:

- "A cruise ship is quarantined after an outbreak — and mutiny brews inside."
- "A mining crew trapped deep underground after a quake must survive each other as well as the collapse."
- "An isolated boarding school becomes its own brutal society after communication cuts off."

Small, closed environments crank up tension fast and let character dynamics explode.

Ninth: Generational Disaster Stories

Sometimes survival isn't about one desperate sprint — it's about living *long enough* to see hope again.

Generational prompts:

- "Three generations of survivors pass down a legend about a safe place that might not exist."
- "Children born after the disaster discover hidden truths their parents refused to share."
- "A survivor becomes the founder of a new village—but old rivalries threaten to tear it down again."

Long-term disaster survival adds depth and heartbreak to every success and failure.

Tenth: Psychological Disasters

Sometimes the world doesn't break.

Sometimes it's the people.

Psychological collapse prompts:

- "After surviving a major disaster, the protagonist can no longer tell what is real — and what they made up to survive."

- "The survivors create myths to explain what happened — but someone knows the truth is much worse."
- "Isolation in a 'safe zone' drives the last survivors slowly into paranoia and violence."

Internal disasters mirror the external collapse—and sometimes are more terrifying.

Bonus Category: Hybrid Disasters

Who says you have to pick just one?

Hybrid disaster prompts:

- "A flood releases an ancient virus buried under glaciers."
- "A chemical fire triggers a massive blackout that leads to a city falling into anarchy."
- "An earthquake damages nuclear facilities across a continent, unleashing chain-reaction fallout zones."

Mixing disasters multiplies tension—and creates layered survival challenges.

Because great disaster story ideas aren't just about destruction.

They're about the small stubborn things that survive:

- A battered wedding ring.
- A photo of a city that no longer exists.
- A lullaby sung over crackling radios to children born in the ruins.
- A single light blinking in the dark, daring the end of the world to come closer.

A great disaster story doesn't just destroy the world.

It asks: *What's left?*

What matters?

What's worth saving—even if it costs everything?

And if you ask the right questions?

Your story will leave readers gasping, aching—and burning to come back for more.

Your One-Day Disaster Story Writing Game Plan

So you've got the ideas, the world, the characters, the emotional stakes. You've been through disaster plotting, survival dynamics, structure tricks, emotional layering, and story testing. Now it's time for the real challenge: sitting down and **writing an entire disaster story in one day**.

Sounds impossible?

It's not.

It's brutal, thrilling, and wildly addictive once you feel the momentum.

All you need is a plan that pushes you through the chaos—and today, you're the survivor.

Writing a full disaster story in a single day isn't about perfection. It's about pure narrative survival.

You're not building a polished, publish-ready book here—you're building **a living, breathing, bleeding story skeleton** that you can refine later.

Here's your game plan—from the first idea to the final emotional gut punch—in just one fierce, relentless day.

Step One: One-Hour Disaster Storm (Idea + Structure)

You start by grabbing the core.

In your first hour, you need to make three simple, unbreakable choices:

- What is the disaster?
- Who is trying to survive it?
- What is emotionally at stake?

Quick prompts to keep handy:

- "What breaks the world?"
- "What does the protagonist refuse to lose?"
- "What would crush them even if they survive?"

Once you have those, sketch a rough three-act structure:

- **Act 1:** Disaster hits. Life tilts into survival mode.
- **Act 2:** Survival costs grow. Trust fractures. Hope wavers.
- **Act 3:** Final choice. Sacrifice or salvation. Something is lost. Something survives.

Sketch fast. Ten minutes per act. No stalling. No second-guessing.

Step Two: Two-Hour Character Crucible

Now you make your people bleed (emotionally).

Spend an hour hammering out your protagonist:

- What are they most afraid of?
- What guilt, shame, or secret do they carry?
- What small hope keeps them fighting when it's easier to give up?

Spend the second hour sketching three to five supporting characters:

- A friend they might lose.
- An enemy they might rely on.
- A stranger who changes everything.

You don't need full bios.

You need emotional grenades ready to go off halfway through the story.

Step Three: One-Hour World Smash

Now, quickly, brutally, you world-build only what you need.

Focus on:

- What's immediately dangerous (floods, fire, gangs, disease).
- What's scarce (water, food, medicine, safe ground).
- What's emotionally iconic (abandoned schools, burnt-out hospitals, silent cities).

Jot down five sensory snapshots you want to hit during the story:

- The smell of melting plastic.
- The sound of sirens fading into nothing.
- The feel of ash sticking to wet skin.
- The sight of ruined playgrounds under burning skies.
- The taste of canned peaches eaten on a rooftop full of broken glass.

Done. World is ready.

Now burn it down.

Step Four: Five-Hour Survival Sprint (Writing the Story)

This is the big chunk of your day—and it's where you let the chaos flow.

Write fast.

Write messy.

Write *like survival depends on it.*

Here's your rhythm:

- **Hour One:** Write Act 1. Disaster hits. Characters make terrible choices under pressure.
- **Hours Two and Three:** Write Act 2. Everything goes worse than expected. People die. Trust crumbles. Hopes shatter.
- **Hour Four:** Write Act 3. The last stand. The final sacrifice. The small, stubborn heartbeat that survives.
- **Hour Five:** Crash through the ending.
  Let it hit hard.
  One image.
  One final decision.
  One last line that echoes.

Don't stop for typos.

Don't stop to rethink scenes.

Don't stop to reread.

Forward. Forward. Forward.

Step Five: Two-Hour Rapid Edit

You made it through the disaster. Now patch up the worst wounds.

- Read through your draft ONCE, straight through, no stopping.
- Mark scenes that feel slow or confusing.
- Tighten opening paragraphs. Sharpen dialogue. Clarify action.
- Make the last page punch harder.
- Fix only what you can in two hours.

If a scene isn't broken? Leave it.

If you see a clear fix? Make it fast and move on.

The goal is not perfection.

The goal is survival—and emotional truth.

Step Six: One-Hour Closing Reflection

Before you end your writing day, **capture the heart** of what you just made.

Ask yourself:

- What scene hurt the most to write?
- What moment surprised you while you were sprinting?
- What line or choice felt *real* in your gut?

Write down a one-paragraph emotional summary of your story.

Capture the raw feeling while it's still burning inside you.

This will guide your deeper edits later—or remind you why the story matters when you need to rework it.

Survival Tips for a One-Day Sprint:

- **Set a timer.** Sprint in 25- or 50-minute blocks, short breaks between.
- **No phone, no internet surfing.** Your only "net" is your imagination.
- **Write on rough paper, Notepad, Scrivener, Word—whatever flows fastest.**
- **Don't apologize to yourself.** A messy story full of heart beats a polished story with no soul.
- **Breathe. Hydrate. Snack. Keep moving.**

Remember: you're writing a disaster story.

It should feel like survival.

It should hurt.

It should leave you breathless.

But if you finish?

If you make it to the final line, battered and burning and somehow still standing?

You didn't just write a story.

You *lived* it.

And that's what readers will feel too—every desperate heartbeat, every broken prayer, every stubborn breath after the sky falls.

You Did It: Your Next Disaster Story Starts Today

You made it.

You sprinted through the end of the world.

You survived the wreckage of ideas, structure, emotions, twists, sacrifices, collapses, rebirths, edits—and somehow you kept your story alive all the way to the final breath.

That's not small. That's not ordinary. That's **rare**.

Because writing a disaster story isn't just an act of creativity—it's an act of resilience.

It's a survival test in itself.

You built characters who fought through flood, fire, betrayal, hunger, heartbreak.

And while you did it, you fought through doubt, fatigue, second-guessing, plot holes, lost threads, and the temptation to give up.

But you didn't.

You finished the story.

Or you're about to finish.

Or you're standing right at the edge, breathing hard, seeing the road ahead, knowing you *can*.

And here's the best part:

You're just getting started.

Disaster stories aren't one-shot wonders.

They're a way of seeing the world, a way of cracking open what it means to survive, to lose, to love, to rebuild.

Now that you know how to do it once, you can do it again—and every time you do, you'll get stronger.

Faster.

Braver.

You'll dig deeper into human emotions.

You'll create wilder, sharper, harder stories that leave readers gasping and scarred in the best way possible.

Your next disaster story starts today.

It might start with a whisper.

A creaking sound in an empty house.

The first drop of rain in a sky too dry for years.

A strange transmission on an abandoned radio.

Or it might start with a scream.

A fire racing up a mountainside.

A siren blaring in the middle of a wedding.

A hand reaching through the floodwaters—and slipping away.

Wherever it starts, you'll know the signs now.

You'll feel the ground tilt under your characters' feet.

You'll hear the silent clock ticking down in the background of every scene.

You'll see the moment when a choice, once small, turns deadly.

And you'll write it.

Because you know that survival isn't clean.

It's not about winning every battle.

It's about crawling, bleeding, grieving, hoping anyway.

It's about broken hands building something new.

It's about stubborn hearts refusing to stop beating.

If you ever get stuck—remember what you survived to get here.

- The messy first drafts.
- The fear of bad ideas.
- The pressure of pacing and tension.
- The heartbreak of killing a character you loved.
- The thrill of watching a broken hero stand up one more time when the world said stay down.

You've already beaten doubt once.

You can beat it again.

And remember:

Every disaster story you write teaches you something new.

Maybe your next story will be about a slow-burn drought, and how a girl becomes a legend leading survivors across poisoned fields.

Maybe it's a cold, bitter nuclear winter where two enemies become unlikely allies.

Maybe it's a micro-story—one hour, one shelter, one hard choice that echoes forever.

Maybe it's a sweeping saga—generations rebuilding on the bones of fallen cities.

Whatever it is, it starts now.

It starts today.

It starts with that strange, stubborn little voice in the back of your mind whispering:

What if...

What if the dam broke?

What if the last plane never landed?

What if the last radio broadcast wasn't telling the truth?

What if the real danger wasn't the virus, but the cure?

What if...

Grab the "what if."

Run with it.

Crash into it headfirst.

Let it shake your story loose, scene by scene, moment by moment, until the world falls apart again—only for something stronger to rise from the ruins.

Because you are not the same writer who started this journey.

You're a survivor now.

A creator of worlds that crack and bleed and still somehow find the will to beat again.

The next story is already waiting inside you.

The next characters are already reaching out across the dust and darkness, begging you to tell their broken, beautiful, terrifying, unforgettable story.

So don't wait.

Don't second-guess.

Don't apologize.

Write it.

Survive it.

Finish it.

Again.

And again.

And again.

Because the world will always need stories of survival.

And the best stories?

They come from the writers who know exactly what it feels like to fight for the light—and carry it through the darkest storms.

And today,

that writer

is you.

I hope you found inspiration here for your next project. If you liked this book, please leave a review where you bought it. Thank you from the author.

Disaster Story Survival Kit Checklist

When everything's collapsing—when you're deep in the heart of your next disaster story—it's easy to get overwhelmed, to lose track of what matters most.

This Survival Kit is here to drag you back to your feet, dust you off, and shove you forward again.

Print it. Copy it. Keep it taped to your desk or stuck in your notebook.

Whenever you're writing your next disaster story—whether in one day or one furious week—use this as your **battle map**.

1. My Core Disaster

☐ What broke the world? (Specific event, accident, slow collapse?)

☐ How does it *keep* breaking beyond the first shock?

☐ What small daily dangers make survival brutal?

2. My Protagonist

☐ What do they fear most?

☐ What secret guilt, mistake, or loss haunts them?

☐ What stubborn hope keeps them fighting when logic says quit?

3. My Supporting Cast

☐ Who will help—and hurt—the protagonist along the way?

☐ Which relationships will crack under pressure?

☐ Who changes the story more than expected?

4. My World-Building Must-Haves

☐ Immediate sensory details (What does it smell, sound, and feel like?)

☐ Resources: What's scarce? What's priceless?

☐ Danger zones: Where's safe today—but deadly tomorrow?

5. My Emotional Core

☐ What personal stakes matter most?

☐ What memory or vow drives survival?

☐ What internal journey mirrors the external disaster?

6. My Pacing and Structure

☐ Act 1: Life tilts into survival mode—quick, brutal, no long setup.

☐ Act 2: Rising danger, broken trust, impossible choices.

☐ Act 3: Final test—survival means loss, sacrifice, or transformation.

☐ Final image: One line, one scene, one emotional gut-punch.

7. My Disaster Set Pieces

☐ At least one "pressure cooker" scene (trapped, desperate, against time).

☐ At least one breathtaking collapse or turning point.

☐ At least one silent, emotional moment to contrast the chaos.

8. My Survival Themes

☐ Hope vs despair

☐ Loyalty vs betrayal

☐ Sacrifice vs selfishness

☐ Remember vs forget

9. My Symbols and Echoes

☐ One object, place, or phrase that means something early—and changes by the end.

☐ One repeated image that grows heavier with every scene.

☐ One small act of humanity that survives even after everything else dies.

10. My Disaster Story Commitment

☐ Write fast and fierce.

☐ Chase emotion, not perfection.

☐ Accept the mess—it means you're alive inside the story.

☐ Finish, even if it's ugly and broken and bloody.

☐ Trust that you can survive the collapse—and come out with something powerful.

Quick Reminder:

It doesn't have to be perfect.

It just has to be real.

Optional Survival Boosts:

☐ Use a timer (25-min or 50-min writing sprints).

☐ Turn off internet distractions during writing sessions.

☐ Let your characters make messy, terrible, unforgettable choices.

☐ Remember: when it feels hopeless, you're getting close to something great.

Because disaster stories aren't about perfect plans.

They're about surviving the unexpected.

They're about walking into the ruins with nothing but a broken heart—and somehow finding a way to make it beat harder than ever before.

And with this kit by your side?

You'll survive every single story you write.

www.ingramcontent.com/pod-product-compliance
Lightning Source LLC
LaVergne TN
LVHW082334200926
848481LV00012B/3346